Decentralization, Democratization, and Informal Power in Mexico

Decentralization, Democratization, and Informal Power in Mexico

Andrew Selee

The Pennsylvania State University Press
University Park, Pennsylvania

Library of Congress Cataloging-in-Publication Data

Selee, Andrew.
   Decentralization, democratization, and informal power in Mexico / Andrew Selee.
       p.   cm.
   Includes bibliographical references and index.
   Summary: "Explores the democratization and decentralization of governance in Mexico and finds that informal political networks continue to mediate citizens' relationships with their elected authorities. Analyzes the linkages between informal and formal power by comparing how they worked in three Mexican cities: Tijuana, Ciudad Nezahualcóyotl, and Chilpancingo"—Provided by publisher.
   ISBN 978-0-271-04843-7 (cloth : alk. paper)
   ISBN 978-0-271-04844-4 (pbk. : alk. paper)
   1. Decentralization in government—Mexico.
   2. Democracy—Mexico.
   3. Mexico—Politics and government.
   I. Title.

JL1229.D42S45 2012
320.972—dc22
2010049709

Copyright © 2011 The Pennsylvania State University
All rights reserved
Printed in the United States of America
Published by The Pennsylvania State University Press,
University Park, PA 16802–1003

The Pennsylvania State University Press is a member of the Association of American University Presses.

It is the policy of The Pennsylvania State University Press to use acid-free paper. Publications on uncoated stock satisfy the minimum requirements of American National Standard for Information Sciences—Permanence of Paper for Printed Library Material, ANSI Z39.48–1992.

Contents

List of Figures vii

Acknowledgments ix

1 Introduction: The Paradoxes of Local Empowerment 1

PART 1 STATE FORMATION AND POLITICAL CHANGE

2 Centralization and Informal Power 27

3 Decentralization and Democratization 47

PART 2 A TALE OF THREE CITIES

4 Chilpancingo: The Continuation of Corporatism? 73

5 Tijuana: Liberal Democracy? 98

6 Ciudad Nezahualcóyotl: Social Movement Democracy? 130

PART 3 CONCLUSIONS

7 Pathways of Democratic Change 163

Index 179

Figures

2.1 Total public sector income by level of government, 1900–1980 *38*
3.1 Governors by political party, 1983–2006 *55*
3.2 Mayors by political party, 1983–2006 *56*
3.3 Percentage of the population governed by each political party at a municipal level, 1983–2006 *57*
3.4 Public sector spending by level of government, 1980–2006 *62*
3.5 Sources of municipal revenue, 1989–2006 *63*
3.6 Real increase in municipal income by source, 1989–2006 *63*
4.1 Municipal elections by political party, Chilpancingo, 1977–96 *81*
4.2 Real municipal income by source, Chilpancingo, 1989–2006 *86*
4.3 Municipal elections by political party, Chilpancingo, 1996–2005 *89*
5.1 Municipal elections by political party, Tijuana, 1954–89 *107*
5.2 Real municipal income by source, Tijuana, 1989–2006 *110*
5.3 Municipal elections by political party, Tijuana, 1989–2004 *113*
6.1 Municipal elections by political party, Ciudad Nezahualcóyotl, 1978–96 *143*
6.2 Real municipal income by source, Ciudad Nezahualcóyotl, 1989–2006 *146*
6.3 Municipal elections by political party, Ciudad Nezahualcóyotl, 1996–2006 *148*

Acknowledgments

The research for this book began more than eighteen years ago, long before I ever realized it might one day be published or even publishable. In 1992, I moved to the city of Tijuana to work with a Mexican nongovernmental organization on migration and local development projects. The city was, at the time, in the midst of profound changes brought about by a still incipient process of political opening and a simultaneous empowerment of local government. I lived in Tijuana for almost six years in the midst of these changes and began to document some of the transformations on the ground that would later become the material for this book. I am grateful for all those individuals with whom I worked during those years, and I am still proud to consider Tijuana a second home.

I am particularly grateful to Jonathan Fox, Rod Camp, and Carol Wise, as well as two anonymous readers, all of whom reviewed this manuscript and made extensive comments that greatly improved the final product. Sandy Thatcher at Penn State University Press was the best editor an author could ever want. Peter Smith, Tonatiuh Guillén, Phil Oxhorn, Enrique Cabrero, Jesse Ribot, Tomila Lankina, Arturo Alvarado, Ariel Armony, David Crocker, Mac Destler, Raúl Benítez, Lorenzo Meyer, John Bailey, Jesús Silva-Herzog Márquez, Rossana Fuentes-Berain, Leonardo Avritzer, Enrique Peruzzotti, Richard Stren, Marcus Melo, Blair Ruble, and Stephanie McNulty all helped shape my thinking on specific ideas raised in this book, and they have all pointed out issues that later found their way into the text. I am also grateful to Patricia Rosas for her work in editing the manuscript, which greatly improved the book.

For several years now, I have been fortunate to work at the Woodrow Wilson Center, which has allowed me to continue researching issues related to Mexico and the quality of democracy in the hemisphere. This book has been influenced by several research collaborations over these years, including projects with Jonathan Fox, Phil Oxhorn, Enrique Peruzzotti, Jacqueline Peschard, Cindy Arnson,

Raúl Benítez, Xochitl Bada, David Shirk, Eric Olson, Rossana Fuentes-Berain, Joe Tulchin, Robert Donnelly, Jorge Hernández Díaz, Leticia Santín, and Heidy Servin-Baez.

I am indebted to David Crocker and Mac Destler at the University of Maryland School of Public Policy, where I completed my Ph.D., as well as Mary Kay Vaughan, Bill Galston, and Roberto Patricio Korzeniewicz. I am also indebted to Christine Hunefeldt at UCSD (where I completed my M.A. a number of years ago) for introducing me to much of the theoretical literature that helped me begin to make sense of the issues in this book, and to Peter Smith for his many comparative insights.

In completing the research for this book, I benefited from a period of residency in the Center for Sociological Studies at El Colegio de México and from a fellowship at the University of Maryland's Institute for Philosophy and Public Policy. I am especially grateful to Arturo Alvarado and Gustavo Verduzgo for arranging the residency at El Colegio de México. I am also thankful to Raúl Benítez for receiving us in his home while my wife and I lived in Mexico City, and to Rossana Fuentes-Berain, who kindly lent me her office for a couple weeks as I was preparing the final manuscript.

In Tijuana, I am grateful to Tonatiuh Guillén and Sandra Dibble for their help in understanding municipal and state politics; to Lilia León, a friend and former colleague, for her expert research assistance and analysis; and to José Luis Pérez Canchola, Maricarmen Hernández, Cristina Franco, and Oscar Escalada for insightful analysis of local political developments since I moved away from the city. Above all, my friends Carlos Mendoza and Concepción Aguilar, along with their son Andrés, provided a home away from home in Tijuana, and they also shaped my understanding of the city in countless ways.

In Ciudad Nezahualcóyotl, I benefited immensely from my conversations with Gerardo Salazar, Alliet Bautista, and Alma Aquino and from the expert research assistance of Jessica Hernández. Martha Schteingart, Socorro Arzaluz, Ramón Rivera, and Gerardo Salazar generously shared their research, and my sister-in-law Adriana Vallejo provided us with a shared home a few miles away in Mexico City.

In Chilpancingo, I learned a great deal from Julio César Aguirre, Homero Castro, Silvia Alemán, and Silvia Castillo. I am grateful for the research assistance of Osiel Humberto González and the historical insight of Pety Acevedo, as well as the constant hospitality of Elsa Romero and Edgar Pavía who provided a home away from home when visiting the city and a roadmap through Chilpancingo's past and present.

Most of all, I owe thanks to my wife, Alejandra, the center of my life, who offered not only moral support but also intellectual guidance to this project (and read the manuscript more times than either of us can count). This book is dedicated to her and to our daughter, Lucía, who was born during the writing, with the hope that she may grow up with the promise of a better tomorrow for her two countries.

1 INTRODUCTION: THE PARADOXES OF LOCAL EMPOWERMENT

In the 1980s and 1990s, decentralization reforms swept across Latin America and the developing world, as almost every country implemented measures to strengthen the authority and autonomy of local governments. Mexico was no exception. At least in formal terms, Mexico had been one of the most centralized countries in Latin America. From the 1930s to the early 1980s, a single party dominated almost all aspects of political life, including holding most elected positions. Between 80 and 90 percent of all public resources in the early 1980s were spent through national government agencies despite the nominal existence of a federal system. By the new millennium, however, Mexico had become a multiparty democracy and almost half of all public resources were managed at the state and local level. State and local governments, which had appeared to be mere appendages of an overwhelmingly dominant central state, now had a degree of discretion in spending and policy making they had not enjoyed in decades. Even more important, this process of decentralization took place in the context of a gradual process of democratization in which the country instituted truly competitive elections for the first time in decades.

Proponents have argued that decentralization has the potential to improve democratic governance by making elected authorities more responsive because they would be closer to citizens and better able to discern their preferences. In addition, decentralization would bring citizens closer to government, allowing them to know what their elected officials were doing and to interact with them more frequently. Decentralization would thus reinforce democracy by making government more accountable and ensuring enhanced opportunities for citizen participation in political life. In short, democracy "close to home" would allow citizens a quality of politics that could not be achieved with democracy on a larger scale.

However, much of what we know about the relationship between decentralization and democracy is from the experience of the developed world. In most of those countries, the construction of democratic institutions and the extension of citizenship rights took place during a period of centralization, and decentralization has occurred after these rights and institutions were largely determined.[1] Citizenship rights, of course, are still being negotiated, extended, and restricted in these countries, and political institutions are frequently modified, sometimes to respond to major failings in the institutional structure.[2] However, the greatest expansion of citizenship rights in what are today considered developed countries generally coincided with periods of centralization. Indeed, the struggle for inclusive rights has often led to greater central government intervention to ensure equal access to rights in areas where they are least enforced.

In contrast, in Mexico, as in much of the developing world, decentralization has coincided with a period of democratic transition.[3] Local governments are being empowered at the same time that political institutions at all levels of government are being constructed and citizenship rights negotiated and expanded. We understand too little about how decentralization affects democratic governance in contexts where political institutions are still under construction and citizenship rights are often weakly defined and enforced. Does decentralization

---

1. See T. H. Marshall, "Citizenship and Social Class," in T. H. Marshall and Tom Bottomore, *Citizenship and Social Class* (1950; repr., London: Pluto, 1987).

2. See, for example, Judith N. Shklar, *American Citizenship: The Quest for Inclusion* (Cambridge: Harvard University Press, 1991) on the United States. For a compelling argument about the commonality of problems in "old" and "new" democracies, see Ariel C. Armony and Hector E. Schamis, "Babel in Democratization Studies," *Journal of Democracy* 16, no. 4 (2005): 113–28.

3. For a comparative study of reasons for decentralization around the world, see Philip Oxhorn, Joseph S. Tulchin, and Andrew D. Selee, eds., *Decentralization, Democratic Governance, and Civil Society in Comparative Perspective: Africa, Asia, and Latin America* (Washington, D.C.: Woodrow Wilson Center Press, 2004); and James Manor, *The Political Economy of Democratic Decentralization* (Washington, D.C.: World Bank, 1999). On Latin America, see Alfred P. Montero and David J. Samuels, eds., *Decentralization and Democracy in Latin America* (South Bend: University of Notre Dame Press, 2004); and Joseph S. Tulchin and Andrew D. Selee, eds., *Decentralization and Democratic Governance in Latin America* (Washington, D.C.: Woodrow Wilson Center Press, 2004). In some cases, national leaders used decentralization to maintain or reestablish legitimacy in the midst of popular protest or generalized discontent. For an argument that follows this logic in three countries, see Merilee S. Grindle, *Audacious Reforms: Institutional Invention and Democracy in Latin America* (Baltimore: Johns Hopkins University Press, 2000). This model fits Venezuela and Bolivia particularly well. In other cases, demands from newly empowered local governments or political parties with important regionally identifiable constituencies drove the process. On this, see the chapters in Montero and Samuels, *Decentralization and Democracy*. In a few countries, efforts to settle long-standing conflicts through peace processes also drove decentralization. On the role of these processes in shaping political systems generally, see Cynthia J. Arnson, ed., *Comparative Peace Processes in Latin America* (Washington, D.C.: Woodrow Wilson Center Press; Stanford: Stanford University Press, 1999).

in the context of democratization empower local governments that are responsive and accountable to citizens? Or do the weak enforcement of rights and incipient institutional structures of democracy undermine the few channels that exist to ensure government responsiveness and accountability? In other words, does decentralization reinforce democratization, or does it limit its potential?

It is not easy to arrive at the answer to these questions, but the available evidence from the effect of the most recent round of decentralization on democratic governance in the developing world is decidedly mixed. There are numerous documented examples of more responsive and accountable governments throughout the world. However, the literature is also replete with cautionary tales about how empowering local governments can weaken the state and undermine citizenship rights. In other cases, local governance simply appears to be weak and ineffectual, given local authorities' inability to resolve daily problems as effectively as the central state can.

Although scholars recognize these uneven outcomes, there is no consensus about the reasons for the discrepancies. Traditional explanations have tended to focus on formal political institutions or long-term characteristics of the social structure. Scholars and experts have argued for the need to design adequate institutions to improve coordination among levels of governments. Others have emphasized the need to strengthen local government institutions. Still other scholars have signaled that long-term social characteristics shape outcomes. However, *Decentralization, Democratization, and Informal Power in Mexico* suggests that we need to look beyond formal political institutions or inherent structural qualities to examine the way that informal power relations are constructed between the state and citizens and how these interact with formal political changes during the process of decentralization and democratization.

In the traditional interpretation within the literature, authoritarian states in the developing world were highly centralized, and democratization brought about a process of decentralization.[4] However, as we will see, the Mexican state was

---

4. We will explore the links between democratization and decentralization further in chapter 3. However, it is worth noting that the decentralization of social services—especially health care and education—had far less to do with democratization than it did with the desire to rationalize public expenditures. I am grateful to Iván Finot at CEPAL for pointing out these distinct trajectories. On sectoral reform in education and health care, see Robert R. Kaufman and Joan M. Nelson, eds., *Crucial Needs, Weak Incentives: Social Sector Reform, Democratization, and Globalization in Latin America* (Washington, D.C.: Woodrow Wilson Center Press; Baltimore: Johns Hopkins University Press, 2004). See also some of the chapters in Tulchin and Selee, *Decentralization and Democratic Governance*, especially those on Argentina, Brazil, and Mexico.

never as centralized as the literature generally suggests. As in much of the region, the underlying logic of politics in Mexico was a bit more complex. For its survival during several decades of one-party hegemonic rule, it relied on extensive alliances with power centers outside the state, even while its *formal* institutions were highly centralized.[5] What looked to most observers like a monolithic, centralized authoritarian state was actually a state that was much more diffuse and based on a series of *informal* power arrangements with key veto players in the political system, especially local and regional party leaders who often had their own bases of power. Formal political institutions existed alongside clientelism, particularism, and shared understandings about how decisions could be made at the margins of legal arrangements. Formal power was highly centralized within the state, whereas informal power, which sustained the state's legitimacy and effectiveness, was deeply decentralized. It is a central contention of this book that informal power can be as influential as formal institutions.

On the face of it, this analysis would suggest that decentralizing formal power in the context of weak citizenship rights would simply reinforce channels of informal power and thus strengthen local and regional leaders in the authoritarian system at the expense of government accountability and responsiveness. This might be even more likely since decentralization coincided with a period of economic liberalization or marketization that helped undermine the social safety nets that had sustained families and communities.[6] The rise in poverty during this period is likely to have strengthened informal power at the expense of formal relationships.

However, decentralization and democratization have been largely simultaneous processes in Mexico, as is the case in much of Latin America. Democratization has created new ways of choosing leaders and renewed channels of intermediation

---

5. For excellent analyses of how this process occurred, see Alberto Díaz Cayeros, *Federalism, Fiscal Authority, and Centralism in Latin America* (Cambridge: Cambridge University Press, 2006); and Luis Aboites Aguilar, *Excepciones y privilegios: Modernización tributaria y centralización en México, 1922–1972* (Mexico City: El Colegio de México, 2003). Moreover, in the context of a system dominated by a single party, the president developed extensive extraconstitutional powers that allowed him to name state governors and municipal mayors (when he wished), and they essentially served at his pleasure. Molinar Horcasitas and Weldon refer to these as "metaconstitutional powers." See Juan Molinar Horcasitas and Jeffrey A. Weldon, "Electoral Determinants and Consequences of National Solidarity," in Wayne A. Cornelius, Ann L. Craig, and Jonathan Fox, eds., *Transforming State-Society Relations in Mexico: The National Solidarity Strategy* (La Jolla: Center for U.S.-Mexican Studies, University of California, San Diego, 1994).

6. Philip Oxhorn and Pamela Starr, eds., *Markets and Democracy in Latin America: Conflict or Convergence?* (Boulder: Lynne Rienner, 1999). On the relationships among decentralization, democratization, and economic liberalization, see Philip Oxhorn, "Unraveling the Puzzle of Decentralization," in Oxhorn, Tulchin, and Selee, *Decentralization*.

between citizens and the state. In the process of democratization, citizens have also mobilized to demand accountability from public authorities and developed new repertoires for engagement with them. Although the underlying logic of Mexico's authoritarian system was a dense web of informal power relationships, democratization has provided an impulse for the construction of new formal channels for intermediation with the state. Economic liberalization provided an additional impetus to citizens' efforts to mobilize for democratic change and the strengthening of formal institutions.

Decentralization, Democratization, and Informal Power in Mexico examines how democratic governance has changed in three Mexican cities—Tijuana, Ciudad Nezahualcóyotl, and Chilpancingo. For several consecutive administrations during the period of most intense decentralization and democratization, each city was governed by a different political party: Tijuana by the Partido Acción Nacional (PAN), Ciudad Nezahualcóyotl by the Partido de la Revolución Democrática (PRD), and Chilpancingo by the Partido Revolucionario Institucional (PRI). The formal institutions that shaped decentralization and democratization in these municipalities are quite similar, which lets us examine how informal institutions may have shaped the responsiveness and accountability of local governments. In particular, this book looks at the way that the real channels for intermediation between citizens and their local governments have changed as municipalities have acquired new functions, powers, and resources, and as elections have become more competitive in these three cities. The research looks at the way different political parties are embedded in society, the density of social organizations and their horizontal and vertical linkages, and the structure of clientelism and corporatism as possible intermediate variables that might influence divergent outcomes for decentralization in the context of democratization and shape the way that formal institutional changes take effect.

The research in this book finds important variations in these patterns across cities, which produce significantly different outcomes for democratic governance in the context of decentralization and democratization. It also finds some constants in how informal power is constituted in Mexico that condition this process more generally across municipalities. The past is often prologue: the way the Mexican state was formed through networks of informal power conditions the way formal institutional changes take place today. Yet, at the same time, I find that different pathways of change in each place shape the way formal institutions work from city to city.

Decentralization and Democratization: What Is the Correlation?

The academic literature and publications of multilateral organizations have frequently linked decentralization and democratization as mutually reinforcing processes. However, almost all scholars acknowledge that decentralization produces divergent outcomes within the same country. There are certainly many cases where subnational governments have helped drive democratic change or become centers for democratic innovation. This is the case with participatory budgeting in Brazil,[7] as well as similar participatory experiences in India,[8] the Philippines,[9] and several other countries of Latin America.[10] In Mexico, subnational governments have played an important role in driving innovation in key public policy areas, including justice reform, infrastructure development, and environmental programs, and they have often experimented with participatory forms of democratic governance.[11]

Nonetheless, many of the innovations in Mexico, as elsewhere in Latin America, appear to be fragile and short-lived.[12] Elected officials' brief periods in office

---

7. Leonardo Avritzer, *Democracy and the Public Space in Latin America* (Princeton: Princeton University Press, 2002); Rebecca Abers, *Inventing Local Democracy: Grassroots Politics in Brazil* (Boulder: Lynne Rienner, 1999); and Gianpaolo Baiocchi, "Participation, Activism, and Politics: The Porto Alegre Experiment," in Archon Fung and Erik Olin Wright, eds., *Deepening Democracy: Institutional Innovations in Empowered Participatory Governance* (London: Verso, 2003).

8. Jean Drèze and Amartya Sen, *India: Development and Participation* (Oxford: Oxford University Press, 2002); Patrick Heller, "Social Capital as a Product of Class Mobilization and State Intervention: Industrial Workers in Kerala, India," in Peter B. Evans, ed., *State-Society Synergy: Government and Social Capital in Development*, International and Area Studies Research Series 94 (Berkeley: University of California, Berkeley, 1997).

9. Leonora C. Angeles and Francisco Magno, "The Philippines: Decentralization, Local Governments, and Citizen Action," in Oxhorn, Tulchin, and Selee, *Decentralization*.

10. Andrew Selee and Enrique Peruzzotti, eds., *Participatory Innovation and Representative Democracy in Latin America* (Washington, D.C.: Woodrow Wilson Center Press; Baltimore: Johns Hopkins University Press, 2009).

11. On decentralization and innovation generally, see Tim Campbell, *The Quiet Revolution: Decentralization and the Rise of Political Participation in Latin American Cities* (Pittsburgh: University of Pittsburgh Press, 2003). On Mexico, see Enrique Cabrero Mendoza, *Las políticas descentralizadoras en México (1983–1993): Logros y desencantos* (Mexico City: Miguel Ángel Porrúa, 1998); and Enrique Cabrero Mendoza, ed., *Innovación en gobiernos locales: Un panorama de experiencias municipales en México* (Mexico City: Editorial CIDE, 2002). On innovations in justice reform specifically, see Wayne Cornelius and David A. Shirk, eds., *Reforming the Administration of Justice in Mexico* (La Jolla: Center for U.S.-Mexican Studies, University of California, San Diego, 2007).

12. See Selee and Peruzzotti, *Participatory Innovation*, on the fragility of democratic innovation in Latin America. On Mexico, see Tonatiuh Guillén, "Democracia representativa y participativa en los municipios de México: Procesos en tensión," in Andrew Selee and Leticia Santín, eds., *Democracia y ciudadanía: Participación ciudadana y deliberación pública en gobiernos locales mexicanos* (Washington, D.C.: Woodrow Wilson Center Press; Mexico City: Agora, 2005).

and the poor institutionalization of creative democratic efforts often hamper the long-term viability of many initiatives to deepen democracy. At the same time, authoritarian leaders sometimes take refuge in local governments during democratization, as has happened in some states and municipalities in Mexico.[13] It is hard to find a consistent correlation between decentralization and democratization, either positive or negative, despite a wealth of empirical evidence for both sides of the argument.

Several explanations have been put forth for why decentralization might enhance democratic governance. For scholars of public choice and institutional economics, decentralization can help improve the flow of information between principal and agent, ensuring a closer fit between citizen preferences and government actions. Moreover, decentralization reduces the scale of policy implementation, which can also help tailor a closer fit between citizens' preferences and a government's actions, something that might be difficult to achieve on a larger scale.[14] Although much of the public choice and institutional economics literature focuses on policy outcomes, it has profound implications for democratic governance as well. This literature suggests that decentralization might help the state be more responsive and accountable because the state can respond more effectively to specific citizen demands and citizens can monitor state actions more closely.

Recent scholarship on social capital suggests that decentralization may deepen democracy, but it will do so unevenly depending on the stock of social capital in a given locality or region.[15] According to this theoretical lens, the density of associational life, which changes only slowly over time, affects the ability of subnational governments in democratic societies to assume their new responsibilities effectively and with public oversight. Still others have suggested that the variation in democratic outcomes of decentralization is not just linked to the stock of social

---

13. Edward L. Gibson, "Subnational Authoritarianism: Territorial Strategies of Political Control in Democratic Regimes" (paper presented at the 2004 Annual Meeting of the American Political Science Association, Chicago, Ill., September 2–5, 2004); Jonathan Fox, *Accountability Politics: Power and Voice in Rural Mexico* (Oxford: Oxford University Press, 2007).

14. See, for example, Mariano Tommasi and Federico Weinschelbaum, "Centralization Versus Decentralization: A Principal-Agent Analysis" (Leitner Program in International and Comparative Political Economy Working Paper no. 2003-02, Yale University, 2003); and Wallace E. Oates, ed., *The Economics of Fiscal Federalism and Local Finance* (Northampton, Mass.: Edward Elgar, 1998), xiv. For perhaps the most influential early work on fiscal federalism, see Charles M. Tiebout, "A Pure Theory of Local Expenditures," in Oates, *Economics of Fiscal Federalism*. See also Ernesto Stein, "Fiscal Decentralization and Government Size in Latin America," *Journal of Applied Economics* 2, no. 2 (1999): 357–91; and Jennie Litvack, Junaid Ahmad, and Richard Bird, *Rethinking Decentralization in Developing Countries* (Washington, D.C.: World Bank, 1998).

15. Robert D. Putnam, with Robert Leonardi and Raffaella Y. Nonetti, *Making Democracy Work: Civic Traditions in Modern Italy* (Princeton: Princeton University Press, 1993).

capital, but rather to the nature of associational life and its horizontal and vertical linkages.[16] In this approach, in localities and regions where social movements have created linkages among citizens and between them and the political system, decentralization is more likely to empower citizens and ensure responsiveness and accountability than it is in places where these linkages are more tenuous.

For scholars of deliberative democracy, decentralization may allow for the strengthening of local arenas where citizens can be more fully engaged with one another in setting public priorities.[17] Theorists of deliberative democracy argue that deliberation should help people go beyond their particular interests to develop a collective sense of the common good. In effect, by debating priorities, citizens can generate a sense of common purpose that is superior to that which emerges from strategic bargaining among them.[18] However, these scholars generally caution that it is vital that power relationships be relatively horizontal; otherwise, decentralization may reinforce existing hierarchies rather than create new opportunities for collective reflection and action.[19] Enrique Peruzzotti and I argue elsewhere that it is important to ensure that deliberative and participatory approaches also reinforce representative democracy rather than creating parallel channels that undermine representative institutions.[20]

Skeptics of decentralization have been quick to point out that local governments may not be able to carry out their new functions and that local arenas may lend themselves to capture by small elite groups. Even if decentralization provides a closer match between citizens' preferences and government decisions, uneven capacities to raise revenue and unequal abilities to provide services may undermine local government's ability to be responsive to citizens.[21] Moreover,

---

16. Sidney Tarrow, "Making Social Science Work Across Space and Time: A Critical Reflection on Robert Putnam's *Making Democracy Work*," *American Political Science Review* 90, no. 2 (1996): 389–97; Heller, "Social Capital"; and Michael W. Foley and Bob Edwards, "The Paradox of Civil Society," *Journal of Democracy* 7, no. 3 (1996): 38–52.

17. For works on deliberative democracy that specifically reference decentralization, see Fung and Wright, *Deepening Democracy*, and Iris Marion Young, *Inclusion and Democracy* (Oxford: Oxford University Press, 2000).

18. David A. Crocker, "Deliberative Participation in Local Government," in Crocker, *Ethics of Global Development: Agency, Capability, and Deliberative Democracy* (Cambridge: Cambridge University Press, 2009); Amy Gutmann and Dennis Thompson, *Democracy and Disagreement* (Cambridge: Belknap Press of Harvard University, 1996); and Daniel Yankelovich, *Coming to Public Judgment: Making Democracy Work in a Complex World* (Syracuse: Syracuse University Press, 1991).

19. Ian Shapiro, *The State of Democratic Theory* (Princeton: Princeton University Press, 2003); Crocker, "Deliberative Participation"; Fung and Wright, *Deepening Democracy*; and Young, *Inclusion and Democracy*.

20. Selee and Peruzzotti, *Participatory Innovation*.

21. Rémy Prud'homme, "On the Dangers of Decentralization," *World Bank Research Observer* 10, no. 2 (1995): 201–20.

some scholars argue that elites can more easily capture local arenas because they lack the crosscutting cleavages that safeguard democracy in larger political communities.[22] In cases where countries transition from authoritarian rule to democracy, authoritarian leaders who have been expelled from national power may find refuge in local and regional governments where there are fewer checks against unrestrained power held by a single faction or group.[23]

Building on these existing theoretical insights, I suggest an alternative approach to understanding the link between decentralization and democratic governance. Although local governments' inherent characteristics may make them propitious for responsive and accountable government and although the structure of formal institutions certainly influences outcomes, the evidence in this book suggests that the way informal power is constructed historically in local arenas helps determine outcomes in terms of responsiveness and accountability during decentralization and democratization. It is also likely that existing patterns of social capital play a role in how informal power is structured. During periods of political change, however, the way informal channels horizontally and vertically link state actors, political parties, and citizens also influences how social capital shapes outcomes. These channels are conditioned, in turn, by patterns of clientelism, histories of social mobilization, and the divergent strategies of political parties. In short, to understand how formal political institutions operate, we need to understand how their operation is shaped by informal channels of intermediation between citizens and the state.

Informal Power and Indirect Citizenship

Most studies that explicitly address decentralization have assumed that developing countries were, in fact, centralized before the 1980s and 1990s, and that

---

22. Grant McConnell, for example, writes, "As Madison observed long ago, the smaller the society, the fewer probably are the parties and interests composing it; the fewer these parties and interests and the smaller the compass in which they act, the more easily do they concert and execute their plans of oppression. Far from providing guarantees of liberty, equality, and concern for the public interest, organization of political life by small constituencies tends to enforce conformity, to discriminate in favor of elites, and to eliminate public values from effective political consideration." McConnell, *Private Power and American Democracy* (New York: Alfred A. Knopf, 1966), 6.

23. On this point, see Gibson, "Subnational Authoritarianism"; Giles Mohan and Kristian Stokke, "Participatory Development and Empowerment: The Dangers of Localism," *Third World Quarterly* 21, no. 2 (2000): 247–68; and Gerd Schönwälder, "New Democratic Spaces at the Grassroots? Popular Participation in Latin American Local Governments," *Development and Change* 29 (1997): 753–70.

those decades saw a dramatic change in the nature of the state, as powers, functions, and resources were devolved to subnational governments.[24] This is partially, but not wholly, true. Many states in the developing world, including most in Latin America and certainly Mexico, were quite centralized in terms of formal institutions.[25] Powers, functions, and resources were concentrated within the central state, which often had significant mechanisms for controlling the actions of subnational governments. However, this centralization of formal powers in these countries conflicted with the diffuse nature of informal power. As Joel S. Migdal has shown, authoritarian governments in the developing world were constructed not by creating a strong central state that was capable of penetrating and organizing society, but rather by striking bargains with power holders within society to allow them a margin of autonomy in exchange for loyalty.[26] In the strong, Weberian states of Western Europe, Japan, China, the United States, Canada, and a few other countries around the world, the state succeeded in limiting arenas of rule-making authority outside the state and imposing a more or less uniform rule of law.[27] However, state formation in most developing countries has involved constructing both strongly centralized formal institutions and highly diffuse networks of informal power relations. Of course, in all developed countries, informal power arrangements continue to exist as well; however, they tend not to be as central to the functions of the state as they are in many developing countries.[28]

24. Most of the studies cited in note 3, including some of this author's previous work, fall into this category.

25. The classic work on centralization in Latin America is Claudio Véliz, *The Centralist Tradition of Latin America* (Princeton: Princeton University Press, 1980). Brazil is, perhaps, a partial exception. See Díaz Cayeros, *Federalism*. For an overview of formal centralization with a comparison among six countries in Latin America, see Andrew Selee, "Introduction," in Tulchin and Selee, *Decentralization and Democratic Governance*.

26. Joel S. Migdal, *Strong Societies and Weak States: State-Society Relations and State Capabilities in the Third World* (Princeton: Princeton University Press, 1988). It is worth contrasting Midgal's analysis of countries in the developing world with the work of Michael Mann on the development of a strong state capable of penetrating and organizing society in Europe. Mann, *The Sources of Social Power: A History of Power from the Beginning to A.D. 1760* (Cambridge: Cambridge University Press, 1986).

27. Eric Hobsbawm, *Nations and Nationalism Since 1780: Programme, Myth, Reality* (Cambridge: Cambridge University Press, 1990), 81; Stein Rokkan and Derek W. Urwin, *The Politics of Territorial Identity: Studies in European Regionalism* (London: Sage, 1982); and Samuel Huntington, *Political Order in Changing Societies* (New Haven: Yale University Press, 1968), 135. See also Max Weber, *Economy and Society: An Outline of Interpretive Sociology*, ed. Guenther Roth and Claus Wittich, trans. Ephraim Fischoff, vol. 3 (New York: Bedminster Press, 1968).

28. Even a cursory look at developed countries' states will show the use of informal power networks, but these tend to be secondary rather than central to the state's effectiveness. However, this was not always the case. On the history of patronage politics in the United States, for example, see Robert Dahl, *Who Governs?*

These informal networks not only buttress the state and ensure its survival, but also serve as mechanisms for state agencies to deliver services, enforce the rule of law, and respond to citizen demands. In Mexico, for example, patronage has provided a means both for political leaders to manipulate voters and for the state to target and deliver programs. Clientelistic networks also provide vital channels for citizens' voice about their preferences for government action, often in lieu of or in parallel to formal representative channels. Moreover, in many cases, informal politics plays a role in ensuring the rule of law. Through diverse modalities, local leaders can enforce understandings about permitted behavior and influence the application of justice against infractors. In most cases, these informal mechanisms for enforcement, program delivery, and representation exist alongside the formal mechanisms, and there is a symbiotic relationship between formal and informal institutions. Informal power is not a sign of the lack of institutionalization of the state, but rather a particular form of institutionalization that serves to link the state with society.[29]

What is informal power? The concept is linked to patronage politics and clientelism, that is, the unequal exchange of resources for votes, but the term, as I use it here, goes a bit beyond that.[30] It is closely related to what Frances Hagopian calls "traditional politics" and Guillermo O'Donnell refers to as "particularism."[31] It involves a complex, hierarchical network of political intermediaries, who provide access to influence and distribute resources and favors in return for political support. These exchanges generally imply unequal power. Nevertheless, a web of complicity and mutual dependence often ties those superior in the hierarchy to those who are lower in it.[32] Moreover, in many countries, including

---

Democracy and Power in an American City (New Haven: Yale University, 1961); and William F. Whyte, *Street Corner Society: The Social Structure of an Italian Slum*, 4th ed. (Chicago: University of Chicago Press, 1993). Developing and developed countries lie along a continuum, with some developing countries (e.g., China) having more formal capacity and some developed countries (e.g., Italy) having significant relationships of informal power.

29. Cf. Guillermo O'Donnell, "Delegative Democracy?" *Journal of Democracy* 5, no. 1 (1994): 55–69; and O'Donnell, "Illusions About Consolidation," *Journal of Democracy* 7, no. 2 (1996): 34–51.

30. On patronage and clientelism, see Luis Roniger and Ayşe Güneş-Ayata, eds., *Democracy, Clientelism, and Civil Society* (Boulder: Lynne Rienner, 1994); Jonathan Fox, "The Difficult Transition from Clientelism to Citizenship: Lessons from Mexico," *World Politics* 46, no. 2 (1994): 151–84; and Javier Auyero, *Poor People's Politics: Peronist Survival Networks and the Legacy of Evita* (Durham: Duke University Press, 2001).

31. Frances Hagopian, *Traditional Politics and Regime Change in Brazil*, 2nd ed. (Cambridge: Cambridge University Press, 2007); O'Donnell, "Illusions About Consolidation," 35.

32. In the case of Peronism in Argentina, Auyero shows how this mutual dependency goes beyond concrete transactions and involves shared symbols, understandings, and meanings. Auyero, *Poor People's Politics*.

Mexico, not only the urban and rural poor are linked to the state through the web of informal power, but so too are professional organizations, the media, large corporations, and religious associations.

The term "informal power" also refers to a series of shared understandings about how political and resource distribution decisions are to take place at the margin of the formal decision-making channels. All political systems have informal channels; indeed, most important political negotiations take place "off-the-books" in any political system. Such common terms as "lobbying," "log-rolling," and "horse-trading" bear witness to this.[33] However, in countries with strong states, these informal negotiations must eventually be processed through formal institutional channels (for example, a vote in the legislature or a budget appropriation process). When informal politics dominates the system, these negotiations often take place at the margin of formal institutions and may not be processed through any formal political decisions at all. The formal representative mechanisms for making decisions generally exist separately from the most important—and least transparent—channels for decision making, and the influence of political leaders in these decisions in many cases has little to do with their formal titles. Informal politics thrives on the personalistic distribution of resources from political leaders to subordinates and eventually to citizens or organized groups (including not only the poor and marginalized but powerful groups as well) in exchange for loyalty and political support.

We have generally understood clientelism and patronage as unequal exchange of resources for votes between politicians and (usually poor) citizens.[34] I employ the term "informal power" to understand the wider system of hierarchical power relations based on patronage and informal intermediation that serves as an organizational structure linking citizens and groups in society to the state. Unlike Hagopian's "traditional power," there is no assumption here that the political brokers involved in the hierarchical chains of intermediation remain the same

---

33. See Gretchen Helmke and Steven Levitsky, "Introduction," in Helmke and Levitsky, eds., *Informal Institutions and Democracy: Lessons from Latin America* (Baltimore: Johns Hopkins University Press, 2006) for an analysis of the various ways that informal institutions complement, compete with, substitute for, and accommodate formal rules. "Informal power," the term I use here, is primarily a "substitute" for formal rules, although it occasionally complements and competes with the formal rules, particularly as they are modified and strengthened.

34. The classic study of clientelism in Latin America is Luis Roniger, *Hierarchy and Trust in Modern Mexico and Brazil* (New York: Praeger, 1990). On the operation of clientelism in urban areas in Mexico, see Richard R. Fagen and William S. Tuohy, *Politics and Privilege in a Mexican City* (Stanford: Stanford University Press, 1972); and Wayne A. Cornelius, *Political Learning Among the Migrant Poor: The Impact of Residential Context* (Beverly Hills: Sage, 1973).

individuals over time. But although the brokers may change, the basic structure of state-society relations remains the same or strikingly similar. At the same time, unlike usual definitions of clientelism, which predominantly focus on interactions between political brokers and the poor, informal power also includes relationships between political leaders and all potential power centers outside the state, including private businesses, religious organizations, and even nominally "autonomous" organizations.

Although informal power suggests that political brokers are powerful regardless of their formal positions within state institutions, there is clearly a relationship between formal and informal power. Political brokers cycle in and out of formal positions of influence in the state as a means of developing their influence and their access to resources. Political brokers are rarely influential because of their formal titles alone, but they use their participation in formal politics to strengthen their position. Therefore, in many cases, a mutually reinforcing relationship exists between the exercise of formal and informal power. In addition, in Mexico, brokers are generally embedded within specific political parties (although switching parties has become somewhat more common in recent years). Each political party has specific ways of relating to citizens and particular strategies to develop ongoing channels for intermediation with citizens. Political parties thus structure the options that brokers have for exercising their craft.

Moreover, citizens shape informal power as well. Social mobilizations and alliances between civic associations and reformers within the state can empower citizens and alter channels of intermediation.[35] In some cases, this may help build formal institutions for intermediation, strengthen representative democracy, or encourage new formal participatory structures for direct engagement between citizens and the state. In other cases, it may lead to new forms of informal power that produce better responsiveness and accountability without changes in formal institutions.

The predominance of informal power as a means for organizing relations between state and society has profound implications for the nature of citizenship. Citizenship is generally defined as a set of rights and responsibilities that pertain to membership in a political community.[36] The development of modern citizenship is what Charles Tilly calls the rise of "enforceable claims on the

---

35. Fox, "Difficult Transition."
36. J. G. A. Pocock, "The Ideal of Citizenship Since Classical Times," in Ronald Beiner, ed., *Theorizing Citizenship* (Albany: State University of New York, 1995).

state."[37] Most theories of democracy predicate its effective functioning, at least in large-scale societies, on the existence of an impersonal and universal category of citizenship that establishes political equality among members of the political community.[38] However, where informal power predominates as a form of political organization, citizenship becomes primarily contingent on political negotiations through informal channels rather than membership in the political community. Citizens can access their rights only by bargaining with political leaders, who serve as intermediaries between citizens and the state.

One important implication of this is that citizens' responsibilities are also split between their civic duties to the larger political community and their loyalty to the particularistic interests of the intermediaries who assist them. Citizens' demands are also processed not as demands based on rights (which the state should enforce) but as favors from the intermediaries. Demands for public goods are essentially privatized as political favors. For example, citizens concerned about building a new school in their neighborhood will generally need to make this demand via intermediaries, as a petition for a favor from those in power rather than a demand that the state comply with its constitutional obligation to make education available. Similarly, in cases where the judicial system is weak and the enforcement of the rule of law relies largely on informal arrangements, an innocent person accused of a crime is far more likely to beg a politically powerful ally for support in order to get out of legal troubles than trust their luck in the judicial process. This, in turn, limits the construction and enforcement of rights since most demand-making is based on bargaining over concrete, particular demands that can be granted as favors rather than on making overarching claims for the construction and enforcement of rights. The system of informal power is thus self-reinforcing.

Informal power creates a form of citizenship that is highly indirect. Instead of citizens making claims on the state, based on their membership in the political community, they bargain with political intermediaries for resources, favors, and even justice. Mahmood Mamdani has coined the term "indirect citizenship" to explain the form of political organization in many African societies, in which

---

37. Charles Tilly, ed., *Citizenship, Identity, and Social History* (Cambridge: Cambridge University Press, 1996).

38. Robert Dahl, *Democracy and Its Critics* (New Haven: Yale University Press, 1989); Giovanni Sartori, *The Theory of Democracy Revisited*, vol. 1, *The Contemporary Debate* (Chatham, N.J.: Chatham House, 1987); and Norberto Bobbio, *Democracy and Dictatorship: The Nature and Limits of State Power*, trans. Peter Kennealy (Minneapolis: University of Minnesota Press, 1989).

citizens' relationship to the state is determined by community membership and channeled through community leaders, who serve as intermediaries for political demand making.[39] According to Mamdani, colonial regimes and then postcolonial African states legitimized traditional leaders as intermediaries as a means of enshrining indirect citizenship, which guaranteed that the state had both mechanisms for top-down political control and clearly defined channels for bottom-up demand making. Jan Rus has found a similar process in Chiapas, Mexico, where the ruling PRI used community leaders (usually indigenous bilingual teachers) to ensure a carefully calibrated system of control through indigenous intermediaries.[40]

In Mexico, as in many countries of Latin America, indirect citizenship is the most common form of citizenship, and it is not limited to a particular region, ethnic group, or socioeconomic level. Chapter 2 traces the development of indirect citizenship in Mexico, and the particular way it was enshrined as part of a political structure based on informal power. Although these processes reached their most complete and coherent form with the rise of the PRI as the hegemonic party after the Mexican Revolution, the roots can be found much earlier in Mexican history. As later chapters will show, democratization and successive social mobilizations have, in fact, altered the nature of citizenship in important ways, bringing it closer to the normative ideal of democratic citizenship, that is, an impersonal category with rights and responsibilities based on membership in the political community. However, important continuities remain in the way power is structured. Despite important advances, citizenship is still largely indirect for many citizens and mediated by political brokers.

Mexico's political system has largely been based on informal power and indirect citizenship, yet prior to democratization, forms of responsiveness and accountability did exist within the political system.[41] Although informal power is generally structured hierarchically and unequally,[42] it is predicated on a two-way

39. Mahmood Mamdani, *Citizen and Subject: Contemporary Africa and the Legacy of Late Colonialism* (Princeton: Princeton University Press, 1996).
40. Jan Rus, "The 'Comunidad Revolucionaria Institucional': The Subversion of Native Government in Highland Chiapas, 1936–1938," in Gilbert M. Joseph and Daniel Nugent, eds., *Everyday Forms of State Formation: Revolution and the Negotiation of Rule in Modern Mexico* (Durham: Duke University Press, 1994).
41. Fox, *Accountability Politics*.
42. There may be cases where relations of informal power are not clearly hierarchical and unequal. The relationships between the Mexican state and several powerful groups, including the Catholic Church, Televisa (Mexico's sole television network until the early 1990s), and the largest corporations, were structured through informal negotiations and networks of power relationships, but at any given moment, it was not always clear who had the upper hand.

relationship at all levels. Political leaders who serve as intermediaries generally gain power by delivering favors to those below them in the hierarchy and providing benefits (usually demonstrations of political support and loyalty) to those above them. As Beatriz Magaloni has shown, one-party hegemonic systems like Mexico depend on elections—even when their outcome is known ahead of time—as a means for shoring up their legitimacy by mobilizing voters and showing the weakness of the opposition.[43] Even authoritarian governments use informal power as a means of ensuring two-way communication with citizens, by creating controlled channels for demand making and service delivery.[44] Therefore, although informal power privileges "upward accountability" to those above in the political hierarchy, it also creates a degree of "downward accountability" to those below. And although it fragments demand making into petitions for favors, it still provides channels for citizen voice.[45] In the case studies, I will explore the specific ways that voice and accountability were structured under authoritarian rule in different Mexican municipalities and how this may have subsequently influenced the ways these processes are have come to be structured today after democratization.

Design of the Study

This study seeks to understand how decentralization in the context of democratization has transformed democratic governance in Mexican municipalities. More specifically, it tries to determine what factors explain different outcomes for responsiveness and accountability. There is a substantial body of work on decentralization in Mexico.[46] By decentralization, I mean *the increase in subnational*

43. Beatriz Magaloni, *Voting for Autocracy: Hegemonic Party Survival and Its Demise in Mexico* (Cambridge: Cambridge University Press, 2006).
44. Hagopian, *Traditional Politics*.
45. On this point, see Michelle M. Taylor-Robinson, "The Difficult Road from *Caudillismo* to Democracy: The Impact of Clientelism in Honduras," in Helmke and Levitsky, *Informal Institutions and Democracy*. The concepts of "upward accountability" and "downward accountability" are explored extensively in Jesse C. Ribot, *Waiting for Democracy: The Politics of Choice in Natural Resource Decentralization* (Washington, D.C.: World Resources Institute, 2004).
46. For example, Díaz Cayeros, *Federalism*; Cabrero Mendoza, *Las políticas descentralizadoras*; Peter Ward, Victoria Rodríguez, and Enrique Cabrero Mendoza, *New Federalism and State Government: Bringing the States Back In*, U.S.-Mexico Policy Report no. 9 (Austin: University of Texas, 1999); Wayne A. Cornelius, Todd A. Eisenstadt, and Jane Hindley, eds., *Subnational Politics and Democratization in Mexico* (La Jolla: Center for U.S.-Mexican Studies, University of California, San Diego, 1999); Tonatiuh Guillén López and Alicia Ziccardi, eds., *Innovación y continuidad del municipio mexicano: Análisis de la reforma municipal de 13 estados de la República* (Mexico City: Miguel Ángel Porrúa, 2004); Yemile Mizrahi, "Twenty

governments' authority over functions, powers, and resources and in their autonomy in decision making relative to the national government.[47] By democratization, I mean simply the establishment of free and fair elections and the institutionalization of the other requirements of polyarchy.[48] Several excellent studies have explored democratization in Mexico, at either a national or local level, primarily focused on explaining the transition process itself[49] or its functioning after the emergence of competitive elections.[50] This book, in contrast, will look at the effect of

---

Years of Decentralization in Mexico: A Top-Down Process," in Oxhorn, Tulchin, and Selee, *Decentralization*; and Mauricio Merino Huerta, *Fuera del centro* (Xalapa: Universidad Veracruzana, 1992).

47. This definition departs slightly from traditional usage, which generally sees decentralization as the transfer of responsibilities to subnational governments. Dennis Rondinelli has been particularly influential in creating this definitional framework, although he and his co-authors often include devolution to local agencies of the central government as well as transfers to subnational governments. See Dennis A. Rondinelli and G. Shabbir Cheema, "Implementing Decentralization Policies: An Introduction," in Cheema and Rondinelli, eds., *Decentralization and Development: Policy Implementation in Developing Countries* (Beverly Hills: Sage, 1983), 18; Dennis A. Rondinelli, John R. Nellis, and G. Shabbir Cheema, *Decentralization in Developing Countries: A Review of Recent Experience* (Washington, D.C.: World Bank, 1983); and Dennis A. Rondinelli, "What Is Decentralization?" in Jennie Litvack and Jessica Seddon, eds., *Decentralization Briefing Notes* (Washington, D.C.: World Bank Institute, 1999). Most recent studies of decentralization, both by scholars and by multilateral institutions, focus their discussion on devolution exclusively, even if they reference a broader concept. Among the World Bank studies, see Shahid Javed Burki, Guillermo E. Perry, and William R. Dillinger, *Beyond the Center: Decentralizing the State* (Washington, D.C.: World Bank, 1999); Litvack and Seddon, *Decentralization Briefing Notes*; Litvack, Ahmad, and Bird, *Rethinking Decentralization*; George E. Peterson, *Decentralization in Latin America: Learning Through Experience* (Washington, D.C.: World Bank, 1997); Anwar Shah, *Balance, Accountability, and Responsiveness: Lessons About Decentralization*, Policy Research Working Paper no. 2021 (Washington, D.C.: World Bank, 1998); Anwar Shah and Theresa Thompson, *Implementing Decentralized Local Governance: A Treacherous Road with Potholes, Detours, and Road Closures*, Policy Research Paper no. 3353 (Washington, D.C.: World Bank, 2004); and Manor, *Political Economy of Democratic Decentralization*. Among the academic studies, see Tulia G. Falleti, "A Sequential Theory of Decentralization: Latin American Cases in Comparative Perspective," *American Political Science Review* 99, no. 3 (2005): 327–46; Richard C. Crook and James Manor, *Democracy and Decentralisation in South Asia and West Africa: Participation, Accountability, and Performance* (Cambridge: Cambridge University Press, 1998); Oxhorn, Tulchin, and Selee, *Decentralization*; Tulchin and Selee, *Decentralization and Democratic Governance*; Arun Agrawal and Jesse C. Ribot, "Accountability in Decentralization: A Framework with South Asian and West African Cases," *Journal of Developing Areas* 33 (Summer 1999): 473–502; and Ribot, *Waiting for Democracy*, as well as many others cited in this chapter.

48. According to Dahl, the requirements of polyarchy are elected officials, free and fair elections, inclusive suffrage, the right to run for office, freedom of expression, alternative information, and associational autonomy. Dahl, *Democracy and Its Critics*, chap. 15.

49. Magaloni, *Voting for Autocracy*; Mauricio Merino Huerta, *La transición votada* (Mexico City: Fondo de Cultura Económica, 2003); Kevin J. Middlebrook, "Introduction," in Middlebrook, ed., *Dilemmas of Political Change in Mexico* (London: Institute for Latin American Studies, University of London, 2004); and Kenneth F. Greene, *Why Dominant Parties Lose: Mexico's Democratization in Comparative Perspective* (Cambridge: Cambridge University Press, 2007).

50. Andrew Selee and Jacqueline Peschard, eds., *Mexico's Democratic Challenges: Politics, Government, and Society* (Washington, D.C.: Woodrow Wilson Center Press; Stanford: Stanford University Press, 2010);

democratization and decentralization on municipal governance.[51] Chapters 2 and 3 explore in depth the dynamics of democratization and decentralization and how these two processes relate to each other.

The large-scale formal institutional changes entailed in decentralization and democratization hold fairly constant across municipalities. Therefore, the study looks for intervening variables that might explain divergent outcomes in terms of responsiveness and accountability within the informal structure of power. In particular, I look at two that have been the dominant explanations given in the literature and an alternate hypothesis. The first is the possibility that formal institutions may in fact diverge during decentralization and democratization, even if it looks as though they are the same across localities. Because both decentralization and democratization are iterative processes, what looks like a common set of institutional changes might actually hide small but significant differences in institutional structure.[52] In particular, the institutions for representative democracy

---

Roderic Ai Camp, *Politics in Mexico: The Democratic Consolidation* (Oxford: Oxford University Press, 2006). For works on the political party system, see Joseph Klesner, "The 2006 Elections: Manifestation of a Divided Society?" *PS: Politics and Political Science* 40, no. 1 (2007): 27–32; José Antonio Crespo, *PRI: De la hegemonía a la oposición: Un estudio comparado, 1994–2001* (Mexico City: Centro de Estudios de Política Comparada, 2001); Kathleen Bruhn, *Taking on Goliath: The Emergence of a New Left Party and the Struggle for Democracy in Mexico* (University Park: Pennsylvania State University Press, 1996); Yemile Mizrahi, *From Martyrdom to Power: The Partido Acción Nacional in Mexico* (South Bend: University of Notre Dame Press, 2003); and David Shirk, *Mexico's New Politics: The PAN and Democratic Change* (Boulder: Lynne Rienner, 2005). For works on the Mexican Congress, see María Amparo Casar, "Executive-Legislative Relations: Continuity or Change?" in Selee and Peschard, *Mexico's Democratic Challenges*; Luis Carlos Ugalde, *The Mexican Congress: Old Player, New Power* (Washington, D.C.: Center for Strategic and International Studies, 2000); and Jeffrey Weldon, "Changing Patterns of Executive-Legislative Relations in Mexico," in Middlebrook, *Dilemmas of Political Change*. On the rule of law, see Cornelius and Shirk, *Reforming the Administration of Justice*. For media, see Chappell Lawson, *Building the Fourth Estate: Democratization and the Rise of a Free Press in Mexico* (Berkeley: University of California Press, 2002). For public opinion, see Roderic Ai Camp, *Citizen Views of Democracy in Latin America* (Pittsburgh: University of Pittsburgh Press, 2001); Alejandro Moreno, "Citizens' Values and Beliefs Towards Politics: Is Democracy Growing Attitudinal Roots in Mexico?" in Selee and Peschard, *Mexico's Democratic Challenges*; and Jorge I. Domínguez and James A. McCann, *Democratizing Mexico: Public Opinion and Electoral Choices* (Baltimore: Johns Hopkins University Press, 1998).

51. The one comparable study is Merilee S. Grindle, *Going Local: Decentralization, Democratization, and the Promise of Good Governance* (Princeton: Princeton University Press, 2007). However, Grindle's study looks at a large number of municipalities to survey policy outcomes, whereas this study looks at three, in depth, to examine the process of policy making. The research by Fox in *Accountability Politics* touches on many of the same issues explored in this book and has some methodological similarities, though in a rural context.

52. Kent Eaton, for example, has shown that considerable recentralization also takes place in the midst of decentralization processes. In fact, the process moves both ways, and it can occasionally move both ways at once, as one level of government (e.g., state or provincial) is strengthened while another (e.g., municipal) loses strength. Eaton, *Politics Beyond the Capital: The Design of Subnational Institutions in South America* (Stanford: Stanford University Press, 2004).

might differ slightly from municipality to municipality, or municipalities might assume different kinds of powers, functions, and resources or different degrees of autonomy for exercising these.

Second, social capital may vary significantly from municipality to municipality. Although we do not have the tools to measure this rigorously over time, the case studies selected appear to show significant variations in associational activity, which allows for an approximation in each case. It is possible that each municipality may have started with a different set of associational resources, and this would predetermine the degree to which decentralization and democratization will produce responsive and accountable governance.

Third, different patterns of informal power may shape the outcomes of decentralization and democratization on democratic governance in these municipalities. It is possible that the way the political party in power links to citizens; the structure of civil society, including the horizontal and vertical linkages that civic associations have to the state; and the nature of clientelism all shape outcomes related to responsiveness and accountability. This study will look at the real channels that link citizens and the municipality in each case to see whether informal channels of intermediation play a role in linking citizens and the municipality and whether different patterns of informal power influence democratic governance outcomes.

The dependent variable in this analysis is democracy and its practice, which we refer to as democratic governance. Democracy is, of course, a normative ideal based on the notion that all members of the community are political equals and that they should be the ultimate arbiters of public authority.[53] The exigencies of modern democratic societies require that citizens assign authority for most major decisions to elected representatives who act on their behalf; however, the normative ideal of democracy as rule by the people is preserved to the extent that citizens regularly elect representatives who are responsive to voters' prospective preferences and accountable to voters for their actions retrospectively.[54] The case studies therefore look at whether existing representative institutions in Mexican municipalities—both elections themselves and the public authorities they produce—actually help ensure responsiveness and accountability after decentralization and democratization.

53. Dahl, *Democracy and Its Critics*; Bobbio, *Democracy and Dictatorship*.
54. Bernard Manin, Susan C. Stokes, and Adam Przeworski, "Introduction," in Przeworski, Stokes, and Manin, eds., *Democracy, Accountability, and Representation* (Cambridge: Cambridge University Press, 1999). Cf. Sartori, *The Theory of Democracy*, 156.

However, formal representative systems are not the only guarantee of responsive and accountable government. Elections are largely a "blunt instrument" for ensuring responsiveness and accountability, especially given asymmetries of information and contradictory imperatives built into elections systems.[55] Effective democratic representation needs to be embedded in ongoing communication between citizens and elected authorities over priorities and decision making, with a two-way information flow about citizens' preferences and authorities' decisions and actions.[56] Even under conditions of free and fair elections, informal power may undermine responsiveness by reducing citizens' preferences for policy or public goods to private bargaining over private concessions.[57] Similarly, informal power may also undermine accountability by requiring citizens' loyalty to political leaders regardless of their actions. Therefore, it is vital to look at the channels that link citizens and the state in a democracy to understand how these support or undermine responsiveness and accountability.

To do that, the case studies examine whether traditional informal channels are being replaced by formal channels as decentralization and democratization take place. The case studies pay particular attention to the way elected representatives interact with citizens between elections and, especially, to whether citizens and politicians understand that representative institutions are real channels through which demands are made and public actions are monitored and sanctioned. In addition, to see whether they have strengthened democratic governance, I look at innovations in participatory governance, which have become widespread in Mexico and elsewhere in Latin America.[58] I am interested in assessing the potential for participatory innovations to generate a more responsive and accountable form of government, by strengthening representative institutions, and whether these channels replace old practices of informal power. Finally,

---

55. Bernard Manin, Adam Przeworski, and Susan C. Stokes, "Elections and Representation," in Przeworski, Stokes, and Manin, *Democracy, Accountability, and Representation*.

56. Enrique Peruzzotti, "Two Approaches to Representation" (paper presented at the Latin American Studies Association, San Juan, Puerto Rico, March 15–18, 2006); Fox, *Accountability Politics*, 4–7.

57. One study finds that in regions of Brazil where clientelism is more prevalent, political parties are less programmatic in their behavior since they are dedicated to producing private goods for clients rather than policy decisions for citizens. See Scott W. Desposato, "How Informal Electoral Institutions Shape the Brazilian Legislative Arena," in Helmke and Levitsky, *Informal Institutions and Democracy*.

58. There is a large literature on participatory innovations in Latin America and elsewhere around the world. We return to this debate in the concluding chapter. Comparative studies include Selee and Peruzzotti, *Participatory Innovation*; Avritzer, *Democracy and the Public Space*; Fung and Wright, *Deepening Democracy*; and Andrea Cornwall and Vera Schattan Coelho, eds., *Spaces for Change? The Politics of Citizen Participation in New Democratic Arenas* (London: Zed Books, 2007).

the case studies also look specifically at how informal channels themselves are being transformed and whether they present possibilities for responsiveness and accountability, even if these exist at the margins of formal institutions.

It is worth noting that I take a process-oriented approach that looks at how municipal institutions actually work and whether they generate channels that link to citizens in a way that promotes responsiveness and accountability. Several studies of decentralization have sought to account for divergent effects on democratic governance by using proxy variables that quantify tangible outcomes, especially regional and municipal governments' effectiveness in implementing specific policies.[59] Over time, there should be a correlation between democratic governance and good government, but other factors may well intervene in this relationship. Therefore, taking a process-oriented approach helps us understand how responsiveness and accountability are changing over time regardless of tangible, short-term outcomes for policy.

The evidence for this study is based on between twenty-five and forty interviews with political leaders and citizen leaders in each municipality, as well as a detailed review of municipal documents and participant observation of the political processes.[60] In each case, the key questions revolved around the way that citizens interact with the municipality, including transformations in the channels for demand making and monitoring of public decisions at the municipal level. The case studies analyze whether there are formal institutional differences that could account for divergent outcomes. The case studies also look at the density of civic associations as a possible cause for different patterns of political change. Finally, each case study looks at the way that citizens and civic associations relate to the state, the political parties, and the key political leaders with influence in public decision making in order to understand differences in formal and informal channels.

The three cities studied in this book all have significantly different historical patterns of state-society relations and recently, different political paths. Chilpancingo in the state of Guerrero, the subject of chapter 4, is one of the largest cities of which the PRI has managed to retain control. Because Mexico's twenty-five

---

59. For example, Putnam, *Making Democracy Work*, and Grindle, *Going Local*.
60. The interviews included former mayors and council members, municipal officials, leaders of nongovernmental and popular organizations, and a sample of neighborhood leaders in each city. The research was conducted in 2004 and 2005. Because documentation on municipal politics is limited in Mexico, I have included extensive information on each city in the footnotes for those who might want to learn more about them.

largest cities have all experienced partisan changes that left the PRI out of power, Chilpancingo is a slightly smaller city than the other two cases studied here. In a state in which political competition has grown considerably, Chilpancingo has always been known as a corporatist town with strong and seemingly effective PRI base organizations. It was, until very recently, the seat of power in one of the states that is best known for being under the control of a small number of political families. To a large extent, it serves as a baseline for understanding how democratic governance has evolved in cities where the PRI remains the dominant party, something that is true in many of Mexico's municipalities. Because Chilpancingo is a city with low social capital, associations that are overwhelmingly linked to partisan politics through clientelistic channels, and a party in power that is better known for continuity than institutional innovation, we might expect Chilpancingo to have the poorest outcomes for democratic governance of the three cities studied.

Tijuana, presented in chapter 5, was the first major city in which the right-of-center National Action Party (PAN, Partido Acción Nacional) won and then held on to the municipal government. The chapter addresses fifteen years of governance in Tijuana, which has long been characterized as a city with a dynamic economy and citizens who are generally unaffiliated with any political party or social organization. The PRI's clientelistic structure was always fairly weak in this rapidly growing city, far removed from the capital and closely tied to the U.S. economy. The ascendancy and permanence of the PAN, a party that emphasizes individual rights, was no coincidence in a place where citizens had fewer ties than usual to the official party's corporate structure and there were greater individual opportunities for economic advancement. Tijuana is also known for a high density of autonomous civic associations, which have largely operated outside of the sphere of official power. Given the city's high social capital, a significant degree of associational autonomy, and a political party in power known for institutional innovation, we might expect that democratic governance would have evolved here far more than it has in Chilpancingo.

Ciudad Nezahualcóyotl, analyzed in chapter 6, is a large city on the outskirts of Mexico City. It became the first major city won and held by the left-of-center Democratic Revolutionary Party (PRD, Partido de la Revolución Democrática). Neza, as the city is generally called, is known for its poor and working-class neighborhoods and for being a bastion of some of the country's strongest social movements. Although the PRI developed an extensive network of government-affiliated organizations in the town, its residents also created a series of grassroots organizations outside the official party, which often challenged the official organizations for prominence and influence. The strength of the PRD, starting in the mid-1990s, grew out of the dense network of non-PRI popular organizations and the city's long period of social ferment. Neza has high social capital, measured in terms of the number of civic associations, but these have historically always had clear ties to political power, first as opposition movements and later as part of the structure of the governing political party. We might expect Neza to fall between Chilpancingo and Tijuana in outcomes for democratic governance, since it has high social capital and an opposition political party inclined to institutional innovation (like Tijuana) but an associational life largely linked to political power (as in Chilpancingo). We may, however, also be surprised by the results.

These case studies trace highly divergent trajectories of local political transformation, as decentralization and democratization have reshaped both formal political institutions and informal power relationships. The final chapter of this book tries to understand how different patterns of state-society linkages shape the ways in which decentralization and democratization determine the accountability and responsiveness of local governments in Mexico. The final chapter is particularly concerned with the persistence of informal power and its relationship to citizenship within decentralized democratic systems. The conclusion highlights the different paths that these three municipalities have taken in democratic governance. It also finds that the persistence of informal power—a result of the way the Mexican state was constructed historically and is embedded in Mexican society—has significant implications for democratic governance everywhere in Mexico. The nature of state formation historically conditions the outcome of democratization and decentralization in particular ways that are common throughout Mexico, but it also produces specific outcomes that vary according to the nature of state-society linkages in each municipality. These findings, although focused on Mexico, are likely to have broad applicability to other countries that have undergone recent processes of democratization and decentralization.

PART 1

STATE FORMATION AND POLITICAL CHANGE

2 CENTRALIZATION AND INFORMAL POWER

By 1980, Mexico was—formally, at least—one of the most centralized large countries in Latin America. The federal government controlled roughly 80 to 90 percent of public expenditures.¹ In contrast, municipalities accounted for only 1 to 2 percent of public spending, and these local governments had few formal functions, powers, or resources. Then, beginning in the early 1980s and lasting for two decades, Mexico underwent a dramatic process of decentralization.

However, municipalities did not suddenly emerge out of nowhere.² Local spaces have always been an essential element of Mexico's political system. Therefore, before we seek to understand the effects of decentralization on democracy, we need to know something about how state power was constructed historically in Mexico and how the state was embedded in society.³ Although formal power was highly centralized prior to the 1980s, informal power was much more diffuse and contested. The political system that operated in Mexico from the 1920s through the 1990s was designed to channel conflict within a single political party that was closely tied to the state. This system created a set of broadly understood informal rules for settling differences among divergent political leaderships

---

1. See fig. 3.4 for detailed information and sources. Federal expenditures were around 90 percent of all public expenditures if we include semiautonomous companies owned by the government, whereas municipalities controlled only 1 percent. If we factor out the state-owned companies, the federal government spent roughly 80 percent and municipalities around 2 percent.

2. The argument that municipalities were always significant actors in Mexico's political system contrasts markedly with Grindle, *Going Local.*

3. Joel Migdal, Atul Kohli, and Vivienne Shue, eds., *State Power and Social Forces: Domination and Transformation in the Third World* (Cambridge: Cambridge University Press, 1994); Peter B. Evans, *Embedded Autonomy: States and Industrial Transformation* (Princeton: Princeton University Press, 1996).

and allowed each to maintain a considerable degree of autonomy within the party. It effectively linked citizens to the political process through complex chains of intermediation that maintained a tight control on the nature of demands and the degree of dissent.

This single-party hegemonic system, however, was built on a history of attempts to reconcile the need for a strong state with the continued influence of local and regional caciques. It merely represented a more successful and durable attempt to do what national political leaders had sought to do for decades: ensure that the centrifugal forces of political power were loyal to central authority in return for the former's continued dominance as intermediaries between citizens and the state. This attempt finally succeeded in consolidating the national government's dominant role, although it was one built in large part on informal power rather than formal institutions and on indirect citizenship rather than a direct relationship between citizens and the state. Centralization avoided the fragmentation of the country, but the state remained relatively small and severely limited in its ability to promote the kind of development that could benefit the majority of citizens. Indeed, total public expenditures in Mexico remained below the average for Latin America and far below that of more developed countries, suggesting that centralization did not produce a strong central state as much as it did weak subnational governments.

Centralization, State Building, and Citizenship

Both centralism and regionalism have been strong currents in Mexican history since the colonial period. The interplay between these two opposing forces, and the way they have been negotiated over time, have shaped the nature of citizenship and the relationship of state power to citizens. In colonial times, the Spanish crown sought to achieve administrative centralization as a means of control and of optimizing the extraction of resources. This conflicted with the reality of colonists who had been granted control of large tracts of land and indigenous communities, which also maintained a degree of autonomy over their internal affairs.[4] Moreover, the Castilian model of governance, which privileged a strong

---

4. As Lorenzo Meyer has observed, "Great distances and abrupt geography played in favor of local interests, as did the relative weakness of the crown, which always needed resources and had a small army. The disputes among local groups, classes, and races, and the legitimacy of the crown vis-à-vis any other form of authority favored the interests of the center." Meyer, "Un tema añejo siempre actual: El centro y las regiones en la historia mexicana," in Blanca Torres, ed., *Descentralización y democracia en México* (Mexico City: El Colegio de México, 1986), 23.

central bureaucracy located in the colonial capital, conflicted with the legacy of the *municipio libre* (free municipality) as the basic unit of government, ruled by a collegial city council and with a degree of guaranteed autonomy from the colonial authorities.[5] Local power holders, generally acting through municipalities or states, largely controlled fiscal resources, and they raised their own armies.[6] However, the viceroy of New Spain was the ultimate arbiter of public authority during the colonial era.[7] Multiple intermediaries, who included large landowners, bilingual indigenous leaders, military commanders, and even elected municipal authorities, served as a bridge between the colonial authorities and their subjects.

Mexico's independence struggle, which lasted from 1810 to 1821, helped shape a new national identity, at least among some elites.[8] But regional interests also emerged strongly after independence, and they would repeatedly challenge the central state. Between 1829 and 1876, Mexico had thirty-six different presidents.[9] After a brief interlude as an empire, Mexico became a federal state in 1824, in large part to negotiate the tension between an emerging national state and strong regional interests. Federalism in Mexico had less to do with a political ideal for building a great, unified country than with creating a solution to the centrifugal forces of regional governments that wanted to break free from central control.[10] Although the states had existed before independence (as provinces), the decision to imbue them with federal powers at the constitutional convention that drafted the 1824 constitution was not the result of sovereign bodies coming

---

5. Véliz, *Centralist Tradition*, 170; Juan Bruno Ubiarco Maldonado, *El federalismo en México y los problemas sociales del país* (Mexico City: Miguel Ángel Porrúa, 2002), 79–80.

6. Fernando Escalante Gonzalbo, *Ciudadanos imaginarios* (Mexico City: El Colegio de México, 1992), 102–7.

7. According to Fernando Escalante Gonzalbo, "Since its constitution, the colonial state was an apparatus for mediation, not only among competing interests but also among bodies with private privileges." Ibid., 109.

8. John Charles Chasteen and Sara Castro-Klarén, *Beyond Imagined Communities: Reading and Writing the Nation in Nineteenth-Century Latin America* (Washington, D.C.: Woodrow Wilson Center Press, 2003), xvii.

9. "The national state was nothing more than an embryo, a project, during the half century that followed independence," according to Lorenzo Meyer, "Un tema añejo," 24.

10. Riker's classic study argues that federalism is about autonomous political units coming together in a "federal bargain" to face common threats, as happened in the United States. William H. Riker, *Federalism: Origin, Operation, Significance* (Boston: Little, Brown, 1964). However, Mexico, like Brazil and Argentina, followed a different model, which Alfred P. Stepan has called "holding-together federalism." Stepan, "Toward a New Comparative Politics of Federalism, Multinationalism, and Democracy: Beyond Rikerian Federalism," in Edward L. Gibson, ed., *Federalism and Democracy in Latin America* (Baltimore: Johns Hopkins University Press, 2004).

together but rather primarily of regional leaders trying to ensure their base of power through the new constitution.

The 1824 constitution also preserved the concept of the free municipality; however, in practice, the nature of the municipality and its functions were left to each state to decide.[11] Despite this, municipalities often enjoyed far-ranging powers, steady sources of income, and internally democratic procedures. They were generally responsible for providing education and basic services, administering the law in local disputes, and organizing elections. They raised revenues through the *alcabalas*, a local tariff on goods passing through a jurisdiction, as well as through other taxes and fees that they levied. Generally, municipalities were run by municipal councils, elected every year with a prohibition on immediate re-election. Councils usually consisted of a *síndico* and a number of council members (*regidores*), and they would elect the mayor from among their members.[12]

However, municipalities were also checked in their authority by the prefects—or political chiefs (*prefectos* or *jefes políticos*)—officials appointed by the federal or state government to preside over districts that included several municipalities and supervise how they exercised their functions and administered their resources. As often as not, the prefects responded to state governors or to regional power holders, rather than to the distant and ever-changing federal government, and the regional elites used the prefects to check the autonomy of the municipalities.[13] Despite the formally defined and legal functions for each level of government, their real operation was thus often determined by informal relations among key power holders.

The tension between the creation of a strong central state and the maintenance of strong regional interests also played out in the nature of the political rights of citizenship. For most of the period after independence, political rights were granted extensively to all male citizens, regardless of ethnic origin or property qualifications.[14] However, the liberal impulse of universal suffrage was checked

---

11. Meyer, "Un tema añejo," 23.
12. Síndicos were—and are today—municipal comptrollers and the officials responsible for the application of the law. I will generally refer to both síndicos and regidores as city council members.
13. Romana Falcón, "Force and the Search for Consent: The Role of the *Jefaturas Políticas* of Coahuila in National State Formation," in Joseph and Nugent, *Everyday Forms of State Formation*.
14. There were short-lived attempts to impose wealth qualifications from 1836 to 1847. Hilda Sabato, "On Political Citizenship in Nineteenth-Century Latin America," *American Historical Review* 106, no. 4 (2001): 1295–96. Overall, however, suffrage was far more extensive and inclusive in Mexico in the 1800s than in the United States. See Erika Pani, "*La calidad de ciudadano*: Past and Present; The Nature of Citizenship in Mexico and the United States: 1776–1912" (Woodrow Wilson Center Latin American Program, Working Paper no. 258, Washington, D.C., July 2002).

by the application of indirect elections, through which voters selected representatives who would, in turn, elect public authorities. For most of the period between 1824 and 1857, elections involved a three-layer process, where ever-smaller numbers of elected representatives selected the next set of authorities above them. This meant that political citizenship was largely universal but real decision-making authority fell on small, elite groups of citizens.[15] Mexico thus succeeded in simultaneously ensuring both universal political citizenship and elite rule; political rights were widespread but not directly correlated with political power.[16] Citizens had the right to elect intermediaries who voted for political leaders but not to participate directly in the selection process themselves.[17]

After decades of strife between two ideological camps, known as the Liberals and the Conservatives, the Liberals finally emerged triumphant under President Benito Juárez in 1867 and reestablished the Constitution of 1857, which had been ratified a decade before but largely left unimplemented due to civil war and a period of monarchy. The 1857 constitution would remain the law of the land for fifty years. The Liberals believed philosophically in a strong federalism, with municipal autonomy. At the same time, their desire to spur economic development required overcoming the endemic weakness of the central state. These were, by no means, incompatible goals, in theory; however, in practice, a state facing constant challenges from regional elites required centralization to create stability and growth.[18] Almost half of the country's territory had been lost in a war

15. According to Sabato, municipal governments organized the first round of national elections and most male citizens could vote. However, political participation was low, almost always below 5 percent (in one exception, turnout for the 1851 Mexican general election was 20 percent). However, only those individuals with the time and resources to participate in politics and travel to the capital could afford to stand for federal or state legislative positions. Moreover, in some periods, there were also property and literacy requirements for being elected to the second and third tiers of the political structure, even though suffrage was universal to all males in the first tier. Sabato, "On Political Citizenship."

16. The United States, for example, had significantly restricted citizenship (women, African Americans, and many who did not meet economic or literacy tests were excluded), but those included as full citizens wielded a great deal of political power. In Mexico, in contrast, more people were included in full citizenship, but citizenship had less influence overall in the political process. Pani, "Calidad de ciudadano."

17. The limited worth of citizenship as a tool for political empowerment was compounded by the instability of the political system during the first five decades after independence. Although elections for local, state, and national political leaders occurred regularly and all of Mexico's many constitutions in the nineteenth century (save one) reaffirmed a commitment to democracy, real power had less to do with elections than with ongoing skirmishes—some violent, some political—among competing politicians.

18. Meyer, "Un tema añejo," 26–27. Florencia Mallon observes that "this tension between the decentralization and regional articulation of interests, and the need to revindicate the principle of authority and the centralization of power, lay at the center of all Liberal debates and practice from the time of the Ayutla Revolution and the Constitutional Convention of 1856–57. It reemerged during the Restored Republic in the conflict between Juarismo and the defenders of communitarian Liberalism." Mallon,

with the United States in 1846–48, and the economy was stagnant.[19] Juárez succeeded in building a stronger central state by suppressing rival military leaders, taking over land and functions from the Church, and imposing an increasingly centralized structure of local prefects.[20] In addition, the president put down a series of military rebellions in the first years of his government, which established the military superiority of the central government vis-à-vis the regional centers of power.[21]

Despite these moves to concentrate central power, the 1857 constitution also reaffirmed federalism in favor of the states and municipalities, giving them a primary role in raising taxes, recruiting the national army, and running elections.[22] Equally important, not all regional leaders could be suppressed by force. The Liberal leaders had to make deals with many of them to ensure order. In many cases, the prefects ended up responding to the interests of the state governors rather than the central government, even though they nominally represented the president in the district.[23] At the same time, peasant organizations shaped the contours of the new political order, sometimes allying with the federal government against local elites, sometimes with local landowners against an increasingly invasive state.[24] It was a period of political change and the construction of a stronger central state, but the nature of this state-building process was in constant tension with other forms of power outside Mexico City.[25]

These changes in the role of the central state necessarily had a profound effect on the nature of citizenship as well. The liberals replaced the onerous three-tiered election system with one that had only one tier, so citizens were now only one step removed from electing their representatives rather than three steps.

Peasant and Nation: The Making of Postcolonial Mexico and Peru (Berkeley: University of California Press, 1995), 133.

19. Meyer notes that total GDP had contracted 10 percent from the start of the century. See Meyer, "Un tema añejo," 25–26.

20. Liberals expropriated church properties and took over key functions that the church had previously performed, including the registration of births, deaths, and marriage and the provision of education, health care, and social services. Véliz, *Centralist Tradition*, 193.

21. As Enrique Krauze has noted, "Under Juárez, the various states and regions learned a lesson that would always apply in the future. No regional cacique, no caudillo or general could truly oppose the center. Juárez inaugurated an era and an irreversible historical tendency, a fundamental centralism employing federal forms." Krauze, *Mexico: Biography of Power* (New York: Perennial, 1998), 198.

22. Escalante Gonzalbo, *Ciudadanos imaginarios*, 133.

23. Falcón, "Force and the Search for Consent"; Escalante Gonzalbo, *Ciudadanos imaginarios*, 101–2.

24. Mallon, *Peasant and Nation*, 242–43.

25. As Escalante Gonzalbo has written, the state increased its ability to make rules, but ultimately it "did not impose its rules, it negotiated their application" with the range of regional actors who contested state power. Escalante Gonzalbo, *Ciudadanos imaginarios*, 129.

The wars between Liberals and Conservatives had also shaken up the social structure of many towns, creating new community leaderships and new regional caciques.[26] At the same time, laws abolishing communal property led to local landowners buying up newly privatized land from impoverished peasants, which resulted in a dramatic concentration of landholdings and created new forms of control by landowners.[27] Meanwhile, the expanded state bureaucracy created a new urban middle class, largely employed in government, newspapers, and commercial occupations. Members of this middle class also created new forms of civic association in the cities that could be considered an embryonic civil society.[28] The period following the Liberal victory was one of rapid social change and new leadership, but most citizens remained connected to political power through local and regional intermediaries, although the individuals who served as intermediaries often changed due to the turbulence.

After a few shorter periods of rule by other Liberal leaders (and rebellions by still others), Porfirio Díaz, one of Juárez's former lieutenants, seized presidential power in 1876 and ruled uninterrupted, in one way or another, until 1910.[29] He succeeded in the liberal project of creating a strong central state that could generate spectacular economic growth, but he did so at the expense of equity, federalism, and democracy. He created many of the new state institutions, including the central bank; attracted foreign investment at an unprecedented rate; and multiplied the country's roads and railroads.[30] This growth generated an extensive infrastructure that was necessary for modern development, but the economic benefits accrued almost exclusively to a small group of Mexican businesspeople and landowners with ties to the central bank and to U.S. and British investors. By the end of Diaz's government, three-quarters of Mexico's population was rural, of whom 90 to 95 percent were landless.[31] The impoverishment of Mexico's

---

26. Mallon, *Peasant and Nation*, 242–43. *Cacique* is a Mexican term for a local strongman (or woman).

27. This would prove to be a recurring theme in Mexican history: every time the state abolished communal land, peasants would sell their newly privatized plots, leading to a concentration of land in the hands of only a few landowners.

28. Luis Javier Garrido, *El partido de la revolución institucionalizada: La formación del nuevo estado (1928–1945)* (Mexico City: Siglo XXI, 1982), 30; Sabato, "On Political Citizenship."

29. He briefly relinquished the title of president from 1880 to 1884 but retained de facto power even then.

30. During this period, the GDP multiplied 3.2 times; roads increased from 893 km to 19,205 km; silver production soared from 25 million pesos to 85 million; and exports jumped from 60 million to 270 million. Meyer, "Un tema añejo," 28.

31. Nora Hamilton, *The Limits of State Autonomy: Post-Revolutionary Mexico* (Princeton: Princeton University Press, 1982), 48–55. See Peter H. Smith, *Labyrinths of Power: Political Recruitment in Twentieth-Century Mexico* (Princeton: Princeton University Press, 1979), 30, on the role of foreign investors.

rural population was coupled with a tightening of control over local governments and the elimination of any vestiges of democratic rule. Díaz abolished the alcabalas and reinforced the rule of the prefects.[32] He used a heavy hand against many regional caciques, while co-opting others by giving them access to the benefits of the growing economy. Although elections continued to take place, he ensured that he would win reelection repeatedly and that his preferred candidates for Congress and state and local office would do so as well.

By the early part of the new century, dissent had begun to spread. The burgeoning middle class, created by the growing economy and the expanding central bureaucracy, resented the lack of political space left by Díaz's authoritarian rule, and the rural poor resented the loss of land and of economic opportunities. Some regional oligarchs, who wanted greater political influence, joined in the growing discontent. By 1910, these disparate factions had taken up arms against Díaz, and war spread throughout Mexico. Díaz fled. After a brief rule by liberal opposition leader Francisco Madero, followed by a coup in which he was killed, the country descended into anarchy and internecine warfare that continued until 1920. The country's period of most dramatic centralization ended in the complete collapse of the state.

Institutionalizing the Revolution

As North has observed, institutions have an inherent "embeddedness" that can often survive even major regime changes.[33] In Mexico, most of the strong central institutions built by Díaz collapsed during the ten-year civil war known as the Mexican Revolution. The postrevolutionary government that took power after 1920[34] faced a country in economic ruin, with powerful new generals in control of parts of the countryside and a mobilized peasantry. However, within a few

---

32. The alcabalas were eliminated originally by the Ley Lerdo (Lerdo Law) of 1856 and constitutionally banned by the Constitution of 1857, which also nationalized much of the property of the Catholic Church. However, it is unclear how much of an impact this had initially. The Ley Lerdo was revoked in 1862, but it was reinstated in 1884 under Díaz. For more detail on this point, see María del Refugio González, "Debates sobre el régimen del municipio en México en el siglo XIX," in *Estudios Municipales*, no. 13 (January–February 1987): 145–63.

33. Douglass C. North, *Institutions, Institutional Change, and Economic Performance* (Cambridge: Cambridge University Press, 1990), 6.

34. The date is somewhat artificial given that 1920 marks a point when most revolutionary forces had either accepted central rule or been defeated. The new constitution was ratified in 1917.

years, they had succeeded in reconstructing many of the key institutions that had ensured strong central rule, and they created new institutions to complement these. Presidents Álvaro Obregón (1920–24) and Plutarco Calles (1924–29) reestablished the central bank and a professional national army; instituted a national income tax; created a series of government agencies to deal with pressing national challenges; and won passage of an elaborate national labor law to respond to the demands of unionized workers who had participated in the Revolution.[35] Despite these new institutions, the central state faced an ongoing challenge from regional military leaders who had participated in the Revolution.[36] The government benefited from rapid economic growth, influenced partly by the global economic boom of the 1920s, which often allowed them to co-opt regional leaders by giving them a stake in the country's growth.[37] However, the re-creation of strong central state institutions competed with the centrifugal forces of the revolutionary elites who challenged central control at every turn.

Two key institutions also played a decisive role in extending the federal government's central control in this period. The government launched an agrarian reform that granted communal landholdings, known as *ejidos*, to thousands of peasant farmers across the country. This land could not be sold or taxed. Similarly, it started an ambitious program to extend education throughout the country. The Public Education Department (Secretaría de Educación Pública), created in 1921, set about to institutionalize education, which until then had been largely limited to urban areas and dominated by municipality-run schools. It built and staffed schools throughout the country, especially in rural areas.[38]

These measures laid the foundation for greater centralization of the state, but this process needed a political project to complete it and rein in the constant

---

35. The institutions created during the first years after the Revolution's end included the National Power Commission, 1922; National Electrical Commission, 1926; and Central Bank, 1925. The national income tax laws were passed between 1924 and 1927, and the federal labor law was passed in 1931. For an extensive list, see Hamilton, *Limits of State Autonomy*, 79–82; and Kevin Middlebrook, *The Paradox of Revolution: Labor, the State, and Authoritarianism in Mexico* (Baltimore: Johns Hopkins University Press, 1995), 23–25.

36. Vaughan notes that in the first years after the Revolution, "political power was more effectively lodged in the states where civilian and military governors and military zone commanders often vied against one another and correspondingly against the federal government. Some regional power holders opposed structural change and allied with traditional elites against increasing mass mobilization. Others sided with peasants and workers—sometimes on principle and often as a means of building power bases to be reckoned with at the national level." Mary Kay Vaughan, *The State, Education, and Class in Mexico, 1880–1928* (DeKalb: Northern Illinois University Press, 1982), 127.

37. Hamilton, *Limits of State Autonomy*, 76–81; Meyer, "Un tema añejo."

38. Vaughan, *State, Education, and Class*, 271.

challenges from regional power holders. In 1928, the assassination of former President Obregón, recently elected to a new term, created the critical moment for President Calles to launch a bold proposal: the creation of a single political party that would bring together all of the revolutionary elites and "institutionalize" the Revolution.[39] This was hardly a new idea, but the crisis of Obregón's assassination provided the strategic moment to allow this to happen.[40] The party, originally called the National Revolutionary Party (PNR, Partido Nacional Revolucionario), was formed in 1929 with the participation of key revolutionary elites from all over the country, including regional power holders and governors (often, but not always, the same), union and peasant leaders, and federal government officials. It was an elite pact among those who had a claim on the revolutionary legacy, and it specifically excluded business leaders and the Church.

Dissent and disagreement, embodied in the constant and often violent power struggles among competing elites, would now be institutionalized within one official revolutionary family, headed by the president. The PNR, as Lorenzo Meyer has observed, "was born not to fight for power but to administer it without sharing."[41] Everyone could compete for power, as long as each person did so within the confines of the party. Initially, it was almost a "party of parties," with strong local and regional committees receiving campaign money from the central committee, and "a kind of confederation of caciques," who agreed to play by the same rules in competing among themselves.[42] However, Calles clearly saw the party as a means to centralize authority as well as limit conflict.[43]

---

39. Alan Knight, "Mexico's Elite Settlement: Conjuncture and Consequences," in John Higley and Richard Gunther, eds., *Elites and Democratic Consolidation in Latin America and Southern Europe* (Cambridge: Cambridge University Press, 1992), 115.

40. Ibid., 116–18. According to Knight, the assassination proved critical in part because it left only one of the two national leaders (Obregón and Calles) alive and with absolute authority; Obregón's supporters, who distrusted Calles, were happy to have an institutional structure that checked Calles's authority, and Calles's supporters were willing to support the proposal since Calles would lead the new party. According to Knight, "The crisis of 1928 made possible a successful process of settlement, in which elite decisions and conflicts were played out in a situation of flux and uncertainty, but such a settlement was, we might say, latent in the revolutionary legacy" (118).

41. Meyer, "Un tema añejo," 31.

42. Garrido, *Partido de la revolución institucionalizada*, 123–25.

43. According to Knight, "In light of this political panorama, the elite settlement of 1928–9 must be seen as a key element in the central government's battle to assert its power over divergent political and regional interests. The institutionalization that Calles proclaimed implied a further attenuation of independent political movements (of both right and left) in the provinces. The elite settlement thus reflected a clear perception—by Calles and his collaborators—that power had to be centralized, to the advantage of the regime and to the detriment of both popular and regional forces." Knight, "Mexico's Elite Settlement," 128.

In the years after the party's founding, violent power struggles among regional elites and between them and the central government dropped dramatically. Conflict and contestation continued, as they would throughout the twentieth century even as the party consolidated its grip on power, but these took place increasingly within the revolutionary family as delineated by the PNR. Attempts by outside groups to challenge the official party also helped unify party members and solidify the elite pact. Belonging to the revolutionary family entailed obligations to respect the formal and informal rules that would develop within the party and its hierarchies, with the country's president at the apex; however, belonging to the family also ensured members the right to participate in politics and share in the spoils of government.

One of the important banners of the Revolution had been greater municipal autonomy and the abolition of the prefects. The 1917 constitution, which was approved by the main revolutionary factions, recognized the idea of municipal autonomy without giving it much content. It did ban the prefects by forbidding any authority between the states and municipal governments; however, it also granted no specific powers to municipalities, leaving the definition of their role and their fiscal powers to the state constitutions.[44] Article 115 of the constitution, as originally written, simply stated that the municipalities had legal jurisdiction, should have an elected government, and could administer their own treasury based on rules imposed by the state governments.[45] Similarly, the constitution, which is still in effect today, gave few explicit functions to states that were not also shared with the federal government. Institutionally, therefore, the stage was set for the states to dominate the municipalities. Over time, the federal government would do the same to the states and, by extension, to the municipalities.

By 1980, the federal government concentrated around nine-tenths of all public income and left little tax base to the states and municipalities (fig. 2.1). Most of the reduction of subnational finances in favor of the federation came through agreements between the state and federal governments in a series of fiscal pacts

---

44. Lorenzo Meyer, "El municipio mexicano al final del siglo XX: Historia, obstáculos y posibilidades," in Mauricio Merino Huerta, ed., *En busca de la democracia municipal: La participación ciudadana en el gobierno local mexicano* (Mexico City: El Colegio de México, 1994), 237–39.

45. Constitución Política de los Estados Unidos Mexicanos, 1917 (original text). Article 115 would remain virtually unchanged until 1983. There were minor constitutional changes made to the article in 1933 (prohibiting the reelection of mayors and city councillors), 1943 (of little substance), 1947 (allowing women to vote), and 1971 (allowing the federal government to remove mayors in territories), but none touched on the substance of the municipality's functions, resource base, or political structure. Meyer, "Municipio mexicano," 241–42.

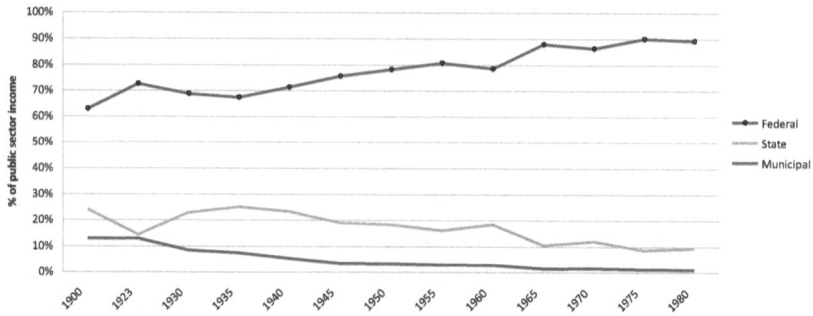

Fig. 2.1 Total public sector income by level of government, 1900–1980

Note: State expenditures include the Federal District.

SOURCE: Alberto Díaz Cayeros, *Desarrollo económico e inequidad regional: Hacia un nuevo pacto federal en México* (Mexico City: CIDAC and Miguel Ángel Porrúa, 1995), 82.

signed between 1942 and 1980. The final pact, in 1980, created the sales tax, collected by the federation and shared with the states through a distribution formula.[46] In an expanding economy, both states and municipalities continued to gain net income over time, which made the pacts palatable, even as these subnational governments had to cede fiscal powers to the federal government.[47]

It was ultimately the political dimension of centralization, more than the structural limitations of the constitution, that permitted the concentration of powers in the central state and also facilitated the creation of an authoritarian political system.[48] Although the PNR began as an elite pact to contain conflict among revolutionary leaders, under President Lázaro Cárdenas (1934–40), it became a true mass party, organized top-down and with the ability to mobilize citizens ideologically by incorporating a discourse (and sometimes a reality) of popular demands. Even though he was Calles' handpicked successor, Cárdenas exiled his mentor and removed most of Calles' allies from his government and from a number of state governorships.[49] He then reorganized the party along sectoral lines, essentially gutting the regional and local structures in favor of four sectors that represented peasants, labor, popular organizations, and the military. Each of these sectors was vertically integrated and responded, at the pinnacle, to presidential

---

46. Alberto Díaz Cayeros, *Desarrollo económico e inequidad regional: Hacia un nuevo pacto federal en México* (Mexico City: CIDAC and Miguel Ángel Porrúa, 1995), 65–67.
47. Aboites Aguilar, *Excepciones y privilegios,* 34–39.
48. Cf. Díaz Cayeros, *Federalism,* especially 96–97.
49. Meyer, "Un tema añejo," 31–32.

leadership. The state and municipal committees remained, but real power negotiations now took place among the sectors and their leaders (although the state and municipal committees would regain a degree of power at other moments in history and compete with the sectors within the party).[50]

Cárdenas was moving the party from a pact among revolutionary leaders to a mass political party that would mediate between citizens and the state. Renamed the Mexican Revolutionary Party (PRM, Partido Revolucionario Mexicano) in 1938, it developed a true peasant and labor base and appropriated the discourses of these organized social sectors.[51] This discourse was backed up by actions. Cárdenas implemented a far-reaching land reform and expropriated foreign oil companies, winning the loyalty of peasants and expanding the resource base for the federal government.

Buoyed by these resources and with a strong base of popular support, the official party dominated Mexico's political life for seven decades. In 1946, it was renamed the Institutional Revolutionary Party (PRI, Partido Revolucionario Institucional), and it would win every election for president, governors, and senators (with one exception in the Senate) from the late 1930s through 1988. The party almost certainly resorted to fraud in the presidential elections of 1940 and 1988 and in many state and local elections as well; however, it remained the undisputed party of power. The PRI lost a handful of municipal elections in these decades, but opposition rule was usually short-lived.[52]

The PRI was bound tightly to the federal government. The president was the de facto leader of the party, although it had its own nominally separate leadership, and in each state, the governor served as the de facto party leader as well. Separate from these state leaderships, the party's sectors (which were reduced to three after the elimination of the military sector in 1940[53]) held influence within the party structure. However, the party was created and shaped by the country's presidents, and the government ran the party more than the party ran

---

50. Garrido, *Partido de la revolución institucionalizada*, 293–95.
51. Ibid., 295.
52. The notable opposition governments were León, Guanajuato, in 1945 and San Luis Potosí, San Luis Potosí, in 1958. However, both opposition victories lasted for only one term. In San Luis Potosí, the mayor ended up in jail after trying to run for governor; in the case of León—an opposition victory that cost numerous lives—the opposition party divided after the federal government starved the municipality for resources and bought off party sympathizers. See Meyer, "Municipio mexicano," 245–48.
53. For a history of civil-military relations in Mexico, inside and outside the PRI, see Raúl Benítez Manaut, "Security and Governance: The Urgent Need for State Reform," in Joseph S. Tulchin and Andrew D. Selee, eds., *Mexico's Politics and Society in Transition* (Boulder: Lynne Rienner, 2003).

the government.[54] The Revolution built on Porfirio Díaz's "bread or bludgeon" method. But whereas Porfirio's order was based on being friends with the president, the PRI was based on negotiating differences within "the system." As Enrique Krauze has written, "The assumption, which came to be widely shared, was that all individuals or groups could rise—or at least not lose hope of rising—in the social and economic scale, provided they did it amicably *within the system*, not independently outside of it."[55]

The one-party dominant state developed several legal and extralegal mechanisms that ensured upward accountability among the ranks of career politicians. Amendments to the constitution in the 1930s outlawed reelection in all elected positions. This reelection ban forced politicians to depend continuously on the will of party leaders—and influential patrons higher in the party—to promote them to new positions once their term had ended. This provision, in theory, served to circulate party elites and instill loyalty to the party, over all else. To some extent, party circulation helped undermine local power holders whose livelihood depended on exclusive control over a jurisdiction; however, as we will see in the coming chapters, this was only partially the case. Many politicians made their careers as political brokers in their hometowns, even if they had brief stints in national office that took them away. Nevertheless, circularity undermined almost any sense of accountability to constituents that politicians might have felt, because their next job depended less on performance in their public duties than on party loyalty.

Similarly, federal and state constitutions allowed the federal Senate to remove governors, as well as for governors or state legislatures to remove mayors.[56] These provisions created powerful incentives for lower levels of government to obey upper levels. Although the Senate removed governors only occasionally—and always at the behest of the president—the dependence of lower-level officials on those above them for eventual promotion to political posts meant that higher-level officials could almost always demand the resignation of officials below them as needed, even without pursuing legal channels. Dozens of governors were forced to resign by the president—as were hundreds of mayors by their governors—during the period of PRI dominance. In time, the PRI developed an institutional

---

54. Smith, *Labyrinths of Power*, 57.
55. Krauze, *Mexico: Biography of Power*, 551.
56. Pablo González Casanova reports that in the early 1960s, thirteen states had constitutional provisions that allowed governors to remove mayors at will. González Casanova, *Democracia en México* (1965; repr., Mexico City: Ediciones Era, 1997), 37–43.

culture where politicians knew they would be taken care of as long as they stayed within the party and obeyed those who were more powerful than they were, even if it meant periods of sacrifice. As one popular joke among politicians ran, "it doesn't matter if the glass is half full or half empty, only that you are in the glass."

Municipalities thus became links in the chain of political power. With few defined functions, limited resources, and almost no fiscal powers, they became primarily stepping-stones for aspiring local politicians and conduits for higher levels of government to maintain control over local affairs. However, this function was no minor matter. Municipalities served as arenas for contesting local political differences and generating demands upward through the party and state leadership. At the same time, a mayor's hope for moving up in politics depended first on maintaining control over dissent and, second, on obtaining from the state or federal government a few funds to carry out projects to benefit his (or, in rare cases, her) constituents. The internal structures of municipalities reflected the profoundly authoritarian nature of their design. The mayoral candidates ran for election with a slate of handpicked candidates for city council. If the PRI candidate won, as he or she usually did, the entire slate of council candidates would be installed in the council.[57] The lack of political plurality within city councils and the nature of their election on a party list chosen by the mayor meant that city councils had few real functions, and most citizens knew little about the council members or about what they did.

The creation and consolidation of the PRI as the party of power, together with the centralization of government functions and resources, successfully replaced the centrifugal forces of regional power holders with a functional structure for negotiating differences among political actors. Whereas the central state in the nineteenth century—and again immediately after the Revolution—had depended on alliances with regional caudillos and caciques for its survival, the state now depended on a complex network of political leaders who were tied together by their common loyalty to the official party. The PRI's promotion of elite circulation helped reduce the dominant control of single families over certain states, eventually ending the era of the true caudillos, who had been the unquestioned

---

57. It is unclear when state constitutions changed to include a single winning slate. In the early period after the Revolution, candidates often ran individually, with or without a party, and the council picked the mayor from among their number. As will be discussed below, opposition candidates were allowed to win seats on some city councils starting in 1977. Blanca Acedo, "Los sistemas electorales municipales en México: La incorporación del principio de representación proporcional," in Jacqueline Martínez Uriarte and Alberto Díaz Cayeros, eds., *De la descentralización al federalismo: Estudios comparados sobre el gobierno local en México* (Mexico City: Miguel Ángel Porrúa and CIDAC, 2003), 281–86.

authority in their states,[58] and making way for multiple families, who would share and compete over regional power.[59] This circularity also gave rise to multiple local caciques, who were important brokers within neighborhoods, rural villages, or specific party organizations (including unions and rural federations) and who held specific power within defined arenas.[60] The way these intermediaries were organized and how they related to those above and below them varied greatly from region to region and locality to locality.

The consolidation of the PRI thus managed to alter many of the bases of political power (and the specific leaders involved), but its functioning was also deeply rooted in the structure of nineteenth-century politics. Although all citizens could participate in elections, they had little ability to decide who was elected. Candidates were selected from above in the political hierarchy, and the PRI candidates were ensured of victory. Therefore, although indirect elections had been abolished, citizens still participated in electoral decisions only indirectly. The PRI became a vehicle for numerous patronage networks that mediated between citizens and the state. This helped channel collective action toward ends that were localized and fragmented.[61] In the nineteenth century, patronage networks had been closely tied to individual leaders who maintained a tight grip on local politics within their domain. Under the PRI, the circulation of leaders meant that individual leaders were more constrained, but party organizations and networks of politicians became increasingly important. Within the PRI, local organizations—whether municipal party committees, neighborhood organizations, or union locals—were linked upward into ever larger second- and third-tier organizations that ultimately were part of one of the party's sectors. Clientelism—the unequal exchange of political support for public benefits—linked citizens to particular organizations and to their leaders at the local level. Corporatism within the national and state PRI connected these organizations within vertical party hierarchies.

---

58. Some states did continue to have a single dominant family, but these generally became political groups that reached out beyond the immediate family, and they had to compete with other political groups within the party. See, for example, the case of the Figueroa family in Guerrero discussed in chapter 4 or the Grupo Atlacomulco discussed in chapter 6.

59. For a detailed account of specific forms of caudillismo and caciquismo in modern Mexico, see Alan Knight and Wil Pansters, eds., *Caciquismo in Twentieth-Century Mexico* (London: Institute of Latin American Studies, School of Advanced Study, University of London, 2005).

60. As Pablo González Casanova has indicated, "all the processes for concentrating presidential power have from their origin, as one of their functions, the control of the *caciques*—of their parties, their followers, their mayors—a phenomenon that does not imply, except indirectly, the disappearance of the caciques." González Casanova, *Democracia en México*, 48.

61. Tulchin and Selee, *Mexico's Politics*, 8.

Political hegemony is never complete, however, and the dominance of the PRI as a single national party masked considerable contestation and negotiation taking place in Mexico. Clientelism was not only a top-down relationship to control dissent but also a bottom-up relationship, which gave citizens regular channels to negotiate demands and express preferences. Although municipal governments and PRI-affiliated organizations were ultimately controlled from above, they also served as sites for struggle and the constant renegotiation of power relationships.[62] Political leaders fought against one another for control of municipal governments and of PRI-affiliated social organizations. Citizens used party structures to mobilize around key demands and needs. The PRI succeeded largely because it was capable of responding to and incorporating demands and discourses from below. Citizens and local politicians had to negotiate demands in an unequal context, in which state and party hierarchies had the last word. The party was sufficiently flexible, however, so that it was able to contain large-scale social discontent for decades, in no small part because it tolerated dissent and contestation within its ranks and was able to incorporate—and co-opt—citizen demands and discourses. The hegemony of the official party (and of the state) was constantly negotiated at local, regional, and national levels.[63]

Contestation also took place outside the party, and the state and its official party allowed a degree of nonofficial opposition. The National Action Party (PAN), founded in 1946, provided a right-of-center alternative to the PRI in many municipalities (and the Federal District) and had an important support base among the middle class. The PAN won a number of municipalities from its creation through the 1970s, including two state capitals (Mérida, Yucatán, and Hermosillo, Sonora) in the 1968 elections.[64] It provided an ongoing challenge to the PRI in several states, especially Baja California, Chihuahua, and Guanajuato, as well as in the Federal District.[65] Two other small "parastatal" parties, the Popular Socialist Party (PPS, Partido Popular Socialista) and the Authentic

---

62. On this point, see Mallon, *Peasant and Nation*; Mary Kay Vaughan, "Cultural Approaches to Peasant Politics in the Mexican Revolution," *Hispanic American Historical Review* 79, no. 2 (May 1999): 269–305; Jeffrey W. Rubin, *Decentering the Regime: Ethnicity, Radicalism, and Democracy in Juchitán, Mexico* (Durham: Duke University Press, 1997); and Joseph and Nugent, *Everyday Forms of State Formation*.

63. For concrete examples, see the discussion of local contestation in chapters 4–6 in this volume.

64. Of Mexico's more than two thousand municipalities, the PAN won one municipality in the 1940s, fourteen in the 1950s, twenty in the 1960s, and thirty-two in the 1970s. Acedo, "Los sistemas electorales municipales en México."

65. Chapter 3 describes the active presence of the PAN in Baja California, where the party almost certainly won the 1968 municipal elections in Tijuana and the state capital, Mexicali, though the victories were never recognized, and consistently presented an electoral alternative to the PRI.

Party of the Mexican Revolution (PARM, Partido Auténtico de la Revolución Mexicana), were also a loyal opposition that gave a façade of democratic competition and occasionally provided a real vehicle for dissent. Mexican leaders were mindful of the importance of the appearance of opposition outside the official party and its utility for creating an escape valve for social conflict. In 1977, following a period of increasing social conflict, the federal government recognized the long-outlawed Communist Party (PCM, Partido Comunista Mexicano). At the same time, a constitutional change required all municipalities of more than three hundred thousand inhabitants to include opposition members on their city councils through seats assigned by "proportional representation." This reform, incorporated into state constitutions as the decade closed, greatly expanded the presence of opposition parties in the councils of major cities, although it still guaranteed the PRI an overwhelming majority in each one. The constitutional change also increased the number of seats assigned to opposition parties in the federal Congress.

Civic movements also often challenged the boundaries of political control. Local social movements developed frequently around specific demands that political leaders failed to meet.[66] The official party was often able to co-opt leaders of social movements and often the whole movement itself.[67] The economy was growing at a dramatic pace,[68] which allowed government leaders a certain margin of discretion to incorporate pressing demands. Larger social movements, which defied government co-optation, developed from time to time.[69] Each of these larger social movements was ultimately repressed violently as it began to challenge state policy and include demands for democratic opening. However, other, smaller movements maintained a degree of autonomy, by making modest claims for democracy rather than fully challenging state authority. Several smaller left-wing political movements particularly developed along these lines, working

---

66. See the discussions in this volume of the Residents' Restoration Movement (MRC) and several smaller movements in Ciudad Nezahualcóyotl in chapter 6; of CUCUTAC in Tijuana in chapter 5; and of the Urban Popular Movement in Chilpancingo in chapter 4.

67. See, for example, the history of the MRC in Ciudad Nezahualcóyotl described in chapter 6 of this book. Cf. Alan Knight, "Weapons and Arches in the Mexican Revolutionary Landscape," in Joseph and Nugent, *Everyday Forms of State Formation*.

68. The economy grew at annual rates of 7 percent in the 1950s, 8.6 percent in the 1960s, and 7.2 percent between 1970 and 1975. Nora Lustig, *Mexico: The Remaking of an Economy* (Washington, D.C.: Brookings Institution, 1998), 15.

69. These included the teachers' strike of 1956, the railroad strike of 1958, the doctors' strike of 1965, and the student movement of 1968. As will be discussed in chapter 4, there were also significant regional armed movements in Mexico, especially (though by no means exclusively) in the state of Guerrero.

quietly but assiduously around local and regional demands while avoiding full-scale confrontation with the state. In the subsequent chapters, several of these movements are discussed in more detail. In the 1970s, with the dramatic explosion of major cities, a series of urban social movements began to coalesce in towns throughout Mexico, and toward the end of the 1970s, they began to form national federations. These movements generally mixed concrete demands for land titles and basic services (electricity, water, sewage) with political demands for democracy. Although sometimes co-opted and occasionally repressed, these movements became one of the most sustained challenges to the hegemony of the PRI. They avoided full-scale repression in large part because they were willing to negotiate with the government around concrete demands.

Overall, the Mexican state and its official party preferred to co-opt, when they could, and adapt, when necessary. They tolerated considerable contestation on specific decisions related to resource allocation, but they did not tolerate challenges to their overall power, the basic outlines of the political system, or major national policy questions considered of vital national importance.[70] For a country with a recent memory of war, this system provided stability and an institutional means for resolving conflict peacefully. For a rapidly growing country, it provided mechanisms for sharing the benefits of economic expansion, albeit unequally, among those involved in politics. For the poor, it provided a small measure of security and even influence in politics, although this was mediated by clientelistic channels. What Mexico's political system could not provide was a more democratic relationship between citizens and the state or an equitable process for national growth and development.

Although the Mexican state by 1980 was extremely centralized, even in comparison to other countries in the Western Hemisphere,[71] the system also required the central government to cede power to informal arrangements between political power holders. The formal centralization of the state thus contrasted sharply with the continued existence of multiple centers of informal power built on interpersonal bargains and clientelistic networks. Political elites had to swear ultimate

---

70. Tulchin and Selee, *Mexico's Politics*, 9. According to Stevens, "Some groups have been permitted to express dissent from the choices of national goals, but this dissent is quarantined so that the disagreement is prevented from spreading. This behavior provides the elite with information concerning the effect of its policies while at the same time it places that kind of information beyond the reach of the bulk of the citizenry." Evelyn P. Stevens, *Protest and Response in Mexico* (Cambridge: Massachusetts Institute of Technology Press, 1974), 12.

71. See the comparison of six Latin American countries in Selee, "Introduction," in Tulchin and Selee, *Decentralization and Democratic Governance*.

allegiance to the party (and, therefore, the hierarchy of the state), but in return they received a certain degree of discretion to manage their own networks of power relationships as they saw fit (as long as they maintained order). A centralized state bureaucracy thus coexisted with a highly decentralized web of power relationships mediated through organizations within the official party.

The result of this apparent paradox—an omnipresent centralized government with a pervasive system of informal power—was a state that could channel major conflicts but was constantly undermined in its efforts to regulate economic activity, provide services, and ensure the rule of law.[72] Not surprisingly, central government revenue as a percentage of GDP grew only slowly and noticeably less so than in a number of other countries in the Western Hemisphere. By 1980, Mexico lagged behind much of Latin America in central government revenue and expenditures as a percentage of GDP, despite the ongoing perception of the Mexican state as one of the strongest in Latin America.[73] Moreover, the nature of the bargains within the party necessarily meant a deficient state capacity to enforce the rule of law or create genuinely democratic institutions. As a result, civil and political citizenship, which had been formally universal since independence, was exercised and constantly renegotiated through informal practices of intermediation and clientelism. Even in 1980, as in 1880 and in 1780, citizenship remained somewhat indirect, legally extended to all, yet constantly renegotiated in the interactions between citizens and a range of political brokers who could mediate between citizens' demands and limited state resources.

---

72. Cf. Migdal, *Strong Societies and Weak States*.
73. See the 1980 figures for Latin America in World Bank, *World Development Indicators* (Washington, D.C.: World Bank, 2004), available on CD-Rom.

3 DECENTRALIZATION AND DEMOCRATIZATION

In the 1980s and 1990s, the Mexican state underwent a gradual decentralization at the same time the single-party-dominant state was giving way to greater political plurality. A massive economic crisis that lasted from approximately 1982 until 1997 helped bring about these changes by undermining the legitimacy of the postrevolutionary political order and unraveling the bases of many of the political pacts that had sustained it. The crisis also strengthened citizen demands for greater democratic space and emboldened opposition parties to challenge the regime. These changes, in turn, drove institutional innovation as the regime sought to hold onto power, and civic and political opposition movements pushed to open new spaces for political contestation.

Among the most important institutional innovations pursued by both sides, for different reasons, was decentralization. Opposition political parties and civic organizations saw empowering local government as a means of expanding their presence in the political process, and as they gained a foothold in local governments, opposition leaders sought to increase the functions, powers, and resources of local governments. At the same time, leaders within the official party saw decentralization as a way of deflecting demands for democracy from the national to the local level and forestalling greater political change. Decentralization became, at different times, a banner of all political parties, though often for very different reasons.

Mexico's gradual process of institutional change helped ensure an orderly transformation from a centralized authoritarian state to a decentralized democracy built on consensus among key political actors. Mexico went into the new millennium with a strong party structure while many countries in Latin America lacked stable political parties. States and municipalities often had time to develop the capacities necessary to assume their new responsibilities, unlike the experience of more rapid decentralization reforms elsewhere. Opposition parties also developed leadership at a local level before taking the reins of national power.

However, the exclusive reliance on pacts among political elites meant that their interests were largely preserved in the political system that emerged, and this happened at the expense of changes that might have further opened the democratic process. The electoral changes, for example, kept the prohibition on immediate reelection to any public office and on independent candidacies, which meant that elected officials continued to owe their future careers to party leaders. The municipal structure, with party list elections for municipal council, also remained largely intact. Few attempts were made to create clear rules and procedures for policy making in the federal Congress or most state congresses, leaving legislation subject to informal rules and backroom procedures that are difficult for citizens to monitor. In short, party elites secured their role in the new order—and the preservation of informal channels for wielding power—even as they negotiated changes to the formal structure of the state.

This chapter analyzes the formal changes that took place in the state's structure, with a specific emphasis on the interplay between democratization and decentralization.[1] It looks at the legacies of this period of institutional change to assess the current structure of subnational governments, particularly municipalities, as the period of rapid change draws to a close. In the subsequent chapters, we will look in depth at the way these changes affected the relationship between citizens and the state and whether they produced more accountable and responsive government at the local level.

Changing to Stay the Same (1982–1994)

Mexico's process of institutional change—that took its first steps in the 1980s and accelerated dramatically in the second half of the 1990s—had its roots in the nature of the system itself. Although the political system that prevailed from the late 1920s through the 1990s was, without a doubt, both authoritarian and

---

1. Several studies have covered Mexico's democratic transition thoroughly, so we will not analyze this process in depth here. The emphasis instead is on the interplay between democratization and decentralization. For studies of democratization, see Selee and Peschard, *Mexico's Democratic Challenges*; Magaloni, *Voting for Autocracy*; Camp, *Politics in Mexico*; Merino Huerta, *La transición votada*; and Middlebrook, *Dilemmas of Political Change*.

highly centralized, there were significant spaces of political contestation both inside and outside the official party, and the centralized structure of the state coexisted with a highly diffuse distribution of real power. Elections were largely meaningless as a method for selecting leaders since the PRI almost always won. Nevertheless, the party allowed for leadership circulation within it and tolerated a degree of popular mobilization outside of it, as well.[2] Although the federal government came to dominate state and municipal governments and assumed almost all their official functions, local political leaders continued to enjoy a degree of autonomy and influence in the political process despite the weakness of local government structures themselves.

The first period of democratic and decentralizing changes—though initially quite limited—began in the early 1980s with the advent of a severe economic crisis that would last through much of the next two decades. As international interest rates shot up and Mexico found itself unable to repay its debts, President José López Portillo (1976–82) declared a moratorium on those payments shortly before leaving office. His successor, Miguel de la Madrid (1982–88), was left to pick up the pieces. He began a period of major austerity measures that reduced public expenditures, and he adopted the first of a series of neoliberal reforms that would dominate economic policy making in years to follow. He also set in motion a very limited political opening, largely an attempt to strengthen municipalities. These efforts were spurred by the growing discontent citizens expressed toward the government's handling of the economic crisis. In the 1983 municipal elections, their frustration produced the first-ever significant losses for the PRI,[3] as the PAN won several state capitals and medium-sized cities, mostly in the north.[4]

During the 1982 presidential campaign, de la Madrid had proposed a constitutional reform to strengthen municipalities, and he submitted this proposal to

---

2. See chapter 2 for a more thorough discussion of these points. It should be noted that elections did serve the purpose of mobilizing the party base, and they provided citizens with some leverage in negotiating for concrete demands around election time, even if the outcome was almost certain. The party's desire for legitimacy meant that ensuring good turnout and a comfortable victory at election time was essential, and citizens could use these moments to advance their specific causes.

3. Victoria E. Rodríguez, *Decentralization in Mexico: From Reforma Municipal to Solidaridad to Nuevo Federalismo* (Boulder: Westview Press, 1997), 1 and 109; Cabrero Mendoza, *Las políticas descentralizadoras*, 17.

4. In the elections of 1983, the PAN won approximately thirty cities, including the state capitals of Chihuahua, Durango, Sonora, and San Luis Potosí, plus the major border city Ciudad Juárez. For an analysis of the 1983 elections, see Carlos Martínez Assad and Jorge Alonso, eds., *Municipios en conflicto* (Mexico City: UNAM, 1985).

Congress within five days of taking office. The changes to the constitution's article 115, which regulates municipalities, passed in 1983 and took effect on January 1, 1984. Under the amended article, municipalities rather than the states could levy property taxes, and they had full ownership over their own property, which state governments had previously held. Municipalities were also given the right to determine their own internal processes for governance, including municipal planning, budgeting, and the passing of regulations on matters within their territory. In addition, municipalities were granted the right to provide and maintain basic municipal services in the areas of water, streets, markets, cemeteries, slaughterhouses, parks and gardens, public security, and local transportation, and to sign agreements with other municipalities or with the state to coordinate efforts.[5] Finally, the reform clarified the procedure for state governments to remove mayors and councils and limited the governor's discretion to do this.[6]

Initially, these reforms made a significant difference only to large municipalities, which could raise new revenues through property taxes and effectively implement their new set of constitutionally protected functions. Smaller municipalities saw little difference in their status. This was especially true in rural places, where tax-exempt communal properties were the predominant form of landownership. Moreover, this period coincided with the most difficult moments of the economic crisis, so that municipal revenue-raising capacity suffered even in the largest municipalities, and rampant inflation undermined the value of existing revenues.[7] The constitutional amendment set the stage for redefining the relationship between municipalities and states.

These reforms were complemented by shifts in both electoral laws and investment procedures, which also set the stage for later developments. A separate electoral reform in 1983 allowed all municipalities to have city council members from minority parties, even while the dominant party retained an overwhelming majority of seats.[8] In 1986, the federal electoral law was further changed to require minority party representation on all municipal councils, which greatly expanded

---

5. According to President Miguel de la Madrid, the changes were "aimed at strengthening the municipality's finances, its political autonomy, and all the faculties that somehow have constantly been absorbed by the states." Cited in Rodríguez, *Decentralization in Mexico*, 74; for an analysis of the reforms, see p. 119. See also Cabrero Mendoza, *Las políticas descentralizadoras*, 108–9.

6. Merino Huerta, *Fuera del centro*, 113–17.

7. Rodríguez, *Decentralization in Mexico*, 119.

8. The 1977 electoral law changes, mentioned in chapter 2, had allowed this for municipalities of over three hundred thousand inhabitants.

the presence of these parties in local politics for the first time.[9] Having gained a foothold in local governments, opposition parties greatly expanded their influence nationally, and this strengthened their desire to compete, even if they won few municipalities outright and rarely held more than one or two seats on the municipal council.

De la Madrid later created a new system for federal government transfers to the states. For the first time, the federal government signed agreements, known as Single Development Agreements (Convenios Únicos de Desarrollo, CUDs), with all states to establish the purpose and amount of transfers from the various secretariats. The federal government still managed most public investments, but in theory, states would now have a say in how those resources were spent. Each state was to have a State Planning Council (Consejo de Planeación para el Desarrollo Estatal, Coplade), which would bring together all three levels of government. Similarly, each municipality would have a Municipal Planning Council (Consejo de Planeación para el Desarrollo Municipal, Copladem or Coplademun), which would bring together key social groups, municipal government officials, and key state and federal officials.[10] Existing evidence suggests that these new systems were rarely used in practice,[11] but they set an important institutional precedent about how the federal government should manage its relationship with states and municipalities, and the Coplade and Copladem structures would be further institutionalized following subsequent reforms.[12]

The election of 1988 shook the political system like no other before it. After six years of deep economic crisis, a coalition of left-of-center parties supported the candidacy of Cuauhtémoc Cárdenas, a popular former PRI governor and

---

9. Enrique Ochoa Reza, "Multiple Arenas of Struggle: Federalism and Mexico's Transition to Democracy," in Gibson, *Federalism and Democracy in Latin America*.

10. Rodríguez, *Decentralization in Mexico*, 73. Coplades were actually created in 1981 under the previous president, José López Portillo, but their functions expanded under de la Madrid. See John Bailey, "Centralism and Political Change in Mexico: The Case of National Solidarity," in Cornelius, Craig, and Fox, *Transforming State-Society Relations*.

11. According to one study, however, only 11–15 percent of federal investment in the states actually was based on Single Development Agreements, and the Coplades had little influence in determining the nature of these investments. Moreover, only 10 percent of municipalities reported that they had created a Copladem, and most planning councils were dominated by the municipal mayor. Cabrero Mendoza, *Las políticas descentralizadoras*, 153–61.

12. The de la Madrid administration also began a gradual decentralization of health care from the federal to state governments, done on a state-by-state basis. It would greatly expand state budgets over the coming years. For a synopsis of this process, see Mizrahi, "Twenty Years of Decentralization in Mexico"; for a full analysis, see Kaufman and Nelson, *Crucial Needs, Weak Incentives*.

son of former president Lázaro Cárdenas. Cuauhtémoc had bolted from the party after failing to democratize its internal procedures. Although PRI candidate Carlos Salinas de Gortari (1988–94) was declared president with just over half the votes, many observers believed that Cárdenas had won the election, and a four-day delay in announcing the election's results stoked suspicion.[13] Salinas started office with limited credibility given his questioned election. To regain legitimacy for the regime, he pursued a series of measures to democratize the political system and decentralize power to local governments without losing control of the political process. His efforts—coupled with divisions among the opposition parties—succeeded in reasserting the PRI's hegemony. However, the measures also created openings that the newly emboldened opposition on both the right and left used to push for changes that were even more ambitious.

The most significant changes were in electoral laws. Among other reforms, the Federal Electoral Institute gained a degree of autonomy by including independent citizen councillors on its board, and it created a hard-to-falsify national voting card. Salinas also recognized the first-ever opposition victory in a state election, when a PAN candidate was elected governor of Baja California (as is discussed in chapter 5). A second PAN governor would win election in Chihuahua three years later. Salinas's administration largely sought to limit the advance of the Democratic Revolutionary Party (PRD), formed by Cárdenas after the 1988 elections, but he opened spaces for the PAN to govern in states and municipalities.

Bent on rebuilding his political base by re-creating the social pact that had existed between the government and the Mexican poor before the crisis, Salinas also initiated an ambitious new social program called Solidarity.[14] In theory, it was to be a participatory, demand-based program, in which the government would provide funds to civic organizations to carry out major public works and productive projects in coordination with the government. Begun in 1989, by 1994, Solidarity accounted for over 6 percent of the programmable budget and around 13 percent of social spending.[15] The program included more than a dozen

---

13. According to official reports, the computer system used for counting votes "crashed" and required four days to start working again. This raised suspicion, because Cárdenas had been ahead in the early vote count before the system went down. For an interesting analysis of these events in the voices of some of the principal actors of the period, see Carmen Aristegui, *La transición: Conversaciones y retratos de lo que se hizo y se dejó de hacer por la democracía en México* (Mexico City: Grijalbo Mondadori, 2009).

14. The full official name was Programa Nacional de Solidaridad (Pronasol), or the National Solidarity Program.

15. Since most of social spending is in education and health care, this is actually a very large number. It represented around 1.08 percent of GDP in 1992. Nora Lustig, "Solidarity as a Strategy for Poverty Alleviation," in Cornelius, Craig, and Fox, *Transforming State-Society Relations*.

separate funds that were managed in different ways and for different purposes. Among them were the Solidarity Municipal Funds, which provided financing directly to municipalities for community-driven, small-scale infrastructure projects. Municipal Funds constituted approximately 14 percent of the total Solidarity budget.[16] These funds noticeably increased the resources available to municipalities for public investment, although the funds had to be approved by the federal government on a case-by-case basis. Other Solidarity funds, though not given directly to municipalities, often required their active involvement for implementation along with state and federal governments.

Solidarity produced contradictory effects for both decentralization and democracy. On one hand, the funds created new synergies between the levels of government in the implementation of projects and provided municipalities with funds for investment that did not depend on the discretion of state governors.[17] Solidarity's demand-driven approach also created new synergies between state and society, at least in some regions where authoritarian control was already weak.[18] On the other hand, the program was also highly centralized and managed discretionally by the federal Office of the President, where the program was located for most of its existence.[19] Critics have noted that although Solidarity had decentralizing elements, it was far from a decentralization initiative. Its real intention was to recentralize power in the presidency and to reestablish the legitimacy of the president.[20] Although it provided funds to municipalities, the transfers were discretional, rather than being institutionalized or ensured in future years.[21] On balance, we might conclude that the intention of Solidarity was to

---

16. This figure covers 1989–92. Jonathan Fox and Josefina Aranda, *Decentralization and Rural Development in Mexico: Community Participation in Oaxaca's Municipal Funds Program* (La Jolla: Center for U.S.-Mexican Studies, University of California, San Diego, 1996), 5n.

17. Rodríguez, *Decentralization in Mexico*.

18. Fox and Aranda, *Decentralization and Rural Development*, 45–50; see also Kerianne Piester, "Targeting the Poor: The Politics of Social Policy Reforms in Mexico," in Douglas A. Chalmers, Carlos M. Vilas, Katherine Hite, Scott B. Martin, and Monique Segarra, eds., *The New Politics of Inequality in Latin America: Rethinking Participation and Representation* (Oxford: Oxford University Press, 1997). Solidarity is believed to have created over 150,000 local committees related to projects. Although many had limited permanence, some achieved a life beyond the original project the committee had set out to implement. See Cornelius, Craig, and Fox, *Transforming State-Society Relations*, 20–21.

19. Starting in 1992, the federal government created the Secretariat of Social Development (Secretaría de Desarrollo Social) to run the program; however, it remained closely tied to the presidency. On the discretional nature, see Molinar Horcasitas and Weldon, "Electoral Determinants."

20. Bailey, "Centralism"; Denise Dresser, "Bringing the Poor Back In: National Solidarity as a Strategy of Regime Legitimation," in Cornelius, Craig, and Fox, *Transforming State-Society Relations*.

21. Cabrero Mendoza, *Las políticas descentralizadoras*, 38. Cabrero finds that most Solidarity decisions, even for Municipal Funds, continued to be made in a top-down manner, with the federal government

recentralize power in the federal executive, and it created few sustainable institutional structures for decentralization or for society-driven development. Nevertheless, the program did generate new practices among levels of government and between government and society, which would later prove important as additional institutional changes were made.[22]

A Period of Rapid Reform (1994–2000)

The election of Ernesto Zedillo as president in 1994 marked a turning point for Mexican democracy and stimulated a period of rapid state reform. Zedillo (1994–2000) appeared far less determined than his predecessor to hold on to power at all costs, and the gains that opposition parties had made in state and local elections placed them in an increasingly strong position to negotiate (figs. 3.1 and 3.2). Zedillo accepted the opposition's demand for the complete autonomy of the Federal Electoral Institute, which would now be run entirely by nonpartisan citizen councillors, whose appointments would be approved by a two-thirds majority in Congress, and a requirement that all states have electoral bodies that met minimum requirements for autonomy and impartiality.[23] During Zedillo's presidency, opposition victories in local elections grew until, by 1996, over half of all Mexicans (excluding those in the capital, who had no elected representatives) had experienced at least one period of opposition-run municipal government.[24] Thus, by the mid-1990s, the country had reached a "tipping point," where citizens voted as often for opposition parties as for the PRI in municipal

---

rather than municipalities making the final decisions on projects (see 169–81). Fox and Aranda, in *Decentralization and Rural Development*, found a more participatory approach in Oaxaca's Municipal Funds program, however

22. The Salinas administration also began decentralizing education to the state governments. Most day-to-day responsibilities for schools were passed from the federal government to the states in this period, although the former maintained tight control over key policy decisions, including curriculum and wage levels. The transfer of education to the states would dramatically increase their share of total public expenditures, and education would come to be one of the central activities of most state governments and one of the most significant components of their annual budget. See Mizrahi, "Twenty Years of Decentralization," and Kaufman and Nelson, *Crucial Needs, Weak Incentives*.

23. Despite significant advances, the autonomy and impartiality of state electoral boards still vary greatly. See Jacqueline Peschard, "Federal and Local Electoral Institutions: From a National to a Fragmented System," in Selee and Peschard, *Mexico's Democratic Challenges*.

24. By 1996, excluding the Federal District's residents, 52.7 percent of Mexicans had previous or ongoing experience with an opposition party governing their municipality. Author's calculations based on the data cited in fig. 3.3.

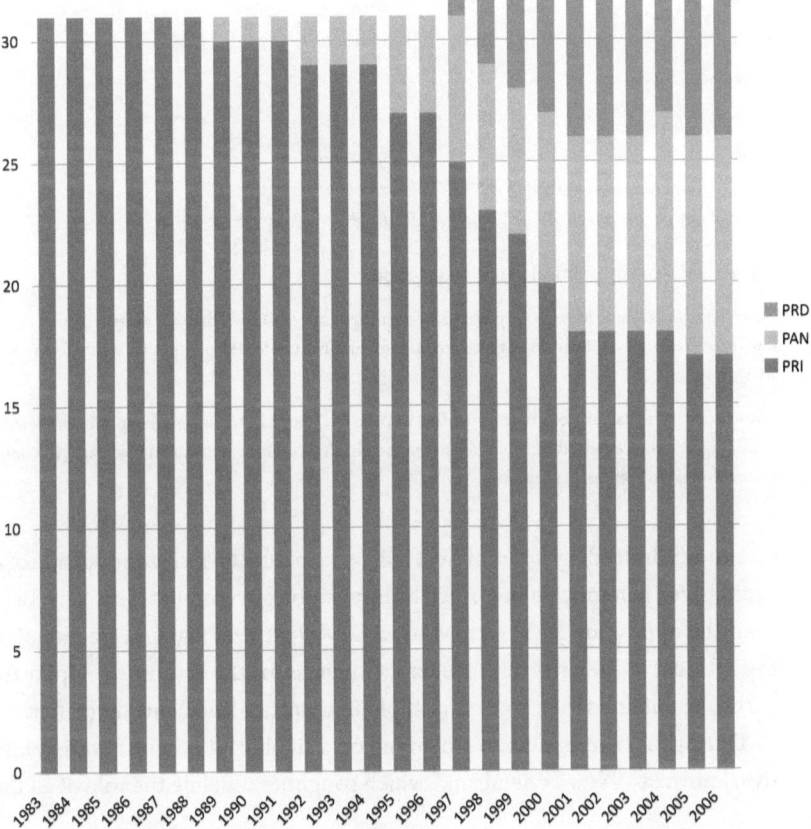

Fig. 3.1 Governors by political party, 1983–2006

Note: After 1997, the chief of the Mexico City government is included in the count, which raises the number of governors from thirty-one to thirty-two. A few coalition governments have been assigned to the strongest party in the coalition.

SOURCE: Author's calculations based on CIDAC, Base de Datos Electorales, available at http://www.cidac.org.

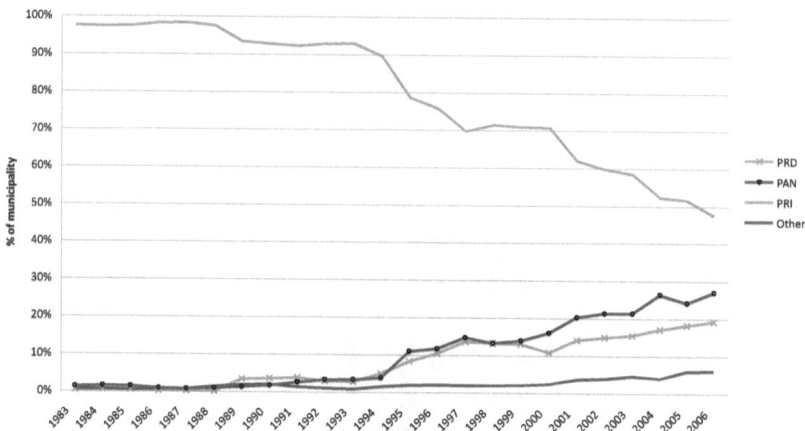

Fig. 3.2 Mayors by political party, 1983–2006

Note: The data exclude Mexico City and those municipalities of Oaxaca that are governed by customary law (*usos y costumbres*). Pre-1989 figures are the sum of the totals for the parties that would form the PRD in 1989.

SOURCE: Author's calculations based on CIDAC, Base de Datos Electorales, available at http://www.cidac.org. When needed, additional information on election results was obtained from state election commissions and newspaper reports.

elections.[25] Indeed, by 1997, almost half (49.9 percent) of citizens outside of the capital lived in municipalities ruled by opposition governments (fig. 3.3). In that year, the opposition PRD won Mexico City's first-ever mayoral election,[26] and the PRI lost its majority in the federal Congress for the first time.[27] Opposition parties maintained their strong foothold in municipal elections thereafter.

During his tenure, Zedillo embarked on a significant decentralization initiative, known as "New Federalism," which sought to redefine the role of all three

25. Alberto Díaz Cayeros, Beatriz Magaloni, and Barry Weingast argue that the mid-1990s constitute the "tipping point," when a critical mass of opposition municipalities was reached and citizens stopped fearing fiscal retaliation from the federal government if they voted for an opposition government in local elections. Díaz Cayeros, Magaloni, and Weingast, "Mexico: Before the Fall," *Hoover Digest*, no. 1 (2001).

26. Author's calculations based on the dataset cited in fig. 3.3. Cuauhtémoc Cárdenas, the former presidential candidate and founder of the PRD, became Mexico City's first elected mayor in 1997. Because of the size of the city, its mayor is generally considered to be the equivalent of a governor and participates in governors' meetings. If we included Mexico City and other states where the PAN held governorships in 1997 in this calculation, well over half of the citizens in the country lived under opposition governments in 1997 at the state or local level.

27. It remained the largest party, however, and only a few seats shy of the majority. The PRI was often able to hobble together majority coalitions with small parties, but it also had to negotiate with the PAN and the PRD on major legislation.

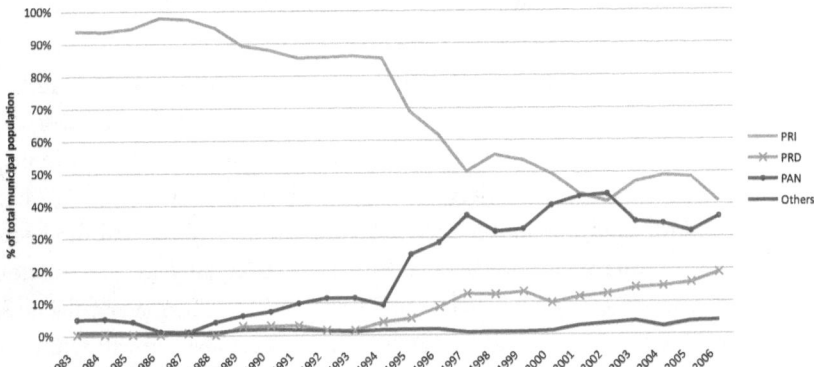

Fig. 3.3 Percentage of the population governed by each political party at a municipal level, 1983–2006

Note: The data exclude Mexico City and those municipalities of Oaxaca governed by customary law (usos y costumbres). Pre-1989 figures are the sum of the totals for the parties that would form the PRD in 1989.

SOURCE: Author's calculations based on CIDAC, Base de Datos Electorales, available at http://www.cidac.org. When needed, additional information on election results was obtained from state election commissions and newspaper reports.

levels of government.[28] This was partially a result of his technocratic approach to governing and a belief that the state should be redesigned to be more efficient, but it also represented a logical response to political realities. The opposition had the ability to force changes that empowered state and local governments at a time when they were growing in influence at these levels. Within this framework, the government converted most of the budget for Solidarity, Ramo 26 (*ramo* is the Mexican word for a budget line), into block grant transfers to state and municipal governments. Instead of administering social programs from Mexico City, many of these would now be administered by subnational governments.[29] Thus, federal transfers showed a noticeable rise in 1995–97 after many years of steady but very gradual growth. The immediate impact of these new transfers was lessened somewhat by the effects of rampant inflation in the wake of the 1994–95 "tequila crisis," which reduced the real value of these funds. However, it began a period of accelerated growth in federal transfers to municipalities.

The PRI's loss of control in Congress set the stage for further decentralization

28. Ward, Rodríguez, and Cabrero Mendoza, *New Federalism and State Government*.
29. Part of the Solidarity funds were transferred into other budget lines to be spent on federal social programs, but the bulk of the funds were converted into the block grants under Ramo 33.

efforts. In the negotiations over the federal budget in 1998, the PAN, which saw subnational governments as its pathway to power,[30] managed to win approval for the conversion of Ramo 26 into Ramo 33, an automatic transfer of funds to states and municipalities. Ramo 33 would be composed of several funds, of which two were specifically for municipalities: the Fund for the Support of Municipal Social Infrastructure (Fondo de Aportaciones para la Infraestructura Social Municipal, FAISM) and the Fund for Strengthening Municipalities and the Federal District (Fondo para el Fortalecimiento de los Municipios y las Demarcaciones Territoriales del Distrito Federal, FORTAMUNDF). FAISM, later called FISM, was designed to provide municipalities with funds for small infrastructure projects in low-income communities. Decisions on spending FAISM/FISM funds were to be made by the Consejo para la Planeación Municipal (Municipal Planning Council, Copladem) or a Consejo para el Desarrollo Municipal (Municipal Development Council, Codemun), which would include key government officials and citizen representatives who would jointly set priorities. FORTAMUNDF would provide unrestricted funds for improving the infrastructure and performance of the municipality itself. Ramo 33 funds now comprise over one quarter of all municipal revenue in Mexico, and they are an even more significant part of discretionary spending.[31]

At the insistence of the PAN, Congress also took up the constitutional framework of municipal governments in 1999, and ultimately it passed an amendment to article 115 of the 1917 constitution that would have far-reaching consequences. Under the 1983 constitutional reform, municipalities had been given *administrative* responsibilities for the provision of services, internal governance, and levying income taxes; the 1999 reform specifically designated municipalities as *political* entities, which, like states and the federal government, could set policy for local affairs within their jurisdiction. The reform also gave them the faculty to assume new powers and functions through agreements with state governments, thus moving beyond the initial list of eight functions reserved for municipalities. The 1999 constitutional changes also required reforms to all of the state constitutions, and a few states surpassed the stipulated federal changes by incorporating additional reforms in their constitutions that granted municipalities even greater powers.[32]

30. Mizrahi, *From Martyrdom to Power*.
31. Calculations are based on the author's analysis of municipal income in the period 1989–2006 from figures available in INEGI, Sistema Municipal de Base de Datos, http://sc.inegi.org.mx/simbad.
32. Baja California, Colima, Tlaxcala, Oaxaca, and Coahuila, for example, included local innovations in the constitutional changes. Guillén López and Ziccardi, *Innovación y continuidad del municipio mexicano*. See especially the introduction by the editors.

The Transformation (2000–2006)

The long-standing one party–dominant regime, which had been slowly eroded throughout the 1990s, collapsed in 2000 with the election of former Governor Vicente Fox of the PAN as the country's new president. Citizens' discontent with the ruling party, their growing familiarity with opposition-led governments at the state and local level, and the increasingly level playing field brought about through changes in electoral laws and institutions finally ended the PRI's seventy-one-year monopoly on the presidency and ushered in an era of multiparty democracy. Indeed, the plurality was impressive after such a long period of one-party dominance. Although the PAN controlled the presidency, the PRD governed Mexico City and the PRI continued to govern the majority of states and municipalities, and no party held a majority in Congress.

This new partisan plurality also dramatically shifted the political calculus of decentralization. Not surprisingly, the PAN, which had fought so hard for decentralization in the previous years, suddenly became increasingly skeptical of it. The Fox administration espoused a commitment to "authentic federalism," but in practice, this largely entailed helping municipal governments work better with the resources and legal framework they already had.[33] The strength of PRI-led state and municipal governments made the Fox administration reluctant to pursue major new initiatives that could embolden its old adversaries. However, municipal finances continued to grow slowly and steadily during the Fox administration. As in the late 1990s, state and municipal governments, working largely through their parties' leaders in Congress, were able to push for these gradual increases during repeated negotiations over the federal budget. Federal government agencies also increasingly transferred resources to states and municipalities through agreements that assigned administration of the resources to the subnational governments.[34] The Habitat program, under the Secretariat of Social Development (Sedesol, Secretaría de Desarrollo Social), was particularly important for large urban municipalities because in cooperation with municipal governments, it has injected resources into poor neighborhoods for basic infrastructure.[35]

---

33. Presentation by Carlos Gadsden, director of the National Institute for Federalism, Secretariat of the Interior, at the meeting of the High-Level Inter-American Network for Decentralization (RIAD, Red Interamericana de Alto Nivel sobre Descentralización) of the Organization of American States, Cancún, Mexico, September 2003.

34. See the data in figs. 3.4 and 3.5 in the section below.

35. The total funds per year have ranged from just under 1 billion pesos in 2003, the program's first year, to just over 2 billion pesos in 2006. See L. A. Jiménez Trejo, "El programa HÁBITAT y la superación

Not surprisingly, PRI leaders became the new converts to federalism and saw this as an opportunity to reinforce their new bastions in state and local governments. In July 2002, PRI and PRD governors formed the National Conference of Governors (CONAGO, Conferencia Nacional de Gobernadores). The PAN governors initially refused to join, since they saw the creation of this organization as an opposition ploy to pick a fight with the Fox administration, but by December 2002, they had relented.[36] The CONAGO's main efforts initially were centered on establishing a National Fiscal Convention in which the rules of fiscal federalism could be reevaluated. The federal government eventually agreed to this, since they were also hopeful of passing a major tax reform to increase revenues and thought they could strike a deal with the governors to push this through. The convention was held from February to August 2004. The three municipal mayors' associations (one for each party) jointly presented a set of proposals at this convention, but partisan interests dominated, and so these associations had little weight in the debates. They thought that the federal government might find common cause with them to stave off the challenge from the governors, but this collaboration never emerged.[37] In the end, the convention reached agreements on a few broad proposals, but there was little momentum behind them, and they never even came up for serious debate in the Mexican Congress.

At the same time, the Supreme Court issued a ruling with far-reaching implications. In a May 31, 2005, decision, the court found that municipal governments had exclusive authority for policy making concerning functions under their control.[38] Traditionally, despite the 1999 constitutional amendments, state governments had reserved the right to supersede municipalities in policy making and regulation when they saw fit. The court's ruling, however, established that the intent of the 1999 reform had been to give the municipalities equal standing with states and the federal government as decision-making bodies, each with separate jurisdictions. It removed—at least in theory—the concept that municipalities

---

de la pobreza urbana en México," *Observatorio de la economía Latinoamericana*, no. 99 (2008), available at http://www.eumed.net/cursecon/ecolat/mx/2008/lajt2.htm; and Mathematica Policy Research, Inc., "Evaluación del programa Hábitat en infraestructura básica" (June 2007), available at http://www.sedesol.gob.mx/archivos/801894/file/habitat/Informe_Resultados.pdf.

36. For one governor's history of the formation of the CONAGO, see Miguel Alemán Velazco, *La revolución federalista* (Mexico City: Editorial Diana, 2004).

37. Rubén Fernández, president of the Association of Municipalities of Mexico (AMMAC), interviewed by the author, March 4, 2005.

38. Jesus Aranda, "Confirma la Suprema Corte potestades jurídicas de los municipios del país," *La Jornada*, June 1, 2005; see also the editorial "Responsabilidad municipal," *El Universal*, June 1, 2005.

were administrative bodies subservient to states rather than a third order of government with separate policy-making jurisdiction. The full effects of this ruling have yet to be felt, but it was one more step in shaping the contours of Mexico's federal system in a period of democratic governance.

The Contours of Federalism and Municipal Autonomy

Mexico has been a federal republic since the 1850s. For most of that time, however, including most of the twentieth century, federalism was merely a statement of good intentions with little content. The institutional structure of the state remained profoundly centralized. Local and regional interests were quite powerful, as we saw in chapter 2, but their influence ran primarily through informal channels, rather than through the state's formal structure. The political changes of the 1980s and 1990s, which democratized the country, have also led to a significant decentralization, which has endowed state and municipal governments with important formal roles and the resources to fulfill them.

States and municipalities now control almost half of all public expenditures, which is a radical departure from the early 1980s. Municipalities, in particular, have grown from being largely ineffective bodies, which accounted for only 1 to 2 percent of all public expenditures in the early 1980s, to important entities that make almost one in ten of all public expenditures (fig. 3.4). Their role has expanded from being primarily links in a chain of political intermediation to an increasingly effective level of government with specific policy-making and implementation functions. States, meanwhile, have expanded their participation in public expenditures to over one third. Education and health-care expenditures are a significant percentage of state budgets, and the transfer of these functions was initially a devolution of responsibilities with only limited discretion. In recent years, however, states have developed greater autonomy for managing these functions and setting policy within their jurisdiction.[39]

This expansion in state and municipal functions has largely been the result of increased transfers from the federal government. For states, this largely took place in the early 1990s with the decentralization of health and education. Since the mid-1990s, their proportional participation in public expenditures has largely

---

39. Merilee S. Grindle, "Interests, Institutions, and Reformers: The Politics of Education Decentralization in Mexico," in Kaufman and Nelson, *Crucial Needs, Weak Incentives*.

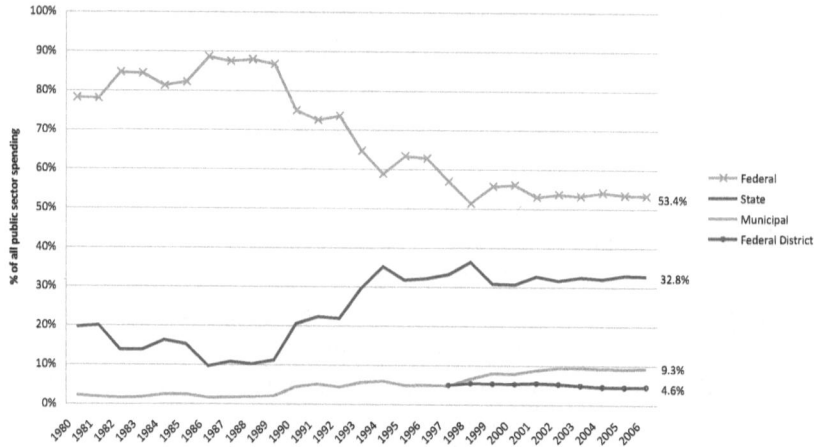

Fig. 3.4 Public sector spending by level of government, 1980–2006

Note: These figures exclude semiautonomous agencies of the federal government, including Pemex, the Federal Electricity Company (CFE), Light and Energy of the Center (LFC), Social Security (IMSS), and the Institute for the Security and Social Services of State Workers (ISSSTE), and many other "parastatal" companies that existed in the 1980s. If these entities are included, the federal government accounted for approximately 90 percent of expenditures in the early 1980s and close to two-thirds today. Municipalities only accounted for 1 percent of total public sector spending in the early 1980s, rising to around 7 percent today. The Federal District is included in the federal spending line until 1997, when Mexico City had an elected government for the first time.

SOURCE: INEGI, *El ingreso y gasto público en México* for 1985, 1988, 1990, 1992, 1995, 1998, 2000, 2003, 2004, 2005, and 2008 (Aguascalientes: INEGI, 1985–2009).

remained constant (though it has expanded in real terms), whereas their discretion over federal resources transferred to them has increased significantly. Municipalities, on the other hand, have seen their revenues expand dramatically since the creation in 1998 of Ramo 33, which now provides over one-third of municipal income. Municipalities and states still remain largely dependent on federal spending.[40] For municipalities, this dependency has increased dramatically since the mid-1990s to reach almost two-thirds (fig. 3.5). However, in absolute terms, municipalities have also continued to expand their revenue bases, though more gradually than the transfers have been expanding (fig. 3.6). In real terms, municipal

---

40. States raise only slightly more than 10 percent of their own revenues and receive the remainder from federal transfers. Municipalities raise between 20 and 30 percent. Figures for 2006 based on INEGI, *El ingreso y gasto público en México 2008* (Aguascalientes: INEGI, 2009). See also Felipe Calderón, *Segundo informe de gobierno, 2008* (Mexico City: Presidencia, 2008), 402.

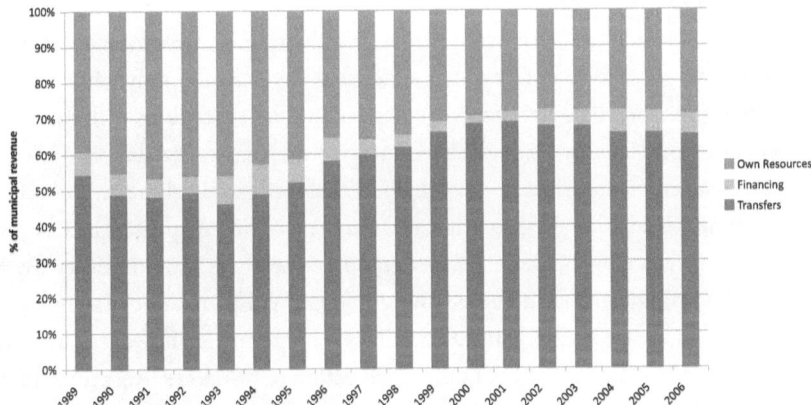

Fig. 3.5 Sources of municipal revenue, 1989–2006

SOURCE: INEGI, Sistema Municipal de Base de Datos, available at http://sc.inegi.org.mx/simbad; the 2006 figures are from INEGI, *El ingreso y gasto público en México 2008*.

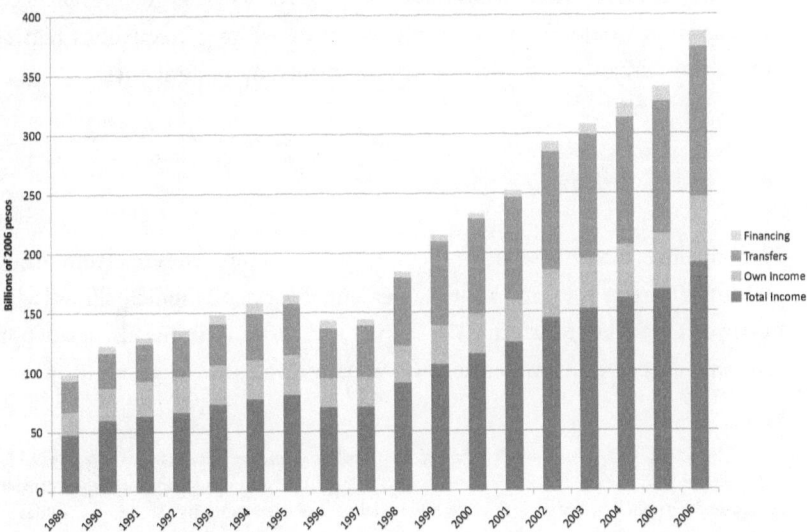

Fig. 3.6 Real increase in municipal income by source, 1989–2006

SOURCE: INEGI, Sistema Municipal de Base de Datos, available at http://sc.inegi.org.mx/simbad; the 2006 figures are from INEGI, *Ingreso y gasto público en México 2008*.

budgets almost doubled in size from 1989 to 1998 and then more than doubled again from 1998 to 2006.

The dependence on transfers may have reduced incentives for municipalities to pursue local forms of financing, and they have created a dynamic through which subnational governments are dependent on negotiations with the federal government (usually through the Congress) on transfer legislation. However, the reliance on transfers has also helped cushion decentralization's effects on economic inequality. In the early 1990s, large urban municipalities had far more financial resources per capita when compared to small municipalities. By the mid-1990s, as transfers increased, this difference had been reduced significantly, and it disappeared entirely by 2002.[41] This does not mean, however, that transfers succeeded in erasing the unequal allocation of resources. According to one study, in poor rural municipalities, federal transfers tended to be spent disproportionately in the municipal capital at the expense of the (usually far poorer) rural districts.[42] This finding suggests a need to pay attention to policy at the submunicipal level.[43] And although the federal government supposedly sets transfers according to transparent formulas, states often exercise their constitutional right to rewrite them to meet their own political needs.[44] However, the overall effect of transfers appears to have been progressive, whereas greater reliance on local taxation would almost certainly aggravate existing inequalities between larger, more urbanized municipalities and smaller, more rural ones.

Municipal Governance

Municipalities have become, for the most part, vibrant arenas of electoral competition. Between 1983 and 2006, 84 percent of Mexico's municipalities (where nearly 90 percent of Mexican citizens live) had had at least one change of political party in power. Competition was most prevalent in large municipalities.

---

41. Based on an analysis by the author of municipal finance data from 1989 to 2002, available in INEGI, Sistema Municipal de Base de Datos, http://sc.inegi.org.mx/simbad. Large urban municipalities are those with a population of more than five hundred thousand inhabitants. By 2002, municipalities of all sizes had similar municipal expenditures per capita.

42. Fausto Hernández-Trillo and Brenda Jarillo-Rabling, "Is Local Beautiful? Fiscal Decentralization in Mexico," *World Development* 36, no. 9 (2008): 1547–58.

43. For an extensive discussion of this point, see Jonathan Fox, *Accountability Politics*, especially chapter 7, "Decentralizing Decentralization: Mexico's Invisible Fourth Level of the State."

44. Hernández-Trillo and Jarillo-Rabling, "Is Local Beautiful?"

Indeed, all but one city with over five hundred thousand inhabitants has had a change of party at least once.[45] However, even small rural municipalities are surprisingly competitive. Fully 76 percent of small rural municipalities had seen at least one change in the party in power by 2006.[46] Clearly, the size and urban or rural condition of the municipality correlates with the likelihood that it has been governed by more than one party; however, competition is now prevalent in municipalities of all sizes. Even in those municipalities where the PRI remains dominant, other political parties regularly compete and often win a significant share of the vote. The introduction of autonomous state electoral institutes and electoral tribunals in the 1990s played an important role in ensuring free and fair elections. Although the autonomy and credibility of the electoral institutes and tribunals varies from state to state, overall they seem to have achieved some credibility in most (though not all) states.[47] Moreover, the ultimate arbiter of electoral disputes in all elections (including municipal and state ones) is the Federal Electoral Tribunal, which has achieved substantial credibility as an impartial judicial institution.[48]

Despite these important gains for free and fair elections, the rules that govern representation in municipalities have barely been updated to respond to the demands of a democratic society. Unlike state and federal legislatures, which are chosen through a mixture of direct district elections and proportional representation, municipal councils are selected via party lists on slates headed by the party's mayoral candidate. Consequently, political parties or mayoral candidates control the selection of candidates for the entire list, and citizens rarely know who the council candidates are, much less, what sort of proposals or profiles they have. Voters cast their ballots for the mayoral candidate they prefer, and the winner brings his whole slate to the council.[49] Under proportional representation

---

45. The one exception is El Centro, Tabasco, where the state capital, Villahermosa, is located. Villahermosa has had some close elections, however. It is also the smallest of the large municipalities, with slightly more than five hundred thousand inhabitants

46. Author's calculations based on a database constructed with the information available in CIDAC, Base de Datos Electorales, available at http://www.cidac.org.

47. See Peschard, "Federal and Local Electoral Institutions."

48. For a dissenting opinion on the tribunal, however, with regard to the 2006 presidential election, see John Ackerman, "The 2006 Elections: Democratization and Social Protest," in Selee and Peschard, *Mexico's Democratic Challenges.*

49. Or very occasionally *her* whole slate: between 2002 and 2004, 96 percent of mayors were men and only 4 percent were women. Among city council members (*regidores* and *síndicos* combined), 16.7 percent were women. INEGI, *Presidentes municipales por entidad federativa según sexo, 2002–2004,* available at http://www.inegi.org.mx; and INDESOL-INEGI, *Encuesta nacional a presidentes municipales sobre desarrollo social 2002* (Mexico City: Secretaría de Desarrollo Social; Aguascalientes: INEGI, 2003), 59.

rules, losing parties always get a few council seats; however, the winning party always receives a majority of seats regardless of the margin of victory.[50] Mayoral candidates thus dominate both municipal campaigns and municipal politics, and the council members have little influence on municipal policy decisions, unless the majority party becomes divided over issues.[51] A system that was built to ensure the dominance of a hegemonic party continues to function even after the advent of a competitive multiparty political system.

The electoral system's deficiencies are compounded by the prohibition on reelection for mayors and council members. This prohibition is a long-standing tradition, which is codified in the 1917 constitution and embedded in the ideological legacy of the Mexican Revolution and its rejection of Porfirio Diaz's repeated reelections as president. Nonetheless, the absence of reelection undermines the accountability of representatives to their constituents because the former have few incentives to fear punishment (or hope for reward) at the ballot box. Indeed, in a system with no reelection for any elected position (as is the case in Mexico), politicians tend to be beholden to party leaders, who determine which elected and appointed positions the party's cadres can aspire to next in their careers. These loyalties are often mediated through informal, rather than formal, channels because the official party representatives do not always choose candidates. Instead, influential party leaders with influence over the factions within their party undertake a series of informal negotiations. Thus, as it was designed to do during the period of single-party dominance, the system creates upward accountability to party leaders rather than downward accountability to citizens.

Municipalities have long had institutional structures to facilitate the participation of citizens in policy decisions and the assignment of municipal resources, including the Municipal Planning Councils (Copladem) instituted in the 1980s; Municipal Development Councils (Codemun), which were required by the Solidarity Program's Municipal Funds in the 1990s; and an array of locally designed neighborhood councils and public works committees. During the decades of single-party dominance, these institutions were generally clientelistic in nature and often closely tied to the PRI's internal structures within the municipality. With the advent of competitive elections, however, some municipalities have tried

50. On the problems inherent in party list systems, see Crook and Manor, *Democracy and Decentralisation*, and Ribot, *Waiting for Democracy*.

51. For a thorough analysis of this, see Guillén, "Democracia representativa y participativa." Exceptions arise when the majority faction in the municipal council has divided and questioned the mayor's proposals (see chapter 5 on Tijuana, for example). Municipal councils, however, are *designed* to be subordinate to the mayor.

to give new life to these bodies and turn them into formal channels for intermediation between the local government and citizens. At the same time, in order to receive the FAIS funds in Ramo 33, the federal government requires municipalities to have a Copladem or Codemun, and several states also have laws that incorporate these structures as part of participatory planning processes.[52]

The available evidence suggests that many municipalities have Copladem or Coplademun, but they tend to be mere formalities, often consisting of an ad hoc group of government officials and program beneficiaries.[53] Few use these bodies to incorporate citizen voices into planning and decision making. Nonetheless, according to one study of municipal mayors, over half of all municipalities have institutions for getting citizen input concerning municipal investment priorities, even though few of these institutions are used to decide on whether to fund a project or for evaluating it after implementation.[54]

Despite these limitations, a few Mexican municipalities have used the Copladem and Codemun in creative ways to open channels for more robust citizen participation in planning and public policy decisions.[55] These experiences have generally taken place in municipalities where opposition parties, usually the PAN or PRD, have won for the first time. Two examples were the small municipality of Cuquío in Jalisco, which, under a PRD government,[56] implemented a twelve-year experiment in participatory planning using an expanded Copladem, and Berriozábal in Chiapas, which did the same during two PRD administrations.[57]

---

52. The legal bases for participatory institutions can take several forms: laws on citizen participation (as in Baja California) or language in a state's municipal code (as in Mexico State). However, many states have no legal framework for Copladem or Codemun. Alison Rowland, "Population as a Determinant of Local Outcomes in Decentralization: Illustrations from Small Municipalities in Bolivia and Mexico," *World Development* 29, no. 8 (2001): 1373–89.

53. Allison Rowland and Edgar Ramírez, *La descentralización y los gobiernos subnacionales en México: Una introducción*, Working Paper no. 93 (Division of Public Administration, CIDE, n.d.).

54. INDESOL-INEGI, *Encuesta nacional a presidentes municipales sobre desarrollo social 2002*, 141–47. Of all municipalities, 58 percent report having a Copladem, 40.8 percent report that they allow citizens to present proposals for the use of Ramo 33 funds, and 43.4 percent report having meetings with citizens on setting priorities for the expenditure of those funds. However, only 8.9 percent involve citizens in actual decision making on how to spend these funds, and 4.1 percent involve their residents in the evaluation of the investments.

55. See Selee and Santín, *Democracia y ciudadanía*; Miguel Bazdresch, "Cambio municipal y participación social," in Enrique Cabrero Mendoza, ed., *Políticas públicas municipales: Una agenda en construcción* (Mexico City: Miguel Ángel Porrúa, 2003); and Alicia Ziccardi and Rolando Cordera, eds., *Participación ciudadana y las políticas sociales en el ambito local* (Mexico City: UNAM, 2004).

56. Miguel Bazdresch, "Consejo democrático en Cuquío, Jalisco," in Cabrero Mendoza, *Innovación en gobiernos locales*.

57. Leticia Santín and Victoria Motte, "Participación ciudadana en Berriozábal, Chiapas," in Cabrero Mendoza, *Innovación en gobiernos locales*.

Two small municipalities in Veracruz, Ciudad Mendoza and Tatahuilcapán, also experimented with far-reaching participatory mechanisms under left governments.[58] Several large cities have also established extensive participatory planning mechanisms, including Ciudad Nezahualcóyotl, under a PRD government, and under PAN governments, Tijuana, Baja California; León, Guanajuato; Hermosillo, Sonora; and Ciudad Juárez, Chihuahua.[59] Nonetheless, the evidence indicates that most of these institutional innovations usually do not survive beyond one or two—or, if very successful, three—periods of government. One extensive study of participatory institutions suggests that most institutional mechanisms for participation tend to be focused on specific projects rather than on policy decisions.[60]

The limited scope and durability of participatory mechanisms in Mexico is perhaps not surprising. The poor quality of representative institutions hardly creates incentives for municipal leaders to reach out to citizens. However, the weakness of participatory channels might also suggest a significant disjuncture between the emergence of a more active citizenry, on one hand, and the structure of the municipality, on the other. In other words, if an autonomous civil society is developing in Mexico as old clientelistic channels within the PRI lose some of their importance, then participation will have to take place at the margin of public institutions because municipal governments have created few durable channels for citizen engagement between elections. Another possibility,

---

58. Carlos Rodríguez, "Experiencia municipales de participación y deliberación en México: Hacia la construcción de una democracia territorial de proximidad," in Selee and Santín, *Democracia y ciudadanía*.

59. Tijuana and Ciudad Nezahualcóyotl are the subjects of chapters 5 and 6, respectively. On Hermosillo, see Leticia Santín, "Planeación urbana en México" (paper presented at the conference on Local Innovation and Democracy at the Woodrow Wilson Center, Washington, D.C., on September 2, 2005).

60. Enrique Cabrero Mendoza, in his analysis of successful municipal experiences nominated for the annual Innovations in Municipal Government prize, notes that most participatory innovations involve forms of citizen consultation (38 percent) or cooperation for project implementation (32 percent), whereas relatively few involve monitoring of government programs (18 percent) or citizen engagement in municipal decisions (12 percent; see fig. 3.20). Of these innovations, Cabrero Mendoza argues that only 14 percent can be considered "high-intensity" participation, where citizens can both influence decisions and monitor outcomes—the kind of participation that engages citizens as deliberators in public affairs in conjunction with public authorities. Another 41 percent of the democratic innovations are "medium-intensity" experiences, where citizens have a consultative say in some aspect of government projects. The remaining 45 percent are "low-intensity" experiences, in which citizens were primarily recipients of government services. His findings suggest that Mexico's municipalities are indeed becoming sources of democratic experimentation, but few of the institutional mechanisms truly allow for ongoing citizen participation and deliberation in public matters. Cabrero Mendoza similarly notes that most of the innovations in citizen participation are weakly institutionalized. They tend to emerge with great "spontaneity and voluntarism" but rarely survive beyond this period of collective social energy. Cabrero Mendoza, "Participación y deliberación en la acción pública local: La experiencia municipal," in Selee and Santín, *Democracia y ciudadanía*.

however, is that there are few participatory institutions largely because traditional forms of informal politics, dominated by clientelism and personalism, remain the dominant means of linking citizens and the state. If this is the case, the absence of participatory institutions might reflect the continued effectiveness of old practices based on political intermediaries. This question will be explored in detail in the three case studies in the following chapters.

Conclusions

Decentralization has given municipalities greater authority and autonomy than they had in previous decades. They now have functions, powers, and resources that were unimaginable in 1980, and the end of one-party rule has freed them from some of the unwritten rules that kept them subservient to higher levels of government. Nonetheless, the actual legal scope of the decision-making power of municipalities is still being negotiated, and their dependence on discretional transfers from other levels of government undermines their ability to be completely autonomous in setting policy and planning investments. Contrary to standard definitions of decentralization (which is generally about the transfer of functions and resources from the national government to subnational authorities), decentralization to municipalities in Mexico has involved both a top-down devolution of functions, powers, and resources from the federal government and the bottom-up development of municipal capacities for revenue collection and service provision, along with the clarification of municipal jurisdiction for decision making. Decentralization is thus a multifaceted process that has involved all levels of government in constant negotiation over both top-down devolution and bottom-up construction of municipal authority and autonomy.[61]

Municipalities served as a tool for democratization in Mexico's long period of political opening, but there have been surprisingly few efforts to democratize local governments since then. As a result, municipalities have structures for representation that hearken back to an older authoritarian era, and they appear to have developed few durable institutions for citizen participation, although there is some evidence of incipient efforts to do this. Political parties have little interest in changing this situation because they have adapted their political practices

61. Cf. Robert H. Wilson, Peter M. Ward, Peter K. Spink, and Victoria E. Rodríguez, *Governance in the Americas: Decentralization, Democracy, and Subnational Government in Brazil, Mexico, and the USA* (South Bend: University of Notre Dame Press, 2008), 249.

to it so well. The structure of Mexican municipalities was developed to privilege single-party rule with limited public oversight or engagement. However, with only minor adjustments, all of the major political parties have learned how to benefit from the status quo even in a competitive political environment. Mexican municipalities appear to be mired in old structures that undermine their accountability and responsiveness. However, the following chapters will explore how these structures affect governance on the ground and whether new channels are emerging between citizens and public authorities despite the municipalities' institutional limitations.

PART 2

A TALE OF THREE CITIES

4 CHILPANCINGO: THE CONTINUATION OF CORPORATISM?

In late January 2005, three weeks before statewide elections in Guerrero, three young men in suits had set up a stand in the central plaza of Chilpancingo, the state capital, to promote the campaign of Héctor Astudillo, the PRI's candidate for governor. A giant television screen broadcast the image of the candidate speaking about progress and development for Guerrero. Astudillo was Chilpancingo's favorite son, and he had done everything a native of the capital could do to prepare himself for the governorship: he had served as a city council member and then mayor before going on to be chair of the state PRI and a senator. Groomed for leadership within his party, he was confident of his victory in a state that had seen no other party in power for over seventy years.

The PRI maintained its power in Guerrero through alliances with local caciques, who controlled their municipalities and helped the state government ensure order and get out the vote at election time. In addition to these strongmen, a few families exercised significant control over regions in the state.[1] The most important was, without doubt, the Figueroa family, which had risen to prominence in the Mexican Revolution and then consolidated its political and economic influence throughout the twentieth century. No fewer than three Figueroas had served as governor, but their power went far beyond that formal title. Although the Figueroa family was the first among cacique families, they were certainly not alone as de facto power holders because several other families had regional influence in the state.

---

1. See Armando Bartra, *Guerrero bronco: Campesinos, ciudadanos y guerrilleros en la Costa Grande*, 2nd ed. (Mexico City: Era, 2000); Carlos Illades, *Breve historia de Guerrero* (Mexico City: Fondo de Cultura Económica, 2000); and Jorge Rendón Alarcón, *Sociedad y conflicto en el estado de Guerrero, 1911–1995: Poder político y estructura social de la entidad* (Mexico City: Plaza y Valdés, 2003).

It is perhaps no coincidence that Guerrero is also one of Mexico's poorest states, with only 1.68 percent of Mexico's GDP but 3.16 percent of the population. It ranks close to the bottom of the list in average levels of education and income and at the top in poverty and extreme poverty. Almost two-thirds of the population earns two minimum wages or less, and fully 36 percent earns one minimum wage or less. On average, students complete 6.6 years of schooling, the third lowest completion rate in the country, and well under the national average of 7.8.[2] Social movements have arisen periodically to challenge the existing political and social order, but these have generally been put down with force. Starting in the 1960s, several social leaders gave up on peaceful protest and founded guerrilla organizations to fight against the state and federal governments. Even today, these rebellions still simmer in the mountains and the coast, the poorest regions of the state. Guerrero has been, without doubt, one of Mexico's most destitute and openly conflicted states.

In the midst of all this, Chilpancingo has been the center of the PRI's political machine in Guerrero. As the capital, the city has been the home of the state bureaucracy and the companies that depend on it to make their businesses profitable. Compared to the rest of the state, the economy was slightly better and incomes a little higher. So despite a growing opposition party presence in Guerrero in the late 1990s, the PRI had never been seriously challenged here. Chilpancingo was, by all appearances, a town where very little had changed even as the rest of the state lived through decades of political turmoil. Indeed, the city had something of a reputation for being a place where everything and yet nothing ever happened. Many of the tumultuous events taking place in Guerrero passed through Chilpancingo yet rarely seemed to disturb its peace.[3] Rebel commanders, army generals, social leaders, union bosses, landowners, peasant organizers, human rights advocates, and political leaders of all stripes had spent time here. Chilpancingo was witness to political negotiations and public debates, to protests and the planning of assassinations. However, the city itself seemed largely

---

2. INEGI statistics, available at http://www.sc.inegi.org.mx.

3. Tomás Bustamante Cruz states, "Chilpancingo is one of those places that, from an early age, has not had much of a local history of its own, rather it has received the influence of other cultures in transition.... In each stage of its history, we find it to be the scene of social processes that have to do with other regions and social groups, which determine the life of the inhabitants of the place." Bustamante Cruz, "Revolución e inmigración, 1910–1940," in *Historia de Chilpancingo* (Chilpancingo: Universidad Autónoma de Guerrero, 1999), 253–54. I largely agree with Bustamante but with a slight difference in emphasis: like any city, Chilpancingo has its own social and political processes that follow local dynamics, but these are also often intertwined with the processes taking place elsewhere in the state. Thus, the former cannot be understood without reference to the latter.

untouched by the dramatic events going on around it and by the decisions outsiders made within its limits.

Every three years the city returned the PRI to power in seemingly uncomplicated elections marked by little real competition. Local contestation seemed muted and easily channeled. Part of the story was city residents' dependence on state government employment and contracts. The other part was that city residents had benefited from the PRI's continued rule; not equitably, of course, but sufficiently so that political dissent could be channeled and contained. The state frequently invested in the city's development, supplementing meager municipal budgets with funds for roads, markets, and parks. In return, the state governor and the state's principal political leaders generally influenced the selection of the city's mayor and intervened periodically in municipal decisions. The municipal government helped maintain peace by creating a loose network of intermediaries in each neighborhood who had ties to the ruling party. These intermediaries provided a channel for community demands and a conduit to assign resources for services and infrastructure. They also helped get out the votes at election time for the PRI.

Something was wrong on this January day, however. No one was stopping to look at the giant screen on which Héctor Astudillo was making campaign promises in a booming politician's voice. Instead, a large group partway across the plaza was gathered around a small black-and-white television that was broadcasting the image of Zeferino Torreblanca, a charismatic businessman and former mayor of nearby Acapulco, who was the gubernatorial candidate of the left-of-center PRD. Two poorly dressed older men, who seemed surprised by the crowd, answered questions and pointed to newspaper articles about the candidate, which were haphazardly taped to the wall behind the television screen. Clearly, something was happening in this city where nothing ever seemed to happen.

Three weeks later, in the state elections, Zeferino Torreblanca of the PRD overwhelmed Héctor Astudillo to end the PRI's rule in the state. It was a stunning defeat for the party that had kept power for more than seven decades. To add insult to injury, Chilpancingo voted overwhelmingly for Torreblanca over its own favorite son and former mayor. Indeed, the PRI managed to hold on to only a few of the poorest neighborhoods around the edges of the city and some of the rural areas farther away.[4] Almost the entire city—the bureaucrats, the

---

4. Based on the author's analysis of the election results by polling station. Detailed election data is available from the state electoral council at http://www.ieegro.org.mx. An electoral map of Chilpancingo, indicating its polling stations, was made available by the Federal Electoral Institute. Torreblanca (PRD) defeated

businesspeople, and even the majority of the poor, all of whom had benefited from the PRI's largesse—voted for the PRD candidate. The old mechanisms for control seemed to have lost their ability to turn out votes for the official party.

The election suggested that the city had never been quite as tranquil and uncomplicated as it had seemed. Underneath the semblance of unity around the dominant political party, dissent and dissatisfaction had been building and new cleavages developing among its citizens. As the authority and autonomy of its local government expanded, the municipality became more plural and contested. The increase in the government's capacity, though still somewhat constrained by state authorities, had perhaps given citizens something to fight over in municipal elections. And perhaps the consolidation of electoral mechanisms had allowed new political actors to emerge and reshaped the channels that linked citizens and their government. Finally, in the 2005 elections, the old mechanisms of control appeared to have failed after years of silent erosion.

The PRI would return to win the mayoral election later that year and again in 2008, suggesting that the change was, at best, partial. While most of the rest of the state turned to the PRD, the PRI in Chilpancingo managed to reassemble its local coalition and continued to govern, although it was now more challenged than it had ever been before. However, as political relationships were changing, the new forms of political mediation were unclear.[5] What implications did these changes have for democratic governance in a city like Chilpancingo, where one party (the same as the state government's) has ruled unchallenged for eight decades? As the municipality became increasingly relevant to citizens' lives, was municipal governance becoming more accountable and responsive to citizens?

Deep Historical Roots, Recent Growth

Chilpancingo was first registered as a municipality in 1693.[6] For most of its existence, it remained a sleepy, primarily rural municipality on the highway connecting

---

Astudillo (PRI) in Chilpancingo 50.8 percent to 47 percent, according to the state electoral council's figures. The margin was notably higher in the city, which makes up three-quarters or more of the municipality.

5. For an excellent analysis of the failure, at a state level, of the old mechanisms for mediation and its impact on the 2005 elections, see Raúl Fernández Gómez, *Elecciones y alternancia: Guerrero* (Mexico City: Nuevo Horizonte Editores, 2004). The book was written slightly before the elections, but it shows in great detail how the PRD had built a coalition out of historical social movements, dissidents from the PRI, and those citizens in the growing urban areas who were no longer connected to the PRI through old clientelistic networks. It does not deal extensively with the city of Chilpancingo, however.

6. There are references to Chilpancingo's legal status as early as 1591, but it appears to have been a ranch rather than a town at the time. Jaime Salazar Adame, "Introducción," in *Historia de Chilpancingo*,

Acapulco and Mexico City. In the nineteenth century, the town periodically emerged from its slumber to take a significant place on the national stage. In 1813, Mexico's independence leader José María Morelos y Pavón called for a constituent congress in Chilpancingo, which was in an area the rebel forces controlled. The Congress of Anáhuac, as it was called, proclaimed Mexico's independence from Spain, and Morelos issued his "Sentiments of the Nation," a statement of principles for the cause of independence. One of Mexico's leading independence advocates, Nicolás Bravo, and his two brothers were also natives of the town. Bravo would go on to become Mexico's first vice president and would serve twice as president and two more times as vice president in the first two decades after independence. In the 1850s, Chilpancingo reemerged as an important military garrison in the midst of the civil war between Liberals and Conservatives. In 1855, as the Conservatives faced defeat, Chilpancingo was the site of the negotiations to end the civil war and install Juan Álvarez as Mexico's first Liberal president. Benito Juárez, Álvarez's personal secretary at the time, carried out the negotiations and later went on to become Mexico's most celebrated president.[7]

Chilpancingo was perhaps best known for being the site of an annual Christmas fair, which attracted regional and national attention, and for serving as a center of commerce along the Acapulco–Mexico City highway.[8] In religious matters, it depended on the neighboring municipality of Zumpango, which was the parish seat. In political matters, it depended on the municipality of Tixtla, which was the district capital and later the state capital. In 1868, however, Chilpancingo became its own parish,[9] and in 1871, the city became the official state capital of Guerrero, which would profoundly alter Chilpancingo's trajectory.[10] At the time, it was centered on four *barrios*, traditional neighborhoods, each with

---

14–15; see also Angélica Gutiérrez y Salgado and Héctor Rodríguez Morales, *Chilpancingo ayer y hoy* (Chilpancingo: Instituto Guerrerense de Cultura, 1987), 30.

7. See Gutiérrez y Salgado and Rodríguez Morales, *Chilpancingo ayer y hoy*, chapter 2.

8. Teresa Pavía Miller, "Centro de poder, 1821–1870," in *Historia de Chilpancingo*, 178. Starting in 1825, Chilpancingo was the first city in modern-day Guerrero authorized to have an annual fair without the participants paying state and federal taxes; in 1857, its fair was still one of only fifteen in the country, and it still operates today.

9. Pavía Miller, "Centro de poder," 186; Gutiérrez y Salgado and Rodríguez Morales, *Chilpancingo ayer y hoy*, 37.

10. An 1870 rebellion by the leaders of Tixtla against the state governor convinced him to move the state capital to Chilpancingo on an emergency basis. In 1871, the state congress formally decreed Chilpancingo the new state capital. The governor cited two reasons: the rebellion in Tixtla (which he had successfully contained) and Chilpancingo's advantageous location on the Acapulco–Mexico City highway. Pavía Miller, "Centro de poder."

its own church and annual religious festival,[11] although most of the municipality's population lived in rural localities.

With its new political status, the city attracted a new elite of landowners from elsewhere in the state, who moved to the city to take part in politics.[12] The emergence of Chilpancingo as a state capital coincided with the Porfiriato, the administration of Porfirio Díaz (1877–1910), a period that was marked by rapid economic growth, which helped the city's expansion. Chilpancingo's growth slowed considerably, however, due to major earthquakes in 1902 and 1907 and the ravages of the Mexican Revolution, and it would remain a mostly rural municipality well into the twentieth century. Starting in the 1950s, Chilpancingo's population growth accelerated. The expansion of both the state bureaucracy and Guerrero's autonomous university was a magnet that attracted new residents. At the same time, the endemic poverty in the rest of Guerrero pushed people out of their own localities in search of new opportunities, generally to one of the state's larger cities (Acapulco, Chilpancingo, Iguala, and Taxco). By 1960, just over half of the municipality's population lived in the city itself (rather than in the rural villages within the municipal limits), and this trend intensified in the following decades, until almost three-quarters were living in the city in 2000. The municipal population also grew, more than quintupling, from 35,838 in 1960 to 192,947 in 2000, and then to more than 200,000 by 2004.[13] Throughout the 1970s and 1980s, the number of urban *colonias* exploded, and by 2004, there were more than four hundred. Many of these were initially irregular neighborhoods that were the product of "land invasions."[14]

---

11. For a description of city life in the four barrios—San Mateo, San Antonio, Santa Cruz, and San Francisco—and the city's gradual urbanization, see Gutiérrez y Salgado and Rodríguez Morales, *Chilpancingo ayer y hoy*.

12. According to Bustamante in "Revolución e inmigración," "The majority of members of the new political elite who came to power in the different levels of the state government came from the class of landowners formed in the shadows of the policies of the *Porfiriato*" (255). He continues, "In Chilpancingo, several families emerged that began to create the new social power tied to the institutions of government; they continued to be the landowners, ranchers, farmers, traders, and so forth, but they were increasingly integrated into the institutions of government" (288).

13. The municipality is much more urban than the 74 percent figure suggests, if we include many of the small villages that the city has effectively absorbed. Less than 10 percent of the municipality's population is involved in agriculture (INEGI, *Cuaderno estadístico municipal: Chilpancingo de los Bravo, Guerrero* [Aguascalientes: INEGI, 2002]). The city's first map, which covered the four barrios and twenty-nine *colonias* (low-income neighborhoods), was not drawn until the late 1960s. See Zaida Falcón de Gyves, *Chilpancingo: Ciudad en crecimiento* (Mexico City: UNAM, 1969), for a facsimile and discussion of the map (appendix and p. 7, respectively).

14. By 2004, approximately four-fifths of the colonias had land titles, according to official figures (Ayuntamiento de Chilpancingo, *Informe municipal 2004* [Chilpancingo: Ayuntamiento de Chilpancingo, 2004],

The residents of the growing city largely remained dependent for employment on the government and services related to it. A significant secondary source of jobs was in commerce and business, often tied to the commercialization of agricultural products from other municipalities in Guerrero.[15] There was little local industry.[16] The city had achieved higher income levels than the average for the state (and close to national averages), but it had far more low-wage workers than most medium-sized cities.[17] In short, Chilpancingo was well-off compared to other municipalities in Guerrero but poor compared to other cities of its size in Mexico.

Hegemony and Resistance (1960–1995)

Among Chilpancingo's first inhabitants in colonial times were people with the family names of Adame, Leyva, and Alarcón.[18] Three hundred years later, those family names still resonate: between 1986 and 2005, the city's mayors included Florencio Salazar Adame, Efraín Leyva Acevedo, and Saúl Alarcón Abarca. This highlights one of the central truths of politics in the city: family names, *apellidos*, matter. The elite of the city has hardly been static over the centuries; it has grown and changed with migration and especially with the movement of elites from the rest of Guerrero to Chilpancingo after it became the state capital. However, there is little doubt that the city's elite has been composed almost exclusively of a

---

66). However, José Luis Lozena, the municipal chief of the city's Barrios and Colonias Office (procurador de Barrios y Colonias), noted that there were over one hundred irregular colonias (Lozena, interviewed by the author, April 20, 2005).

15. A study in the 1960s suggested that around 45 percent of the workforce was employed in either the city and state governments or services directly tied to them. Falcón de Gyves, *Chilpancingo*, 37–39. By 2000, a full 29.4 percent of the population worked in government (including teaching and medical services) and another 15.2 percent worked in sales and small businesses. Less than one-twelfth of the workforce in the municipality was in agriculture (7.9 percent) and manufacturing (7.8 percent), while most other workers were in service occupations that depended directly or indirectly on government and business: construction (10.3 percent), transportation (4.8 percent), hotels and restaurants (5 percent), professional services and service to business (3.1 percent). The remaining occupations are all in the service sector as well. Data are from INEGI, *Cuaderno estadístico municipal: Chilpancingo*.

16. The city's municipal development plan for 1999–2002 notes that "manufacturing has not managed to develop as an industry; the activity is limited to small economic units, usually family based, even though there is a large demand for products of this type" (*Plan de desarrollo municipal 1999–2002* [Chilpancingo: Ayuntamiento de Chilpancingo, 1999], 8).

17. INEGI, *XII censo de población y vivienda 2000* (Aguascalientes: INEGI, 2003).

18. Gutiérrez y Salgado and Rodríguez Morales, *Chilpancingo ayer y hoy*, 30.

small set of families with recognizable apellidos.[19] These families live in the city, generally in one of the four traditional barrios, and often have ties to other elites throughout the state. There have been times when the popular sectors have risen to prominence. In the aftermath of the Revolution, for example, a group called the "Greens," composed of leaders from the popular sectors, faced off against the traditional families, known as the "Reds," in election after election. But until recent times, the apellidos have dominated politics. The selection for municipal office has often required a negotiation among these families, mediated and sanctioned by powerful state-level political leaders all within the official party.

In the nineteenth century, Chilpancingo was ruled by a *cabildo* (municipal council) elected for one-year terms, with the mayor chosen from the collegial body.[20] A prefect, who served the district of Tixtla and reported directly to the governor, had the ability to review the finances of the municipality and intervene in local decisions on the governor's behalf. The postrevolutionary governments canceled the figure of the prefect, but the tradition of a rotating city council with one-year terms continued until the 1940s. In 1936, Aurora Meza Andraca was elected mayor of Chilpancingo, making her the first female mayor in Mexico's history, ten years before women's suffrage for local elections was enshrined in the constitution. Eventually, the terms were extended to three years with no re-election allowed, and the members of the city council were elected on a joint slate with the mayor. The number of council members varied over the years; however, one constant until 1989 was that all members were part of the mayor's slate, ensuring mayoral dominance over the council and single-party rule. Indeed, the PRI has won all elections in Chilpancingo with little effort from the 1940s until today (fig. 4.1).

Through the governor's office, powerful political families in the state also maintained tight control over municipal elections. At least by the 1950s, it was common for the state government, in consultation with key local caciques, to

---

19. The key family names include Adame, Memije, Calvo, Alarcón, Acevedo, Tapia, and Leyva. Time after time in interviews, political leaders noted the importance of apellidos in the political process, although they often recognized that this was now changing (as I will discuss later).

20. The municipal government was responsible for organizing elections, resolving misdemeanors (but not felonies), maintaining elementary schools, taking care of public buildings and the cemetery, maintaining roads, and carrying out basic improvements to municipal infrastructure. The municipality had funds from fines and taxes on public spectacles, sales, real estate, and the transport of goods through the jurisdiction. Pavía Miller, "Centro de poder," 165–66. For a detailed description of the number of municipal council members over time, see Jaime Salazar Adame, "De ciudad a capital," in *Historia de Chilpancingo*. At several points throughout the nineteenth century, Chilpancingo, like most other Mexican towns, had auxiliary mayors who governed the rural localities outside a municipality's main city.

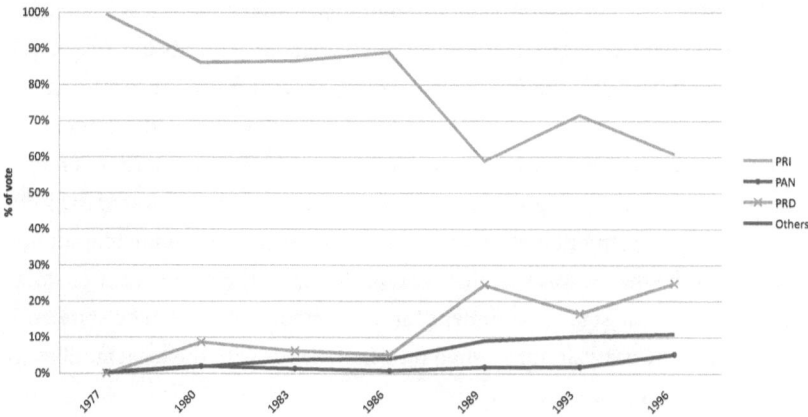

Fig. 4.1 Municipal elections by political party, Chilpancingo, 1977–96

Note: The pre-1989 part of the PRD line is based on figures for parties that would join the PRD at its founding in 1989: the PCM (1980) and the PSUM (1983 and 1986).

SOURCE: Consejo Estatal Electoral de Guerrero, available at http://www.ieegro.org.mx/.

name the candidates for mayor and city council in most of the state's municipalities. The state frequently removed mayors as well, either by decree or through unofficial pressure. Even though the prefects had been eliminated and the Mexican Constitution forbade any intermediate authority between the state and municipality, the state constitution allowed the governor to appoint inspectors to "examine accounting, verify entrance and exit of funds, oversee public services, and report on the labors of the municipal government."[21] Mayors were thus elected at the will of the state governor and had to serve at his pleasure as well.[22] However, these appointments were generally consulted with powerful families that held sway in the municipalities in question. In the case of Chilpancingo, governors generally consulted with the leading families on any appointments or removals.

21. Moisés Ochoa Campo, *Guerrero: Análisis de un estado problema* (Mexico City: Editorial Trillas, 1964), 35–41; quote from the state constitution in force in 1960 on p. 35.
22. See also Armando Bartra, "Donde los sismos nacen," in Tomás Bustamante Álvarez and Sergio Sarmiento Silva, eds., *El Sur en movimiento: La reinvención de Guerrero del siglo XXI* (Mexico City: Editora Laguna, 2001), 45. In turn, the state's leaders were not free from federal interference. From 1925 until 2005, only seven governors served their entire term in office. In other words, out of eighty years, elected governors served for only forty-two. The federal governor had formal and informal mechanisms for forcing governors to resign, similar to mechanisms used by the state governor to remove mayors (see chapter 3). In Guerrero, where conflict often spiraled out of control, the president frequently saw that it was in his interest to remove elected governors. See Illades, *Breve historia*, 120.

The symbiosis between the state and municipal governments was even more noticeable in Chilpancingo than in most municipalities. The city had little own-source revenue and few possibilities for investment in infrastructure.[23] Soon the state government began playing a conspicuous role in upgrading the city's infrastructure.[24] In the mid-1990s, the state government continued to carry out major investments in Chilpancingo, even producing a small report to boast of the state government's investment in the city.[25] The dependence of the municipal administration on the mayor was therefore compounded by the mayor's almost total dependence on the state government for investment resources. The state government and the party, in turn, relied on their alliance with the local families to ensure order and guarantee support.

The control of the state government and of state political elites over municipal politics was never complete, however, and a great deal of controversy and contestation did take place in municipalities, including in Chilpancingo. In the case of the capital, the most visible moment in which the dominant system was challenged was in 1960, when a popular protest spun out of government control and set off a series of events that transformed life in the city and in the state. A confluence of factors, including a tax hike and increasing political repression, led to protests

---

23. As one study noted, "Chilpancingo, despite being a capital, remains in the worst state of abandonment.... The lack of resources and aid is translated into a shortage of drinking water, sewers, pavement, and schools" (Ochoa Campo, *Guerrero*, 122).

24. Between 1981 and 1987, for example, Governor Alejandro Cervantes Delgado undertook a major investment strategy for the capital, primarily focused on roads, water, and sewer infrastructure. This initiative, known as Plan Chilpancingo, transformed the physical appearance of the city (Gutiérrez y Salgado and Rodríguez Morales, *Chilpancingo ayer y hoy*, 72–75). When Florencio Salazar Adame took over as mayor in 1987, he recognized that many of the functions that the municipal government should have been performing were actually being carried out by the state government. He noted in his first yearly report, "We received a public administration ... with modest public functions, without decision-making authority in the execution of public works, constrained from providing sufficient services, and always leaning on the support of the State Government, which largely replaced the municipality regarding its responsibilities.... We would greatly appreciate the respectful decision of the Governor not to interfere in municipal responsibilities.... We have proposed to overcome the inertia that made our citizens see in the State Governor also the Mayor. For that reason, we have assumed all of our functions, which has meant ... setting out to perform our tasks with our own resources. The inhabitants of Chilpancingo now know that municipal matters are dealt with and resolved in the Municipality" (*Informe municipal 1987*). Despite this bold declaration, municipal finances remained fragile, and over 78 percent of Salazar's municipal budget the following year was still composed of federal and state transfers (*Informe municipal 1988*).

25. The report notes, "From the beginning of this [state government] administration, it has been a priority objective to improve the image of the city of Chilpancingo." The report only mentions the municipal government in passing. *Construyendo un nuevo Chilpancingo* (Chilpancingo: Gobierno del Estado de Guerrero, 1995), 12.

throughout Guerrero in that year. Students and faculty of the Autonomous University of Guerrero, based in Chilpancingo, soon joined in, and they added a demand for full university autonomy. The state government cracked down, killing eighteen protestors.[26] The federal Congress quickly forced the governor to resign, and the new state government granted autonomy to the university. The events of 1960 have remained a powerful symbol in the collective consciousness of Chilpancingo, as well as "a turning point in the history of Guerrero . . . a symbolic reference to popular mobilization, and a point from which some of the central actors in the conflicts to come emerged."[27]

These events also produced divergent responses from protest leaders. The most visible, Genaro Vásquez, tried for some time to lead a political struggle outside the PRI, but toward the end of the 1960s after considerable repression, he founded a guerrilla organization in Guerrero's mountains. Vásquez's efforts would also spawn a second guerrilla organization, the Party of the Poor, which began in the late 1960s and continues today, through a new organization, the Ejército Popular Revolucionario (EPR), which sees itself as an heir to Vásquez and the Party of the Poor. Other leaders of the protest, like Jesús Araujo Hernández and Josefat Acevedo, remained with the official party and went on to serve in positions in the public administration in the following decades.[28]

The PRI managed to reassert control over most dissent in the state, but the illusion of harmony had been broken. Over the years, several other forms of protest and contestation outside of the official party would emerge. In the mountains and coast of Guerrero, rural unions became especially influential, and the 1990s saw the emergence of human rights organizations to defend rural activists who were often threatened, jailed, or killed.[29] In Chilpancingo, as the number of colonias grew, so too did organizations that represented the urban poor in the city. Some of the strongest organizations, such as the Unión de Colonias Populares de Chilpancingo (Union of Popular Neighborhoods of Chilpancingo), were affiliated with the PRI.[30] Others, like the Consejo Popular de Colonias (Popular

---

26. Alba Teresa Estrada Castañon, *El movimiento anticaballerosta: Guerrero 1960: Crónica de un conflicto* (Chilpancingo: Editorial Universidad Autónoma de Guerrero, 2001), 49–90.

27. Illades, *Breve historia*, 131.

28. Araujo would go on to be chief justice of the State Superior Court and Acevedo an interim mayor of Chilpancingo. On Araujo, see Illades, *Breve historia*, 136; on Acevedo, see Felix J. López Romero, *Del mundo chilpancingueño* (Chilpancingo: Ayuntamiento de Chilpancingo, 1995).

29. See Bartra, *Guerrero bronco*, for a more detailed discussion of these movements.

30. The union later changed its name to Movimiento Territorial de Chilpancingo (Territorial Movement of Chilpancingo). Clementino Navarrete, one of the organization's former leaders and former president

Council of Neighborhoods),[31] were close to the Trotskyite Workers Revolutionary Party (PRT) and to other left-wing parties. The Urban Popular Movement (Movimiento Urbano Popular, MUP), as the non-PRI organizations were called collectively, created concern among PRI leaders and forced them to invest in regularizing land titles and providing services to undercut the strength of these organizations.[32] At the same time, a dissident teachers' movement within the official National Union of Education Workers (Sindicato Nacional de Trabajadores de la Educación, SNTE), Mexico's largest union, caught on in Guerrero and won adherents among teachers in Chilpancingo. Although the dissidents never broke completely with the national union, they openly challenged the state and federal government on teacher pay and education investments. In the process, they received ongoing support from the PRD, and in turn, they provided one of its most consistent bases of support.[33]

In Guerrero, left-wing political parties and the right-of-center PAN developed small but loyal followings and competed in state and municipal elections starting in 1980. The candidacy of Cuauhtémoc Cárdenas struck a chord with the population in 1988. He officially won 36 percent of the state vote in the presidential elections of that year (with the PRI's Salinas de Gortari at 60 percent in the official tallies), though Cárdenas's real support may have been much higher.[34] From that point on, the left in Guerrero became particularly successful in challenging the PRI in local elections and in gaining a foothold in the state Congress. However, in Chilpancingo, the opposition parties lagged behind their performance elsewhere in the state, and through most of the 1980s and 1990s, the PRI seemed immune from the winds of change blowing elsewhere in Guerrero.

---

of the Development Committee of the Tatagildo neighborhood, interviewed by the author, April 10, 2005. Unless otherwise noted, all interviews cited in this chapter took place in Chilpancingo.

31. This was the major alliance of non-PRI neighborhood organizations begun in 1988. In 1989, in a merger with other organizations, it became the Frente de Lucha de las Colonias Populares (Front for the Struggle of the Popular Neighborhoods). Daniel Acatitlán Ramón, interviewed by the author, April 10, 2005; "Se integró el Consejo Popular de Colonias," *Expresión Popular,* January 11, 1988; "Colonos acusan a funcionario municipal," *El Sol de Chilpancingo,* May 26, 1989; "Constituyen aquí el Frente de Lucha de las Colonias Populares," *El Sol de Chilpancingo,* September 12, 1989.

32. The *Informe municipal 1990* of Mayor Efraín Leyva Acevedo is particularly clear in this regard.

33. On dissidence in the SNTE, see Joe Foweraker, *Popular Mobilization in Mexico: The Teachers' Movement, 1977–87* (Cambridge: Cambridge University Press, 1993).

34. Alba Teresa Estrada Castañon, "Guerrero en los 90s: Realineamiento electoral y movimiento social," in David Cienfuegos and Humberto Santos Bautista, eds., *Guerrero: Los retos del nuevo siglo: Politica, cultura, educacion, economica, ecología y demografía, derechos humanos* (Chilpancingo: Fundación Académica Guerrense, 2000), 44; Bartra, *Guerrero bronco,* 141–42. The vote total for Cárdenas was probably much higher than the official calculations.

Strengthening the Municipality (1996–2005)

Like all other municipalities in Guerrero, Chilpancingo has long struggled to raise local revenues to finance municipal government expenditures. It lacks revenue-generating industry, although the proliferation of commercial enterprises, services related to government, and the annual fair provide some opportunities for taxation. Overall, by diversifying its revenue sources, Chilpancingo fares better than many other municipalities in Guerrero, but not when compared to other municipalities of the same size elsewhere in Mexico.[35] Chilpancingo has historically depended on revenue transfers from the federal and state governments, complemented, especially in the mid-1990s, by loans for major projects (fig. 4.2), and this dependency has increased over time. The creation of Ramo 33 and later Habitat has bolstered the city's revenues, and its capacity for investment; nonetheless, even with the growth in federal transfers, Chilpancingo has remained a poor city, in terms of per capita municipal revenue when compared to other medium-sized cities.[36]

The state government has taken a particular interest in improving the infrastructure of its capital city, but this has come at a price to the municipal government's autonomy. This was particularly noticeable during the early 1990s under the Solidarity Program, which gave Chilpancingo far more per capita resources than most other municipalities received.[37] Although the state government continues to provide occasional investments out of its budget,[38] transfers to most of Guerrero's municipalities appear to be far more equitable than before. The arbitrariness of transfers has been reduced over time with the implementation of Ramo 33, which is based on a formula. Indeed, Chilpancingo received around 6

---

35. This was true in 1960 and is still so today, based on a review of financial statistics in the national municipal financial database (INEGI, Sistema Municipal de Base de Datos, http://sc.inegi.org.mx/simbad). For 1960, see Ochoa Campo, *Guerrero*.

36. Medium-sized municipalities (those with 100,000 to 500,000 inhabitants) spent an average of 1,367 pesos per inhabitant in 2002; Chilpancingo, in contrast, spent only 895 pesos per inhabitant. Author's calculations are based on figures available in INEGI, Sistema Municipal de Base de Datos.

37. Despite being one of the three wealthiest municipalities in the state, Chilpancingo received more Solidarity funds than any other municipality, except Acapulco, and more funds per capita in the period 1990–92, except for two small municipalities. Indeed, Chilpancingo concentrated 10.09 percent of all Solidarity investments in this period, despite having only 5.2 percent of the state's population. See Isabel Osorio Salgado, *Eradicación o radicación de la pobreza? PRONASOL y territorio en el Estado de Guerrero* (Chilpancingo: Universidad Autónoma de Guerrero, 1995), especially the charts on 126 and 185.

38. City council member Rigoberto Ramos (PAN), for example, noted the state government's direct investment in the reconstruction of a major city market in 2004.

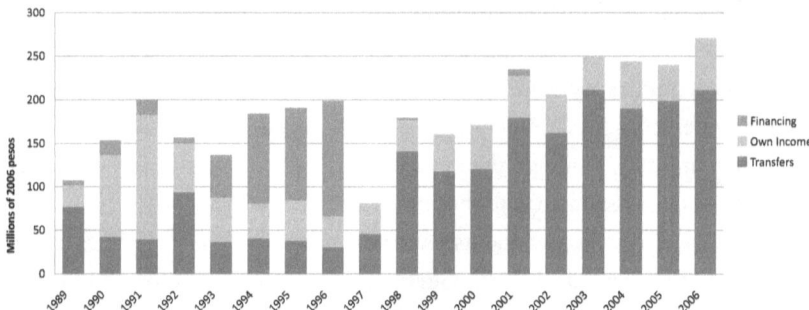

Fig. 4.2 Real municipal income by source, Chilpancingo, 1989–2006

SOURCE: INEGI, Sistema Municipal Base de Datos, available at http://sc.inegi.org.mx/simbad; the 2006 figures are from INEGI, *Ingreso y gasto público en México 2006*. Additional data on transfers are from INEGI, *Finanzas públicas estatales y municipales, 1996–1999* (Aguascalientes: INEGI, 2001).

percent of all federal and state transfers in Guerrero in 2002, roughly in line with its population, which is now around 6.3 percent of the state's overall population.[39]

Although state leaders take a great deal of interest in the municipality's well-being, they also have traditionally paid close attention to the selection of the PRI candidate for mayor, and governors have been known to intervene regularly in local decision making.[40] The lack of municipal autonomy is confirmed by interviews with major political leaders. Former PRI Mayor Saúl Alarcón (2002–5), for example, recognized that he occasionally had to negotiate with the governor about the municipality's priorities.[41] Opposition council members were more direct. One observed, "Since it is the capital of the state, there is total interference by the governor."[42] Another stated, "Who governs in Chilpancingo is the governor."[43] The truth probably lies in between the two positions. On most issues, the municipal government sets priorities and conducts business without the

---

39. Author's calculations, based on figures from INEGI, *XII censo*, and INEGI, *Finanzas públicas estatales y municipales de México, 1999–2002* (Aguascalientes: INEGI, 2004). This figure includes Ramo 33; *participaciones*, a regular transfer to all states and municipalities based on revenue sharing formulas; and Habitat, a small specialized fund for urban areas. Not surprisingly, the city received slightly less than its population share in transfers because the Ramo 33 formula includes calculations based on poverty indicators, which are relatively low in Chilpancingo compared to other municipalities in the state.

40. It should be noted that the state administration has gradually moved most of its functions to the city's southernmost side, creating a greater physical distance than that which existed when both municipal and state offices were concentrated around the central plaza.

41. Mayor Saúl Alarcón Abarca (PRI), interviewed by the author, March 11, 2005.

42. Rigoberto Ramos Romero (PAN), interviewed by the author, March 11, 2005.

43. Julio César Aguirre (PRD), interviewed by the author, March 11, 2005.

governor paying much attention, but he is still able to influence priorities when he wants to. This is facilitated by his control over the resources the city needs and on the metaconstitutional powers that the governor has enjoyed through his political connections to the mayor and other leaders in the city.[44] Although the municipality officially enjoys considerable autonomy, the relationships of informal power that link it to the state government often undermine that autonomy. The election of a PRD governor almost certainly has changed this dynamic, but this new period falls outside the research for this study.

Weak Representative Institutions (1996–2005)

Historically, Chilpancingo was run not only by the PRI but also by a small number of traditional families, which were the city's economic elite and dominant in the party. Every three years, state political elites, who had a direct interest in the capital, and city elites would negotiate over who would be the candidates for mayor and city council, drawing the names from the ranks of these privileged families. Even a cursory look at the apellidos of members of the city council and high-level municipal officials gives a sense of some of the leading political families: Memije, Abarca, Calvo, Tapia, Adame, Acevedo, and Leyva. The poor were not excluded entirely, however. Grouped into the official party's corporate organizations, they turned out the vote every three years and influenced decisions between elections through the PRI's affiliated organizations and their links to individual politicians. Nonetheless, by the beginning of the new millennium, the political rules had begun to change, albeit slowly.

State and municipal elections became increasingly competitive in Guerrero in the 1990s, especially after 1996. Indeed, of the state's five large cities, the opposition has won four—Acapulco, Iguala, Taxco, and José Azueta (Zihuatanejo)—at least once since 1996. The fifth city, Chilpancingo, remained the only major city in the state solidly in the hands of the PRI, but even there, the electoral climate began to change after 1997 (fig. 4.3). In that year, one of the PRI's leading figures in the city, Píoquinto Damián Huato, broke away from the party after not being selected as its congressional candidate. The historical leader of the city's storeowners, a former secretary general of the state PRI, and then the state's

44. Of course, with the victory of the PRD in the state elections in 2005, some of the metaconstitutional powers that the governor has always exercised in municipal decisions may be on the wane, but it is outside the temporal scope of this chapter to test that assumption.

secretary of education, he bolted to the PRD and ran for Congress in the 1997 federal elections.[45] He won election as a federal congressman, defeating a former city mayor, 44.6 percent to 40.7 percent, the first defeat ever for the PRI in the city.[46] The PRI's municipal structure remained largely intact after these events, and the PRI would continue to win every other election afterwards (including the 1999 mayoral race against Damián).[47] Nonetheless, his departure from the official party gave the PRD a boost by adding more teachers and some neighborhood leaders to the PRD's base of support. Even though the party failed to repeat its success in subsequent years, it came to be seen as a major alternative to the PRI in the city for the first time.[48]

As political competition increased, the rules that governed elections also improved dramatically. In 1996, the State Electoral Council of Guerrero (Consejo Estatal Electoral de Guerrero, CEEGRO) was created as an autonomous body with citizen councillors to oversee elections.[49] Although opposition parties have sometimes questioned its credibility, its creation effectively removed election organizing from the governor's direct control. Electoral law changes also expanded the number of seats held by opposition parties in the municipal councils throughout the state. Until 1989, opposition parties had no representation at all within the city council;[50] after 1996, this representation grew substantially, to a point where the winning party was only slightly overrepresented and the second party slightly underrepresented.[51]

Moreover, faced with competition, the PRI was increasingly forced to look for candidates from outside the traditional families, candidates who could appeal

---

45. For news coverage, see Héctor Gutiérrez, "Pioquinto Damián Huato 'candidato popular,'" *Vértice*, March 20, 1997; Daniel Genchi Palma, "Pioquinto Damián renunció al PRI y se fue al PRD," *Vértice*, March 20, 1997.

46. Election results for the seventh district of Guerrero, available from the Federal Electoral Institute (http://www.ife.org.mx).

47. Píoquinto Damián, interviewed by the author, April 13, 2005, and April 20, 2005; Miguel Ángel Mercado Durán, director of the PRI's Training Institute, interviewed by the author, April 15, 2005.

48. Municipal council members Julio César Aguirre (PRD), interviewed by the author, March 11 and April 19, 2005; Ramos (PAN), interview; and Bertín Cabañas (PRI), interviewed by the author, March 11, 2005.

49. For the history of the CEEGRO, later called the State Electoral Institute, see its web page, http://www.ieegro.org.mx.

50. See *Informe municipal 1990*, 41–42.

51. In the three elections between 1996 and 2002, the PRI, as majority party, was overrepresented by 4 to 7 percent, and the PRD, as the second party, was underrepresented by 7 to 12 percent. Author's calculations based on data supplied by the Office of the Municipal Secretary (Ayuntamiento de Chilpancingo, 2002–2005, Secretaría de Gobierno), checked against records of the PRI, PRD, and PAN municipal party offices.

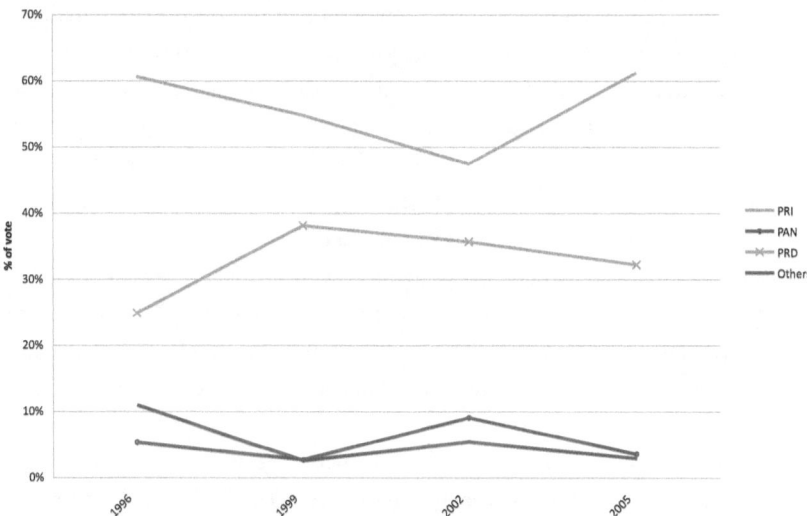

Fig. 4.3 Municipal elections by political party, Chilpancingo, 1996–2005
SOURCE: Consejo Estatal Electoral de Guerrero, available at http://www.ieegro.org.mx.

to the growing number of low-income communities around the city and compete against the opposition party candidates, who often were not members of the traditional families. One rising star in the municipal PRI in recent years was Mario Moreno, a charismatic federal congressman, who had come from one of the low-income communities himself and who had been active in the party's corporate organizations.[52] After threatening to bolt the party if the PRI turned to one of the old families when nominating its mayoral candidate, Moreno succeeded in winning the nomination and becoming mayor in October 2005.[53]

The municipal council appears to play only a minor role in policy making. Overall, no more than 12 percent of meetings are public (and usually fewer), and most of the council's business is conducted behind closed doors.[54] In questions of municipal investment in public works, the mayor seemed to have the final say

---

52. Aguirre (PRD), interview, March 11, 2005.
53. This victory came after the end of the author's research in Chilpancingo.
54. This is based on an analysis of municipal reports (*Informe municipal* for 1988, 1999, 2003, and 2004). One PRD council member, who publishes his own annual report, stated that he "proposed that the sessions of the council be held openly, with the purpose of making the work and actions of the municipality transparent, something that was achieved on only one occasion during the year." Julio César Aguirre, *Informe de actividades 2002–2003* (Chilpancingo: Reguiduría de Educación, Cultura, Recreación y Espectáculos, 2003), 7.

despite the legal requirement that city council members decide these matters. Council members, in turn, function largely as conduits for demands from organizations affiliated with their parties. These demands were generally channeled to the mayor to be negotiated as part of the municipality's expense budget. In general, opposition council members felt they had little influence over these decisions, although they could occasionally get projects approved for their constituencies.[55]

However, despite their minority position, the PRD and the PAN council members had started to make some inroads in influencing municipal decisions. Opposition council members noted that they were able to use their influence with the federal and state lawmakers and federal government agencies to affect key decisions. In this sense, they were playing a sort of two- or three-level game, in which their influence in municipal decision making derived from their influence in other spheres of government. This was the case with the municipal revenue budget for 2004. The PRD and PAN joined together in order to block it by going to their party delegations in the state Congress, where the PRI was a minority after 2002. The two major opposition parties were able to get Congress to deny approval of the municipality's budget until technical errors were corrected, which gave the opposition council members some limited room to negotiate with the mayor in revising the budget.[56] By appealing to their party colleagues in the Congress, the two leading opposition parties also played a role in stopping that body from privatizing the water system in Chilpancingo.[57] In this case, the PAN and PRD turned out to be key allies of the mayor, who was also opposed to the privatization. And the two PAN members of the city council found they could play an

---

55. "There is a deep-seated presidentialism," one PRD council member alleged. "Public works are negotiated with the mayor, not with the council." He and a colleague from the PAN each noted that they had been promised funding for certain public works in 2004 but that this pledge had not been honored. In 2005, they were reduced to negotiating not for funding but for material—tons of cement for projects. This comment was supported by PRI council members and officials of the municipal administration, who noted that public works requests from communities were generally made directly to the mayor himself and occasionally copied to council members. One PRI city council member, who chaired the public works committee, noted, "The mayor is in charge of the relationship with the neighborhoods, but I help as a council member." Mayor Saúl Alarcón Abarca (PRI), interviewed while still in office, confirmed this pattern. When asked how citizens make requests for public works, he answered, "They come to me as mayor with requests" (Me gestionan a mi como presidente municipal). He added that once the proposal for public works was ready, the council could comment on it, but it was basically his responsibility to decide these matters.

56. Interviews with Aguirre (PRD) (March 11, 2005) and Ramos (PAN). For the congressional decision, see Congreso del Estado de Guerrero, "Ley no. 119, de los ingresos de los municipios del Estado de Guerrero para el ejercicio fiscal del año 2004," December 19, 2004, especially 3–4. Available on the website of the Guerrero State Congress, http://www.congreso.gob.mx/.

57. Ramos (PAN), interview.

important role as liaisons with the federal Secretariat of Social Development (Secretaría de Desarrollo, Sedesol) in helping get funds for local development projects and following up when these funds were not adequately apportioned.[58]

Formal and Informal Channels for Political Intermediation

Citizen participation has long been a central term used in PRI-run municipal administrations in Chilpancingo, so much so that in 1991, the municipality published a book on "participatory municipal democracy."[59] Indeed, this was one of the municipal government's two central thrusts between 1989 and 1992 during Solidaridad.[60] It has been echoed, in one form or another, as a major thrust of every recent municipal administration. The most recent municipal development plan notes that the city's first priority is to "promote citizen participation as a fundamental key to consolidate the plans and programs of government."[61] Former Mayor Saúl Alarcón observed that his priority was to "do more with less" by "getting society to participate" (*metiendo a la sociedad que participe*).[62] However, by participation, PRI leaders have generally meant that citizens should be active in authorized political channels, carefully controlled by the PRI, and they should contribute their efforts in order to lower the cost of providing public services.

The primary means for citizen participation in municipal affairs has officially been development committees (*comités de desarrollo*), which are supposed to exist in each neighborhood; an array of ad hoc public works committees convened around specific projects; and the Planning Council for Municipal Development (Coplademun), required for the disbursement of Ramo 33 funds. The development committees have a particularly long history in Chilpancingo, possibly going

---

58. Ramos (PAN), interview. The PAN had only two seats on the city council, but one of the two members was later expelled from the party after he supported the PRD candidate for governor in 2005.

59. This book, *Democracia participativa municipal: Instituciones de participación ciudadana en la vida municipal*, by José Gilberto Garza Grimaldo (Chilpancingo: H. Ayuntamiento Constitucional, 1990), does not deal with the city specifically. See the review by Beatriz Parra in *Crítica Jurídica*, no. 10 (1992): 217–18.

60. This is according to the *Informe municipal 1990*, reporting on the first full year of the administration of Efraín Leyva Acevedo. The two axes were "consolidation of municipal autonomy and reduction of the social need in marginal zones" and "strengthening participatory democracy through solidarity and co-responsibility between people and government," a clear echo of the federal Solidarity program (ibid., 2).

61. *Plan municipal de desarrollo 2002–2005* (Chilpancingo: Ayuntamiento de Chilpancingo, 2002), 38. See also the previous plan, *Plan municipal de desarrollo 1999–2002* (Chilpancingo: Ayuntamiento de Chilpancingo, 1999), especially 3 and 24.

62. Alarcón (PRI), interview.

back several decades, and in the early 1980s, the first law was published to regulate their activities and the election of their members, with an updated law published in 1999.[63] The law requires a nonpartisan election, in the presence of the responsible municipal authority, every two years in every neighborhood, and the council should "motivate citizens to unite, to achieve social development for the benefit of the population."[64]

In detailed interviews with neighborhood leaders,[65] it became clear that most had neighborhoods with active committees. All the committee members had been elected in public assemblies witnessed by the municipal chief of the Barrios and Neighborhoods Office (procurador de Barrios y Colonias), as the law requires. However, they varied a great deal in their degree of support, level of activity, ways of functioning, and length of service. Some seemed to be minimally active, while others had several ongoing projects. Some committees served for the full two-year term; others for up to seven years. Some assemblies to elect the committees had generated a large turnout; others did not even meet the legal quorum.

Most committees seemed to be primarily concerned with basic services, such as electricity and water, where these services were lacking, or secondary infrastructure, such as pavement and access roads. Several of the committees were involved in issues around public security and transportation. For the most part, they seemed to operate in almost complete isolation from one another, except in rare cases where there was a demand for better transportation services or a common access road or bridge. This style was in sharp contrast to the late 1980s and early 1990s, when large organizations both inside and outside the PRI had brought together neighborhood committees.

The Coplademun, on the other hand, is convened each year merely to approve the proposal for public works under Ramo 33, as required by law. In 2004, 245 people attended the meeting.[66] However, the municipal government invites the

---

63. Lozena, interview.

64. The actual functions are not terribly specific, however, despite considerable detail about the structure and form for electing the committees. Various municipal documents refer to the development committees, though not all neighborhoods have them. The *Informe municipal 1999* referred to the election of 115 development committees, but there are more than four hundred neighborhoods in the city. The *Informe municipal 2003* mentions having had contact with seventy-four development committees during that year. And the *Informe municipal 2004* notes that forty-two committees were "renewed" in 2003. The regulation was passed on April 23, 1999, as "Reglamento de la procuraduría de barrios y colonias y para la organización de barrios, colonias, unidades habitacionales y fraccionamientos del municipio de Chilpancingo de los Bravo, Guerrero," and it was published in the *Gaceta Muncipal* in May 1999.

65. Author's interviews with sixteen neighborhood leaders from six neighborhoods in March and April 2005. Care was taken to interview at least one PRI and one PRD leader in each neighborhood.

66. Ayuntamiento de Chilpancingo, *Boletín no. 56* (April 2, 2004).

presidents of only those neighborhoods that have been selected by the mayor to receive project funding.[67] Development committee leaders confirmed that the only times they were invited to the Coplademun was after they had negotiated a public works project from the municipality.[68] The body is thus not an institutional framework to discuss and negotiate demands, let alone deliberate and decide on policy. Instead, it is a ceremonial occasion to bring together the beneficiaries of public works projects and representatives of the three levels of government responsible for funding and implementing those projects.

Indeed, according to both community leaders and municipal officials, the only institutional channel that exists to bring demands to the attention of municipal authorities is through a written letter (*oficio*), either preceded or followed by informal political negotiations.[69] Most of the development committee leaders interviewed indicated they maintained close relationships with city council members or municipal officials because that was necessary if they were going to have their petitions heard. In several cases, they cited direct communication with the mayor himself, but they also noted the role played by several of the PRI city council members, the secretary of the municipality (the mayor's second-in-command), the director of public works, and even the popular congressman (and later mayor) Mario Moreno in securing support. They reported different levels of responsiveness from the municipality, however. Expressing frustration, one committee president noted that "the people from the municipality only show up in the neighborhood when they want us to support some candidate." Others seemed to have a much more fluid relationship with the municipality, but these leaders were largely the same ones whom opposition supporters accused of campaigning for the PRI during the 2005 state election. Indeed, those leaders who reported a close relationship to the municipality correlated strongly with those who were singled out by their opponents as partisan. Being politically connected helped get demands met, but it also meant using the development committee for partisan purposes.

All of the committees in the six neighborhoods studied were run by members of the PRI, as are most committees in the city.[70] It was particularly evident, however,

67. Interviews with council members Cabañas (PRI), Aguirre (PRD) (March 11, 2005), and Ramos (PAN).
68. Based on three interviews in which leaders noted that they had been invited to Coplademun meetings.
69. Lozena, interview.
70. Lozena and council members Cabañas (PRI) and Aguirre (PRD) noted in interviews that most official development committees were run by PRI leaders.

that competition had increased significantly in recent years. Although committee presidents had been historically imposed by municipal officials, elections are now increasingly competitive between the PRI and the PRD.[71] In all of the neighborhoods studied, the PRD (and in some cases, dissident PRI factions) had competed actively and, in at least two neighborhoods, won in past elections. Even the Colonia del PRI, the largest and oldest neighborhood in the city (with the exception of the four traditional barrios), had elected a PRD development committee at one point. However, the municipal official in charge of development committees explained that the PRI's dominance was due to its leaders being "better at getting results" than were the PRD leaders. He pointed out that when the PRI lost a neighborhood, it would form an alternate committee using the PRI's section structure (the party's grassroots neighborhood unit) to compete with the official committee for funds and projects.[72] Of course, the PRI's control of resources for community investments through the mayor's office might also help explain the party's continued dominance of the committees.

Opposition sympathizers (and dissident PRI members) often claimed that the municipal government had formed the official committees as structures of control and partisan promotion. One former committee president (and local PRI official) noted that his neighborhood's committee was put together "through the intervention of the municipal government." They noted that before elections, the PRI would often visit neighborhoods with handouts for residents (food, cardboard, and cement). In four of the six neighborhoods, citizens sympathetic to the PRD had formed their own organizations, which usually brought together several families across different neighborhoods. Each of these organizations was linked to a PRD leader (a city council member or a leading political figure), except for one that included PRD, PAN, and dissident PRI members, perhaps a product of the 2005 governor's election. Since these organizations had little influence with the municipality, they tended to find high-profile issues (lack of transportation services in one case; an access road in another) around which they could protest and pressure the public authorities. In the new climate of plurality, these organizations appeared to have had a degree of success in achieving their objectives.

71. The PAN has little neighborhood-level organization. PAN council member Rigoberto Ramos noted, "We do not have a social base [but rather] the image of a serious party.... There are no PANista neighborhoods." Instead, he noted, the PAN has often drawn support from the city's professionals. PRI council member Bertín Cabañas simply stated that "the PAN is a club of friends." Interviews with Ramos and Cabañas.

72. Lozena, interview.

Conclusions: The Slow Evolution of Corporatism

The municipal government of Chilpancingo was once mostly a caretaker of day-to-day local issues, with the state government making the major decisions for the municipality. Local administrations—and local political leaders more broadly—played an important role in political control and in channeling demands, but they operated within the shadow of state leaders who saw the capital as an extension of their responsibilities. The informal ties of political power trumped the formal responsibilities of the municipal administration. Decentralization has partly changed this relation of subordination. The municipality still lives in the shadow of the state government (and the state governor in particular), but increasingly the former has its own functions, powers, and resources and sufficient discretion to decide what to do with these. With the election of an opposition party to the state governorship in 2005, it appears that the municipality is breaking away from some of the remaining informal constraints on its autonomy, although perhaps others will emerge.

However, democratization and decentralization clearly have not fully produced the kind of accountability and responsiveness that theory might suggest. The form of governance that still dominates in Chilpancingo is, on the face of it, the same that was set up during the period of one-party hegemonic rule. For the most part, the mayor is all-powerful, and he controls the agenda of the city council. The council members, in turn, serve primarily as an occasional conduit to the mayor's office for petitions from community organizations. Council meetings are closed, and citizens have few ways of knowing what their municipal government does between elections. The PRI controls most spaces of social organization, including a broad array of neighborhood organizations that belong almost entirely to the same party and serve as tools for partisan mobilization as much as conduits for citizen demands. Indeed, demand making usually involves citizens approaching their authorities through intermediaries, either neighborhood leaders tied to the PRI or PRI city council members who can serve as conduits to the mayor. In a state where political competition has become the norm, Chilpancingo still seems, on the surface, like a relic from the past. Informal power, structured through old clientelistic channels, continues to form the basis for governing, despite the construction of new formal institutional structures.

However, under the surface, a great deal of contestation has developed, and alternate forms of conducting politics are beginning to appear. Opposition city council members have found new strength in allying with representatives of their own parties in the state Congress and in federal agencies. The PRI is increasingly turning to its leaders from low-income communities rather than to representatives of a tight-knit group of wealthy families. At a community level, considerable competition takes place for some neighborhood committees, and opposition groups are building broad (though not yet deep) coalitions across neighborhoods.

Nonetheless, all of the new ways of doing politics share one key element of the old ways of doing politics: they rely on informal institutions. They are more means for partisan lobbying than for collective problem solving. The underlying structure of politics has changed, but the institutional channels for processing these changes remains the same. Opposition parties need to rely on two-level games—playing off other federal and state institutions against municipal institutions—to make their voices heard. Citizens must rely on well-placed political intermediaries or pressure through numbers to make their demands known to the authorities or to obtain information about the government's activities.

In a city where poverty is widespread, public services limited, and the application of justice often arbitrary, political brokers serve a vital purpose for people's everyday survival. Little, if any, public debate takes place, and those spaces of citizen participation that do exist serve only to mask the top-down nature of political decision making. The city lacks independent organizations, a strongly autonomous media, or even consistently competitive opposition parties. Much is changing in Chilpancingo, but bringing government closer to people through elections and decentralized governance has done little to make it more accountable or responsive to citizens' voices. The permanence of old political institutions that create upward accountability, coupled with the weakness of a horizontally linked civil society that could push for further democratic opening, have conspired to undermine the possibilities for real change.

On October 2, 2005, the inhabitants of Guerrero went to the polls to elect their municipal authorities and state Congress. As in the gubernatorial election in February, the PRD emerged triumphant, winning forty of the state's seventy-three municipalities and seventeen of the twenty-eight congressional districts. Of the five largest cities, only one went to the PRI—Chilpancingo, where the PRI trounced the PRD by an almost two-to-one margin.[73] Once again, the city's traditional party had reasserted its power to win the local elections decisively, even as the rest of the state was turning against the once dominant PRI.

---

73. The final vote was 61.11 percent for the PRI, 32.33 percent for the PRD, with the PAN and smaller parties winning a handful of votes. Statistics available from the state electoral council, http://www.ieegro.org.mx.

The PRI won, in large part, because it remains the only political party with a broad base in the city. Its leaders have skillfully prevented the emergence of other political options and controlled most of the existing social organizations. The PRI also won because it was willing to adapt in order to survive. For the first time in recent memory, the party ran a candidate who did not come from one of the city's elite families. The winner, Mario Moreno, is a PRI leader who came out of the party's popular organizations and who has his own political base in the city's poorer communities. Faced with pressures from the opposition (and perhaps the fear that Moreno might defect to the PRD), the PRI turned to its most popular candidate, even though it meant that the city's elite families had to give up their historical monopoly on mayoral candidacies.

So, although everything in Chilpancingo remains the same on the surface, there are subtle changes under way that may portend a larger shift in the future nature of the municipality's political processes.

5 TIJUANA: LIBERAL DEMOCRACY?

Shortly before midnight on August 1, 2004, Jorge Hank Rhon, millionaire casino owner, accused smuggler, and (at least for some) suspected assassin, came out on stage in front of his supporters to declare victory in the mayoral race in Tijuana, Baja California.[1] His claim was supported by the official electoral results, which gave him a slim lead of one percentage point over his opponent from the ruling National Action Party (PAN). Hank's followers went wild. After fifteen years in the opposition, the PRI was finally returning to power in Tijuana, Mexico's largest and most modern city on the northern border.

To many observers, Hank's victory seemed startling. Tijuana had been the greatest urban bastion of the center-right PAN for the past decade and a half. In 1989, it had become the first city of its size—then close to a million inhabitants—to throw out the long-ruling PRI and keep them out in subsequent elections. In the same election, Tijuana supplied the votes to elect a PAN governor in Baja California, the first opposition governor in Mexico since 1929. National politics certainly influenced the outcome of the election: then-President Carlos Salinas de Gortari was looking to boost his legitimacy after a contested presidential election and burnish the country's image internationally. Recognizing an opposition victory in a distant border state seemed like good politics.[2] However,

---

1. It should be noted that Hank has never been convicted of any crime and was only charged once (and later cleared) with smuggling rare animal skins across the border. However, accusations against him have been legion in the city, and two of his bodyguards were convicted of killing the city's most popular journalist, Héctor Gato Felix, co-editor of the *Zeta* newspaper. Since the killing in 1988, the paper has run a weekly statement asking Hank to clarify whether he ordered the assassination.

2. A few months later, Salinas would pursue a free trade agreement with the United States. At the time of the 1989 elections, he was already looking at his options for expanding Mexico's commercial relationships, hoping originally for a trade agreement with Europe.

unquestionably, Tijuana's particular characteristics also played a role in creating a margin of victory for the PAN that even the president felt obligated to respect.

Tijuana's motto is "the fatherland begins here," and city residents are proud of being the entry point to the nation. However, for many people in Mexico, including the country's political leaders, Tijuana was always a distant city and one of the hardest to control. Rapid demographic and economic growth further complicated political control. In only four decades, Tijuana's population increased seven times, leaping from 165,000 inhabitants in 1960 to more than 1.2 million by 2000. Although this rapid growth led to a dramatic deficit in urban infrastructure, it was fueled by economic opportunities in tourism, trade, and foreign-owned factories, as well as in the construction boom that these activities generated. As a result, a chronic shortage of basic urban services coexisted with a comparatively well-off population that felt it had real opportunities to get ahead economically.

The right-of-center PAN, which advocated individual rights, efficient government, and free markets, seemed ideally suited to this individualistic, dynamic city. The party consistently won one-quarter to one-third of the votes in municipal and state elections starting in the late 1950s—at the same time that it barely registered significant votes elsewhere in the country—and the PAN almost certainly won the municipal elections of 1968, although the PRI-controlled state legislature canceled the election. So it was hardly surprising that as Mexico took its first steps on the path to democratic opening, Tijuana, in 1989, would become the first major city to elect a PAN government and then reelect it three years later.[3]

The new PAN governments set about to destroy the legacy of corporatism implanted by the PRI and to create a new model of democratic governance based on individual citizenship, civic participation, and transparency. Carlos Montejo, the first PAN mayor of Tijuana, summed up his party's commitment to these values in his inaugural address: "I understand that true politics should be directly oriented toward organizing social activity, but never absorbing it. Political realities should always be at the service of society. That is why every citizen has the right to have his voice heard by the authorities, to express his opinions freely, to monitor the actions that the government engages in, and to know the real results of the government's performance."[4] This was a bold declaration of the principles

---

3. Ciudad Juárez, another border city of comparable size, had elected a PAN government in 1983, but the PRI returned in the next election.

4. From the 1989 inauguration speech of Mayor Carlos Montejo, cited in the *Plan municipal de desarrollo 1990–92* (Tijuana: Ayuntamiento de Tijuana, 1990), 5.

long cherished by PAN leaders: to create an administration responsive to citizen concerns and accountable to them.

During the fifteen years it governed, the PAN would be given an unprecedented opportunity to implement these principles. This period coincided with the country's gradual process of democratization and decentralization, and at times Tijuana even helped lead it. The city government started the first mayors' association in the country, filed the first municipal lawsuit against the federal government over jurisdictional issues, and created the first project for private bank financing of public investments. One of the city's political leaders would, a few years later, become the main sponsor of the congressional legislation that created the Ramo 33 transfers to municipal governments.

How, then, could the PAN lose an election fifteen years later to one of the city's most controversial and polarizing figures?[5] Part of the answer lies in the way the party governed during its five terms, a style that earned it great success administratively but also failed to build a durable base of support. The first PAN governments tried to implement the lofty principles that Mayor Montejo had articulated, by building a more responsive and accountable local government with clear institutional channels for citizens' direct participation in the democratic process. This may have been done partly on principle, but it was also motivated by their desire to create a political coalition to fend off the PRI. Subsequent municipal governments ultimately lacked the will or the incentives to maintain these channels for communication with citizens. They would fall back on old habits of clientelism, although these would be less intense and ultimately less effective than what had been in place before. Informal politics would survive as the key form of political intermediation in Tijuana, but it would be transformed in the municipal arena by the twin processes of democratization and decentralization and by Tijuana's particular characteristics.

Shaping the Political Terrain: Distance, Mobility, and Dynamism

Tijuana began as a small settlement sometime around 1889, in what was then the Northern District of the Federal Territory of Baja California.[6] It would not

---

5. Hank, the renegade son of a famous PRI leader who had served as mayor of Mexico City, was so controversial that many of the business leaders who had traditionally supported the PRI refused to endorse him when he ran for mayor.

6. The state of Baja California was originally part of the Mexican territory of California, but after the 1848 Treaty of Guadalupe Hidalgo, which concluded a war between Mexico and the United States, the

become a major city until after World War II, when it experienced a sustained period of explosive growth that has made it one of Mexico's largest cities today.[7] Initially, the northern half of Baja California was a federal territory, a status it held until 1953 when it became a state. This federal tutelage and the initially sparse population meant that the region did not develop the same kind of homegrown strongmen and powerful families that dominated most other states after the Revolution. Instead, it was the fiefdom of successive national political and military leaders, who were sent by the president to govern the territory, while these individuals made (or increased) their fortunes. Perhaps the most famous among these was Abelardo L. Rodríguez, a prominent Sonoran revolutionary leader, who later went on to serve as the country's interim president. After the Revolution, the federal authorities' control meant that Baja California was technically far more subordinate to the national government than were other states, but it also meant that there were no local leaders capable of exerting hegemony over the state's political process, as was the case elsewhere in the country. Baja California only developed its own dominant political class in the second half of the twentieth century, and it was highly fragmented, with no single leader, family, or cohesive political group standing out over the others.

Distance from Mexico City also shaped political attitudes toward centralization and generated a sense of self-reliance. Until the late 1930s, the territory was poorly connected to the center of the country, and standing at Mexico's northwesternmost point, it developed something akin to a frontier mentality. Distance also weakened the ability of federal authorities—and the PRI—to establish the kinds of political arrangements that made control possible in other Mexican states. Although Baja California had PRI-affiliated corporatist organizations, they often were weakly linked to the national organizations, and they maintained a greater degree of autonomy than similar organizations elsewhere in Mexico. Baja California only briefly had municipal elections, from 1915 to 1927, and it had no

---

northern region of California was ceded to the United States, and Baja California was divided into the Northern and Southern Districts, under direct tutelage of the federal government. The Northern District became the Northern Territory of Baja California in 1930, still under federal jurisdiction, until it achieved statehood in 1953. The southern district of Baja California, which remained a federal territory for most of the twentieth century, became a separate state, Baja California Sur, in 1975.

7. In the 2000 census, it was the sixth largest municipality in the country. If we include Mexico City, not a municipality but a federal district, Tijuana would be the seventh largest city. Municipalities four through six (Ciudad Nezahualcóyotl, Ciudad Juárez, and Tijuana) have just over 1.2 million inhabitants each. Since all are cities with large migrant populations, it is hard to know with certainty which of the three is the largest.

territory-wide elections until it became a state. Consequently, in the crucial period after the Revolution, the PRI did not need to mobilize voters regularly, which was a factor central to the political arrangements that built party loyalty elsewhere. As it did throughout the country, the PRI dominated local politics, and organizations affiliated with the party were the primary conduits for resolving daily problems. Nevertheless, because of the lack of local elections, its capacity for political mobilization was less tested, and its membership was a little thinner than elsewhere in the country. It is hardly surprising that opposition parties found fertile ground in Baja California from even the earliest years, when this was uncommon in the other Mexican states. Tijuana's small business owners were particularly drawn to the PAN, though popular movements often gravitated toward smaller parties of the left. The opposition parties were far smaller in membership than the PRI, and far less relevant as conduits for resolving problems, but they attracted votes at election time, something almost unheard of in other states.

Proximity to the United States complemented distance from Mexico City. During Prohibition, the bars and casinos in Tijuana became a major attraction. When gambling was outlawed in Baja California in 1935, the state became a free zone exempt from the tariffs imposed elsewhere in Mexico. During World War II, Tijuana became an industrial city that helped supply the Allied war effort. In 1965, the Mexican and U.S. governments negotiated an agreement to create *maquiladoras*, foreign-owned industrial plants that would process goods for tariff-free export to the United States.[8] Moreover, many city residents have long had family members on both sides of the border, and Spanish-language media generally treat the two sides of the line as a single market, which creates a constant, binational flow of information.[9] The interdependence with the U.S. side of the

---

8. These companies, principally U.S.-owned, produced goods for the U.S. market using low-wage labor in Mexico. However, by the 1990s, other countries, especially Japan, South Korea, and Sweden, had also set up maquiladoras in order to produce goods for the U.S. market. These companies usually had operations in both Tijuana and San Diego. In principle, this program was designed to create jobs in Mexico to absorb excess labor after the termination of the *bracero* program, a guest-worker program that had brought hundreds of thousands of Mexicans to the United States as seasonal workers starting after World War II. The maquiladoras would become an importance source of employment in the city and a magnet for migration to the city.

9. Television stations and most radio stations serve both Tijuana and the Spanish-speaking communities in San Diego. Tijuana newspapers cover San Diego as part of local news; and the San Diego *Union-Tribune* covers Tijuana as local news for San Diego residents, as well. Both the *Union-Tribune* and Los Angeles's two major papers, the *Times* and *La Opinión*, are commonly sold at Tijuana newsstands (and they are far easier and less expensive to acquire than Mexico City papers). When the federal and state governments began to harass one of Tijuana's leading newspapers, *Zeta*, in the 1980s, the publisher began

border served as a partial counterweight to the centralizing pressures from Mexico City.

Population mobility has also shaped Tijuana, making it one of the fastest growing cities in the western hemisphere and a "cultural mosaic" of people from all over Mexico (as well as other countries).[10] The population exploded between 1960 and 2000, rising from 165,690 to more than 1.2 million.[11] Migration to Tijuana was driven by employment opportunities and sometimes by the desire to cross the border into the United States. In 2003, slightly over half of Tijuana's population was born outside of the state, and growth continued at a rate of around 4.9 percent annually.[12] This mobility tied the city culturally to the rest of Mexico—almost all residents have strong ties to places elsewhere in the country—but it made it difficult for the PRI to develop the stable bases it had in other Mexican states.

Finally, Tijuana has long had a pattern of dynamic economic expansion far ahead of the rest of the country, although this is coupled with a deficient provision of basic services to meet the needs of the growing population as well as only limited regulation, which would otherwise ensure that minimal labor and environmental standards are met. Export manufacturing, tourism, and commerce, all a result of the city's location on the border, have provided expanding employment opportunities to successive generations that have arrived in Tijuana.[13] Income has increased noticeably over time, with more than half of the city's residents earning at least three times the minimum wage (compared to only 27 percent nationally).[14]

---

printing the paper in San Diego and importing it to avoid censorship. See Andrew Selee and Heidy Servin-Baez, "Introduction: Writing Across Borders," in Rossana Fuentes-Beraín, Andrew Selee, and Heidy Servin-Baez, eds., *Writing Beyond Boundaries: Journalism Across the U.S.-Mexico Border* (Washington, D.C.: Woodrow Wilson Center, 2005). See also the chapter in the same volume by Sandra Dibble, reporter for the *San Diego Union-Tribune*, "The Stories That Whisper."

10. I borrow the term "cultural mosaic" from Tonatiuh Guillén, "Presentación," in Tonatiuh Guillén, ed., with the collaboration of José Negrete Mata, *Baja California: Escenarios para el nuevo milenio* (Mexico City: UNAM, 2002), 16.

11. INEGI, *Tijuana* (Aguascalientes: INEGI, 2000). The population in 1920 was only 1,028, but it had risen to 21,997 by 1940. Population data for this earlier period can be found in *Monografía Tijuana* (Tijuana: XVI Ayuntamiento de Tijuana, 2000), based on INEGI census data.

12. *Plan estratégico Tijuana, 2003–2025* (Tijuana: Ayuntamiento de Tijuana, 2003), 43.

13. The city remains primarily dependent on the service sector (52.5 percent) but with a sizable percentage of employment in manufacturing (32.5 percent) and construction (7.9 percent). INEGI, *Estados Unidos Mexicanos XII censo general de población y vivienda 2000: Tabulador de la muestra censal cuestionario amplio* (Aguascalientes: INEGI, 2003).

14. INEGI, *Tijuana* and *XII censo*.

However, these figures mask Tijuana's considerable needs. Although incomes are significantly higher than the national average, the cost of living is also much higher, especially because many basic goods are imported from the United States. Moreover, rapid growth has generated a major deficit in basic services, including electricity, water, and sewer lines.[15] Limited environmental controls on factories located near residential neighborhoods create hazardous health conditions in some areas of the city. As a result, relatively greater opportunities for employment and income generation coexist with a high cost of living and serious deficits in urban infrastructure. Citizens are comparatively more able to raise concerns, but they have no shortage of issues about which to do so.

Political Changes: Weak Control, Strong Resistance

The state of Baja California was born out of a long-term struggle for autonomy. A local movement first developed in 1917, during the national constitutional convention, to demand that the territory have a civilian governor who would also be a native of the territory.[16] This movement gained strength in 1931 with the founding of the Committee for a Free and Sovereign State of Baja California (Comité Pro-Estado Libre y Soberano), which also demanded statehood for the territory. As the population and electoral importance of the state grew, the federal government gradually warmed to the idea of statehood, and in 1952, it created the state of Baja California. In the first statewide elections in 1953, Braulio Maldonado, one of the founders of the committee, was elected the state's first governor. His election set off an uninterrupted period of PRI rule in both the state and municipal governments that would last until the 1980s. However, in Baja California, although the PRI remained the dominant political organization, with an ongoing presence in the daily lives of most citizens, it was never as

---

15. Federal government statistics show that the coverage of services is in the 80 percent to 95 percent range (*Cuaderno estadístico municipal: Tijuana, Estado de Baja California* [Aguascalientes: INEGI, 2003]). However, these statistics often fail to take into account many of the newest neighborhoods in the city. More than three hundred neighborhoods in Tijuana have residents who lack legal land titles; most (but not all) of these colonias are of recent creation. The city's long-term strategic plan lists the coverage of sewage services at only 60 percent (*Plan estratégico Tijuana, 2003–2025*, 40), although INEGI indicates that it is more than 80 percent (INEGI, *XII censo*; INEGI, *XI censo general de población y vivienda* [Aguascalientes: INEGI, 2003]).

16. This paragraph draws on the account of Baja California's independence struggle in Lawrence Douglas Taylor Hansen, "La evolución de las instituciones políticas de Baja California," in Guillén, *Baja California*.

dominant as it was elsewhere in the country. As the century went on, the party's weaknesses would be exposed, and its grip on power would seem, at times, to be on the verge of slipping away.

As elsewhere in Mexico, PRI-affiliated organizations were fundamental to daily life and to citizens' ability to have access to public authorities. The PRI maintained affiliated unions for transportation workers, hotel and restaurant employees, and public sector workers, all crucial sectors of the city's economy.[17] A party-affiliated labor organization even owned the popular boxing ring in downtown Tijuana. Moreover, as the city's population began to explode in the 1970s and 1980s, the PRI developed an army of brokers who helped new residents "invade" unoccupied land and press for land titles and eventually public services. These brokers were usually linked to influential political leaders in the municipal, state, or federal government by one of the party's sectoral organizations. The brokers helped give residents access to officials who would hear and perhaps eventually resolve their petitions. As elsewhere in Mexico, the PRI also maintained an army of brokers linked to their municipal party structure. This ran from the party's municipal president at the top, all the way down to block leaders at the bottom. These two structures—often referred to as the "vertical" and "horizontal" structures of the PRI—generally overlapped, with block and neighborhood leaders often affiliated with the sectoral organizations of the party. No other party in Tijuana or elsewhere in the state could play this role of political mediator.

Nonetheless, the PAN, which had only a small membership and extremely limited presence on the ground, attracted significant sympathies at election time. Elsewhere in Mexico it was a small opposition party, designed to do little more than express disagreement with the ruling party; however, in Baja California it acquired a real electoral capacity and a relentless desire to win elections.[18] The party made strong showings in the 1958 presidential and 1959 gubernatorial elections, winning over one-third of the vote in 1959.[19] In 1968, the PAN made another strong showing, almost certainly winning the municipal elections in both

17. For a description of the PRI's corporatist organization in Baja California, see Víctor Alejandro Espinoza Valle, *Alternancia política y gestión pública: El Partido Acción Nacional en el gobierno de Baja California* (Mexico City: Plaza y Valdés; Tijuana: El Colegio de la Frontera Norte, 2000).

18. In 1945, the PAN had only sixty-five members, but it soon spread to all of the major cities of the state, including Tijuana. Although the PRI-affiliated Committee for a Free and Sovereign State of Baja California fought for statehood, the PAN argued for the restoration of municipal autonomy, which had existed between 1915 and 1927. José Negrete Mata, "Historia política y alternancia en Baja California, 1952–1989," in Guillén, *Baja California*, 58–59, especially 59n.

19. PAN leaders claim that they won both elections, including a clean sweep of all Tijuana polling stations in the 1958 presidential elections. Negrete Mata, "Historia política y alternancia," 62–63.

Tijuana and the state capital, Mexicali. The local Congress, however, annulled these elections and appointed a caretaker government in both cities. Although this incident led many supporters to lose faith in the possibility for electoral change,[20] the PAN continued to command significant support at each election (fig. 5.1). Then in 1986, in the midst of a national economic crisis, the PAN won its first recognized municipal election in the state in the small municipality of Ensenada, just south of Tijuana. The winning candidate was a charismatic small businessman named Ernesto Ruffo. His winning margin was large and the municipality was comparatively small, so it seemed safe for the PRI to accept his victory. However, Ruffo would go on to play an important role in state politics three years later when he was elected the first opposition governor.

Through a variety of popular organizations, the Mexican left was also developing a presence in Tijuana, though it initially did not include participation in electoral politics. In addition to an early role in student organizations, the left came to play a decisive part in the 1970s and 1980s in the struggle for land and services for urban migrants. Many of these migrants had established shantytowns throughout the city. These neighborhoods became particularly politicized as the state government repeatedly sought to forcibly remove residents by bulldozing their homes, especially those along the city's river. In 1980, the governor gave orders to open the city's dam without warning during a particularly strong rainstorm, destroying most of the remaining homes along the river.[21] This galvanized a nascent organization of the city's poor, the Comité Unión de Colonos Urbanos de Tijuana, A.C. (Committee Union of Urban Residents of Tijuana, Civil Association or CUCUTAC), which had been founded two years earlier by residents living near the river. CUCUTAC spread throughout Tijuana's low-income communities, and it became an important actor in struggles over land titles and urban services. Some CUCUTAC leaders would eventually run for political office, initially with the Trotskyite Workers' Revolutionary Party (PRT) in the early 1980s, later with other parties of the left, and eventually with the PRD. Although CUCUTAC became one of the city's most combative organizations on behalf of the poor—and it developed a real capacity to represent its communities and to

---

20. Ibid., 64–65.
21. José Manuel Valenzuela Arce, *Empapados de sereno: Reconstrucción testimonial del movimiento urbano popular en Baja California (1928–1988)* (Tijuana: El Colegio de la Frontera Norte, 1991), 104. This book includes detailed descriptions of the removal of Cartolandia (city of cardboard), as the neighborhoods along the river were known, including the state-mandated flooding of it (99–115). The flood remains a well-known story in Tijuana, which residents of low-income communities frequently recounted to me during the almost six years that I lived in the city.

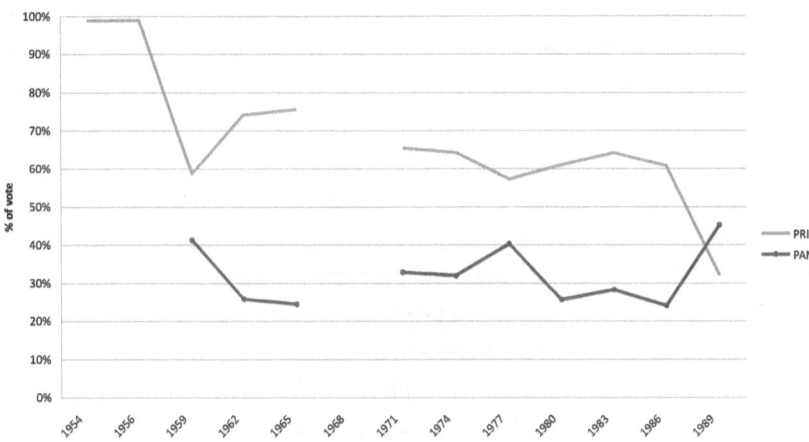

Fig. 5.1 Municipal elections by political party, Tijuana, 1954–89

Note: Percentage for PRI and PAN only. The 1968 elections were annulled and no data ever released.

SOURCE: Instituto Estatal Electoral de Baja California, available at http://www.iepcbc.org.mx/.

pressure the PRI-dominated governments to grant land titles and public services—it remained small compared to the army of PRI brokers who dominated most of Tijuana's communities.

Tijuana entered the late 1980s with considerable competition among diverse approaches to organizing political power. The PRI remained dominant and ensured its continuation in power through effective intermediation and occasional fraud. It possessed a presence on the ground in people's workplaces and in their neighborhoods that no other political force could match, and it ultimately controlled all the levers of political power that could respond to citizens' needs. However, the PAN had developed a real electoral base, with which PRI leaders had to come to terms, and CUCUTAC and other smaller organizations on the left developed the mobilizing capacity to be an alternative path for resolving community needs. Perhaps more so than other Mexican cities, Tijuana also had many citizens who did not belong to any organizations. Much of the employment was in largely nonunionized sectors (maquiladoras, small businesses, tourism, construction, and work on the U.S. side of the border), and the location of the city provided a degree of social mobility beyond the PRI's control. In short, most citizens still dealt with PRI political leaders to resolve their daily needs because they were the most effective brokers who could serve as channels to government decision makers. But the city had a large number of citizens whose true loyalty was up for grabs by any party that could offer a convincing argument. On the strength of its ability to resolve everyday problems and the evidence that no one else could win, the PRI largely captured that vote until 1988.

In that year, however, the campaign of Cuauhtémoc Cárdenas, the presidential candidate of a left-leaning coalition, resonated not only with voters on the left but also with dissidents from the PRI and many of these unaffiliated voters.[22] As the son of Mexico's most revered modern-day president and a powerful former member of the PRI, he seemed like the first candidate who might actually dislodge the ruling party. Baja California gave Cárdenas a majority with 165,497 votes to 157,190 for the PRI's Carlos Salinas de Gortari in the official count.[23] Salinas was declared the winner nationally by the government-controlled elections board despite significant questions about the results, but the PRI had shown its vulnerability. The PAN's presidential candidate ended up a disappointing third in Baja California with 101,164 votes. Within a year, however, the left had divided in Baja California, as elsewhere in Mexico, and could not capitalize on its earlier momentum. With the charismatic mayor of Ensenada, Ernesto Ruffo, as their candidate, the PAN trounced the PRI in the state governor's election in 1989. A largely unknown businessman, Carlos Montejo, became the first opposition mayor of Tijuana, riding Ruffo's coattails to victory.

The PAN was a party that had attracted the votes of unaffiliated citizens, who had individually expressed their rejection of the PRI's corporate style of governance. It was, moreover, a truly liberal party that believed that government should establish a direct relationship between individual citizens and the state rather than one mediated by corporate organizations. A perfect match seemed to exist between the city—distant from the center of power, mobile, and dynamic—and the party—federalist, liberal, and capitalist—that voters had chosen to entrust with their future. How would the PAN go about implementing its new style of democratic governance? Could it create new channels to mediate between citizens and the government and to replace the PRI's old corporatist channels? And if so, would the municipal government have sufficient authority and autonomy for any innovations to be meaningful?

22. The organizers of his campaign in the state included the state's first governor, Braulio Maldonado, who had split from the PRI; Catalino Zavala, the leader of CUCUTAC; and many other local political leaders.

23. Negrete Mata, "Historia política y alternancia," 83.The official tally almost certainly underestimated actual electoral support for Cárdenas.

Empowering the Municipality (1989–2004)

The victory of the PAN in Tijuana in 1989 coincided with a period of expansion of municipal authority and autonomy in Mexico. Under five consecutive PAN mayors, the Tijuana government both benefited from this expansion and, in the 1990s, led the way in promoting it. Municipal finances more than tripled in *real* terms between 1989 and 2004 (fig. 5.2). Increased federal transfers accounted for much of this increase; however, the city government took great pains to exercise its own agency by expanding its locally generated revenue. The first PAN administration, under Carlos Montejo, updated the registry of properties and increased property tax rates.[24] The second administration, under Héctor Osuna Jaime, took out a loan from Banobras, the federal government's bank for subnational governments, to create a comprehensive new system for tracking property taxes.[25] The third administration, under Guadalupe Osuna Millán, created the first detailed city map, which allowed the government to identify property that had not been included in the registry.[26] Overall, compliance with property taxes significantly increased from 47.9 percent in 1989 to 71.3 percent by 2003, and property tax revenue skyrocketed from under 7 million pesos to over 100 million pesos in this same period.[27] At the same time, the city found new sources of locally generated revenue, largely tied to taxation of the city's businesses, so that even while revenue from property taxes increased, other forms of locally generated revenue expanded even faster.[28]

---

24. Property tax rates are the exclusive province of the state legislature. In this case, Montejo used a calculation from an autonomous government commission to determine the rates and then took the proposal to the state legislature. See Tonatiuh Guillén López and José Negrete Mata, "Tijuana," in Tonatiuh Guillén, ed., *Municipios en transición: Actores sociales y nuevas políticas de gobierno* (Mexico City: Friedrich Ebert Stiftung, 1995).

25. For more information on this topic, see Tim Campbell and Travis Katz, "The Politics of Participation in Tijuana, Mexico: Inventing a New Style of Governance," in Harald Fuhr and Tim Campbell, *Leadership and Innovation in Subnational Government: Case Studies from Latin America* (Washington, D.C.: World Bank, 2004). Campbell and Katz argue that municipal governments in Mexico had used loans from Banobras primarily for public works projects, and so the Osuna Jaime administration may have been the first municipal government to use a Banobras loan to increase its own tax-generation capacity.

26. Martín de la Rosa Medellín, former municipal official, interviewed by the author, May 3, 2005. Unless otherwise noted, all interviews cited in this chapter took place in Tijuana. Rosa had served as deputy director of the municipality's social participation department and later went on to head the COMPLADEM in subsequent administrations.

27. Ayuntamiento de Tijuana, *Informe municipal 1998; Informe municipal 2000;* and *Informe municipal 2003* (Tijuana: Ayuntamiento de Tijuana, 1998, 2000, and 2003).

28. For 1989–2002, see INEGI, Sistema Municipal de Base de Datos, http://sc.inegi.org.mx/simbad; for 2003–4, see Ayuntamiento de Tijuana, *Presupuesto de ingresos* for 2003 and 2004, available on the municipal website, http://www.tijuana.gob.mx. See also INEGI, *Finanzas públicas estatales y municipales 2000–2003* (Aguascalientes: INEGI, 2004).

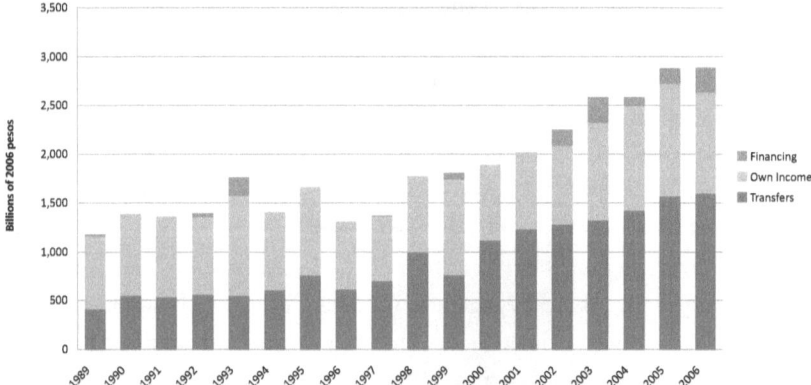

Fig. 5.2 Real municipal income by source, Tijuana, 1989–2006

SOURCE: For 1989–2002, see INEGI, *Sistema Nacional de Base de Datos*, available at http://sc.inegi.org.mx/simbad; for 2003–4, see Ayuntamiento de Tijuana, *Presupuesto de ingresos* for 2003 and 2004, available at http://www.tijuana.gob.mx. See also INEGI, *Finanzas públicas estatales y municipales 2000–2003* (Aguascalientes: INEGI, 2004).

The city also experimented with new approaches to municipal debt. In addition to the Banobras loan to improve the tax-collection infrastructure, the second PAN administration, under Osuna Jaime, created a comprehensive strategy called the Plan de Activación Urbana (Urban Activation Plan) or PAU, which would have allowed for private financing of major infrastructure development. It was the first attempt in Mexico to combine private loans, state and city funds, contributions from business, and a betterment levy to create a major package for modernizing the city's infrastructure.[29] A major flood that devastated Tijuana took more than sixty lives and left entire communities cut off from the city for days was the impetus for the plan.[30] It also responded to a clear political logic: this opposition government wanted to urbanize the city without being dependent on federal government loans that could lead to greater federal control over city decisions.[31] Ultimately, however, Tijuana was forced to scrap its Urban Activation

---

29. The package included forty major infrastructure investments: 70 percent were roads with drainage systems, and 10 percent were flood control projects. A betterment levy on residents who lived near the new infrastructure would cover 20 percent of the payment on the project's US$170 million loan; 40 percent would come from residents who lived further away, 15 percent from business taxes, and 25 percent from state and municipal funds. For a detailed description of the project, see Campbell and Katz, "Politics of Participation."

30. Héctor Osuna Jaime, mayor of Tijuana (1992–95), interviewed by the author, February 25, 2005; Campbell and Katz, "Politics of Participation."

31. Guillén and Negrete Mata, "Tijuana."

Plan. The 1994–95 economic crisis had led to a massive devaluation of the peso against the dollar and had sent interest rates skyrocketing. Nonetheless, this innovative plan set the precedent for later, more modest loan packages from private sources, which were completed under other mayors.

Mayor Osuna Jaime also took a step toward ensuring greater municipal autonomy when he created a national conference of PAN mayors. The organization, which would eventually become the Asociación de Municipios de México (Mexican Association of Municipalities, AMMAC), met for the first time in Tijuana, and Osuna became its first president.[32] During his administration, the city of Tijuana also filed the first municipal lawsuit against the federal government, alleging that the federal Solidarity Program was being used for political purposes in the city. The Supreme Court ultimately found in favor of the federal government, but not before Tijuana had set a precedent of municipal autonomy that dozens of other municipalities would copy in subsequent years.

By the late 1990s, municipal authority and autonomy expanded even further. The creation of Ramo 33 in 1998 led to a dramatic rise in the city's finances under increasingly clear rules. The political and bureaucratic conflicts between the state and city governments sometimes led to financial transfers being delayed, which, in turn, generated problems for the planning and implementation of programs. Nonetheless, the city had a guaranteed source of external revenues in addition to its own-source income.[33] Moreover, because Tijuana comprised almost half of the state population and over half of its economic activity, it had a certain degree of leverage within the Baja California state government's political and policy debates. As a result, the state government recognized its five municipalities as political interlocutors in major policy decisions, and after 1996, it created mechanisms to gather formal input from municipalities in decisions that affected them. A major 2001 reform of the state law on municipalities, which emerged from negotiations among the municipalities and state government, explicitly

---

32. Although at first a relatively small association, the AMMAC would grow to become the most influential municipal association in Mexico. Gradually weakening its relationship to the PAN and expanding its reach to include municipalities governed by other parties, by 2004, AMMAC had more than 250 members, including mayors of most of the country's largest cities. Based on the author's review of AMMAC's website (http://www.ammac.org.mx) in 2005 and an interview with the organization's director, Rubén Fernández, March 4, 2005.

33. An example of a delay due to bureaucratic infighting and political disagreements between the state and city, both PAN-run governments, involved the 2003 and 2004 public security funds. Arnulfo Guerrero, municipal council member (PAN, 2001–4), interviewed by the author, February 24, 2005.

recognized the regulatory authority of municipalities in a range of areas where previously the law had been unclear.[34]

Strengthening Representative Institutions (1989–2004)

After the PAN won both the city and state government, Baja California undertook innovative electoral reforms. In 1991, the state created its own voter registry; in 1992, its own secure election credential with a photograph; and in 1994, an autonomous state electoral institute with citizen councillors elected by the state congress. These measures designed to eliminate vote fraud preceded similar actions by the federal government, which only created an updated registry of voters and a voter credential with photograph in 1994 and a fully autonomous electoral council in 1996. Baja California's 1994 and 1996 electoral reforms also expanded the representation of minority parties in the state legislature and on city councils.[35]

Although the PAN won every Tijuana municipal election and Baja California state election from 1989 to 2001 (see fig. 5.3), the PRI and other parties competed actively. In fact, the PRI won the federal elections of 1994 outright, winning all the state's congressional districts, and it frequently won the other Baja California municipal governments (though never Tijuana). In addition, the PAN only had a majority in the state legislature in 1995 to 1998, so the PRI and PRD had considerable influence over state policies that directly affected the city throughout much of this period.

The PAN had long practiced internal democracy and regularly held conventions to determine its candidates for election. The party's success after 1989 only served to strengthen this process. When Carlos Montejo ran for mayor in 1989, he was unopposed at the party's municipal convention, which barely attracted two hundred PAN members.[36] However, once the party was in power and candidates

---

34. Among other things, the new law transferred full authority for property registry and taxes to the municipalities and allowed for concurrent responsibility in regulating transportation and alcoholic beverage sales. For further discussion of this, see Tonatiuh Guillén López, "Una reforma municipal en dos tiempos: Baja California," in Guillén López and Ziccardi, eds., *Innovación y continuidad del municipio mexicano*.

35. See Espinoza Valle, *Alternancia política*, and Víctor Alejandro Espinoza Valle, *La transición difícil: Baja California 1995–2001* (Tijuana: El Colegio de la Frontera Norte, 2003), for extensive data on state congressional elections and seats and an analysis of the major issues dealt with in each period.

36. Tania Hernández Vicencio, *De la oposición al poder: El PAN en Baja California, 1986–2000* (Tijuana: El Colegio de la Frontera Norte, 2001), 103.

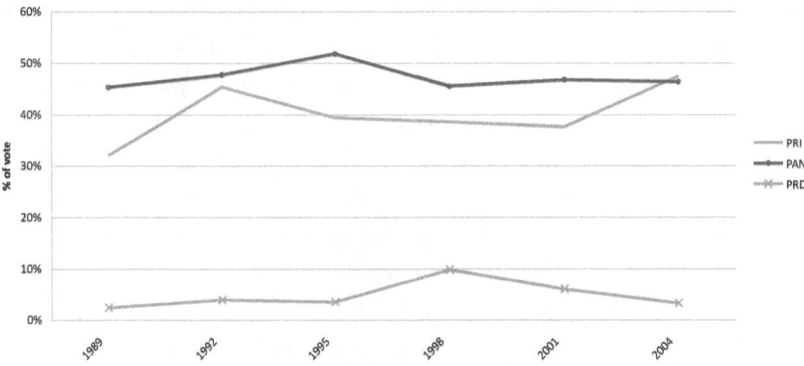

Fig. 5.3 Municipal elections by political party, Tijuana, 1989–2004
SOURCE: Instituto Estatal Electoral de Baja California, available at http://www.iepcbc.org.mx.

had a reasonable expectation of winning the general election, internal elections drew considerably more interest within the party. In both 1992 and 1998, the internal elections proved particularly competitive.[37] They were also quite different from the PRI's method for selecting candidates, which usually involved backroom negotiations among high-level political leaders or government officials.

However, the small number of citizens who could engage in the PAN's internal selection process, less than 1 percent of registered voters, severely limited its democratic potential. The PAN historically had a small number of members, both in Baja California as well as nationally, in order to maintain a clear party identity and avoid PRI infiltration, and this exclusive membership largely remained in place even after the PAN became the governing party.[38] Moreover, once in power, the PAN became increasingly divided into party factions, which formed coalitions around particular candidates.[39] According to former mayor Héctor Osuna Jaime, the PAN's relatively small size meant that a successful

---

37. David A. Shirk, "El PAN, un partido en construcción: Lecciones desde Tijuana," in Tania Hernández Vicencio and José Negrete Mata, eds., *La experiencia del PAN: Diez años de gobierno en Baja California* (Tijuana: El Colegio de la Frontera Norte, 2001).

38. See Mizrahi, *From Martyrdom to Power.* Although PAN membership grew in Tijuana from fewer than 500 in 1990 to 1,581 in 1999 and finally to around 2,400 in 2004, this number was less than 3 percent of those citizens who voted for the PAN in the 2004 municipal elections and a little over 1 percent of all voters. Data on party membership from Shirk, "El PAN, un partido en construcción," for 1990; Hernández Vicencio, *De la oposición al poder,* 113, for 1999; "Estiman depurar a 960 panistas," *Frontera,* February 1, 2005, 1, for 2004. Ironically, the PAN was planning to *reduce* its membership by as much as 40 percent in response to losing the municipal election in 2004.

39. See Hernández Vicencio, *De la oposición al poder.*

municipal candidate only needed to convince "around twenty people" in order to win an internal election, as long as those twenty were the key leaders of the different factions.[40] Internal democratic processes within the PAN were an important innovation that contributed to elections that were more accountable to voters, but this innovation evolved very little as the party itself grew and began to win elections.

Similarly, the Tijuana municipal council gained in stature and profile after the PAN's victory in 1989, but occasional reforms only marginally expanded its relevance as a representative body. The state legislature passed legislation in the early 1990s expanding opposition representation in all the state's municipal councils, but the winning party was still guaranteed a majority of seats regardless of whether they won a majority of the vote.[41] Except for two periods when the PAN delegation in the Tijuana council split among competing factions, the mayor only had to negotiate controversial legislation with his own party to get it passed.[42] The council could shape the mayor's actions through opposition, if the majority party divided, but it had few agenda-setting powers.

Moreover, the changes did nothing to alter the election of council members by party lists, which meant that citizens voted only for the party of their choice but rarely knew the names of the council members. An attempt in 2001 and 2002 to change state electoral legislation to allow half of the council members to be elected in districts ultimately failed because of the opposition of the state's mayors, who enjoyed their dominant position over the councils.[43] Starting in 1995, the PAN began to elect its list of municipal council members through internal

40. Osuna Jaime, interview.
41. This meant that the majority party went from an overrepresentation of more than 30 percent in council seats (above their electoral percentage) to an overrepresentation of only 5 to 20 percent, and the second party's underrepresentation was reduced by an equal amount. This analysis is based on a review of council seats by party, and it includes the *síndico* (syndic) as a council member but not the mayor. Data on elections and seats for 1989–98 from Tonatiuh Guillén, "Gobernabilidad y gestión local en México: El caso de Tijuana, B.C., 1989–1997," in Martha Schteingart and Emilio Duhau, eds., *Transición política y democracia municipal en México y Colombia* (Mexico City: Miguel Ángel Porrúa, 2001), 78. Data for 1998–2001 are from an email communication with Tonatiuh Guillén, December 19, 2005; and for 2001–4, the municipality's web page (http://www.tijuana.gob.mx).
42. This was true during the first PAN administration (1989–92), when a faction of six PAN council members (out of thirteen) disagreed with the mayor on most major policy issues. Consisting of more traditional members of the party, this faction felt that the mayor was not adhering to the party's principles. Guillén and Negrete Mata trace this development in detail in "Tijuana." See also Shirk, "PAN, un partido en construcción." This happened again during the fourth PAN administration (1998–2001). Juanita Pérez, city council member (PRI, 1999–2002), interviewed by the author, February 25, 2005.
43. The reform was scrapped in part because the mayors saw little reason to give up on party control over the selection process for council members. Guillén, "Una reforma municipal."

elections, which ensured a greater degree of inclusion of different party factions and some visibility for the candidates, but this process was only open to the 1 percent of the Baja California electorate who belonged to the PAN.[44]

Finally, in Tijuana, the PAN-dominated council took a few, limited steps toward ensuring greater citizen access to their deliberations. Although most council meetings were not announced in advance and remained closed to the public despite regulations requiring citizen access, the council started filming most of its sessions in the late 1990s and putting these on the municipality's website so that citizens could watch them after the fact.[45] In a 2002 reform, the council also approved a process for "citizen initiatives," which allowed citizens to present resolutions directly to the city council for their consideration.[46]

Overall, elections became much more meaningful after 1989. At least two major parties competed for power under rules that had become increasingly fair and clear, and even smaller parties had a chance to gain seats in the municipal council. However, in other ways, the political transition remained incomplete. Old rules that guaranteed supermajorities for the winning party and elected council members on party lists meant that the municipal council was largely subordinate to the mayor and unknown to citizens. Steps to reduce the supermajorities slightly and guarantee online access to tapes of the meetings were positive but did little to overcome the irrelevance and invisibility of the council. Primaries in the governing party helped to introduce an additional element of accountability into the process, but the PAN's small number of members undermined the effect of these changes. Without question, the electoral process was democratic, but the structural constraints built into the design of representative institutions—which were based on inertias of the past—reduced elected leaders' incentives for accountability and responsiveness.

Reconstructing Channels of Intermediation (1989–2004)

After 1989, PAN state and municipal officials in Baja California held high hopes for reconstructing the channels of communication with citizens in order to treat them as individual citizens rather than as clients of corporate organizations.

---

44. Guillén, "Gobernabilidad y gestión local en México," 80.
45. Guerrero, interview, and an unpublished document by Guerrero, "El Cabildo"; Ayuntamiento de Tijuana, *Reglamento de cabildo*.
46. Ayuntamiento de Tijuana, *Reglamento de participación ciudadana*; Guerrero, interview.

Government officials actively sought to break down the traditional channels of mediation, which had privileged PRI-affiliated unions and community associations. The result of this effort was mixed, however. As former governor Ruffo observed, "When we arrived in the state government in 1989, we expected that a repressed society would take control of its destiny, that it would take the initiative, propose actions, use its new government. We felt the obligation to make the government function . . . ; the responsibility of living up to our promise. But we also felt despair at not seeing an active citizenry who would fight for their rights. Citizen participation was more a slogan than a reality."[47]

The government had partial success with the taxi unions, which had always monopolized the right to ask for operating permits for their members. The PAN state government changed the regulations to require drivers to apply individually for a permit, effectively cutting out the union representatives. Similarly, the governor largely refused to deal with organizations—especially those affiliated with the PRI—representing residents who wanted land titles.[48] The state government accelerated the granting of modestly priced land titles to families, and it jailed leaders who promoted land invasions.[49] These actions largely succeeded in undercutting the strength of both the PRI-affiliated community organizations and, eventually, groups affiliated with parties on the left, like CUCUTAC.

The municipal government in Tijuana followed in the footsteps of the state government in these efforts, refusing to deal, whenever possible, with the corporate organizations. In addition, the city sought to reconstruct its relationship with citizens by creating three new channels for communication, dialogue, and influence: elected neighborhood committees that would replace the traditional clientelistic leaders; a participatory planning structure that employed the legal figure of the Copladem (Municipal Planning Council); and a joint business-government roundtable for long-term planning on economic issues, known as the Tijuana Development Council (Consejo de Desarrollo de Tijuana, CDT). These efforts would initially generate a great deal of creativity, energy, and recognition, but the long-term results were less clear.

---

47. Ernesto Ruffo Appel, "El PAN en Baja California: Su relación con la sociedad," in Hernández Vicencio and Negrete Mata, *La experiencia del PAN*.

48. The notable exception, especially in the early years, was CUCUTAC, since its leader, Catalino Zavala, had become a PRD state legislator and had formed a tacit coalition with the PAN to give the governor a majority in Congress.

49. On the PAN government's attempts to end corporatist intermediation, see Espinoza Valle, *Alternanacia política*, especially chapters 6 and 7; and Espinoza Valle, *Transición difícil*.

The first PAN administration, under Montejo (1989–92), created a system for electing Comités de Vecinos (neighborhood committees). Whenever people from a neighborhood brought a demand to the city, officials would go to the neighborhood and witness the residents as they elected representatives to a committee. Then the officials and the committee would begin working together to resolve the issue the residents had raised. The only requirements were that the members of the committee reside in the neighborhood and that they be elected in a public assembly that had been announced in advance throughout the neighborhood. The approach served to undercut the power of intermediaries from political parties who had served as brokers for neighborhood demands and to establish a direct relationship with citizens.[50] During the first administration, 157 neighborhood committees were created, and the city held the first congress of social organizations to bring these groups together.[51]

The recognition of neighborhood committees—and the requirement that neighborhood demands be channeled through a publicly elected committee— became a hallmark of the PAN governments. The efforts intensified under the subsequent administrations, and by 2004, the city had an impressive total of more than 350 committees.[52] Interviews with residents in two of the fourteen sectors in the city and with municipal officials confirmed that recognizing neighborhood committees had become standard practice, and most appeared to emerge from genuinely democratic neighborhood elections.[53] Many of the committees still

50. Martín de la Rosa Medellín, who served as deputy director of the municipality's social participation department at the time, noted that the city government decided to recognize these committees based on "general criteria but without a legal framework." He also noted that the committees are anchored in the concept of *autogestión* (self-determination). Before serving in the government, Rosa was a Jesuit priest who had created a self-help movement in Ciudad Nezahualcóyotl in the 1970s and a housing cooperative in Tijuana in the 1980s (Rosa, interview).

51. *Informe municipal 1992*; Rosa, interview.

52. This estimate is based on my November 2004 review of the committees in the Comités de Vecinos database. It was not until the fifth PAN administration that the city council finally passed a law establishing the legal framework for neighborhood committees (Ayuntamiento de Tijuana, *Reglamento de participación ciudadana*), but the procedure became well established long before then.

53. Tijuana is divided geographically into six administrative units, known as delegations, each with a *delegado*, an official representing the municipal government. Because of population growth, some delegations have been divided into *subdelegaciones*, each with a *subdelegado* who reports to the delegation. In 2004, the city had fourteen subdelegaciones. In February and March 2005, my colleague Lilia León and I interviewed residents and two former subdelegados from El Florido and La Gloria, two subdelegaciones. We also interviewed the municipal coordinator of citizen participation and the technical secretary of the Municipal Planning Council (Copladem, see below), who had served in the last PAN administration (2001–4). These interviews were conducted shortly after the PRI administration began. However, informal contact with these leaders had been made in early 2004, so the interviews generally corroborated information that we had gathered while the PAN was still in power. Technically the neighborhood committees

operating in 2005 had been established during the second PAN administration of Héctor Osuna Jaime (1992–95), who instituted a short-lived but ambitious community investment program called "Manos a la Obra" (Hands to Work), which provided funds to neighborhood organizations for infrastructure projects.[54]

By 2004, neighborhood committees appeared to be primarily involved in obtaining land titles and basic services, such as pavement, electricity, water, and sewer lines, as well as improvements, such as schools, parks, and community centers. Some committees had long histories and solid organizational structures (especially those that began by getting land titles or basic services in the 1970s and 1980s); others were created recently to deal with a specific set of demands. Almost all had significant leadership rotation. A few committees seemed to be internally democratic with a nucleus of active members; others revolved around a single leader who occasionally called a meeting to get support for his or her initiatives.[55] In neighborhood committee elections, one-fifth to one-third of the families in each neighborhood turned out to vote, which suggests that the committees enjoyed a significant degree of legitimacy.[56]

Unlike the system that prevailed before 1989, by the end of the PAN governments, there appeared to be little partisan involvement in the neighborhood committees in Tijuana. There also appeared to be relatively few leaders in low-income neighborhoods except for those involved in the committees.[57] Several committees reported having had party involvement in the past—with the PRI, PAN, or PRD—but only a handful appeared to have ongoing, though generally tenuous,

---

were still functioning, but their future remained uncertain. The interviews focused only on the period of the PAN governments. Four of its committees had existed prior to 1989 and decided to become official neighborhood committees to facilitate their dealings with the municipality. Eight others were formed when citizens approached the municipality (usually the subdelegado, but occasionally other government agencies) demanding services and were asked to first form a committee.

54. Osuna Jaime developed the program to regain citizens' confidence following the 1994 federal elections, in which the PAN lost all three federal congressional districts in the city. The goal, he believed, was to ensure "that people are satisfied with us," since the elections seemed to suggest that they were not. Osuna Jaime, interview.

55. I have limited information on the internal workings of the committees, because the data are based on interviews with committee leaders. However, in interviews, most of the leaders gave important clues as to whether they saw themselves as part of a community effort or were the ones who got things done in the neighborhood.

56. One larger community reported only a 5 percent turnout, another smaller neighborhood reported that almost every family participated, and others suggested turnout somewhere in between the two extremes. It should be noted that these numbers are approximations based on the memories of the organizations' leaders; however, they appear to represent a significant, though not overwhelming, interest in the committees.

57. It should be noted, however, that in the 2005 elections, Hank Rhon managed to revive some of the old PRI leaderships. This period fell outside the scope of this research.

links to party leaders.[58] Similarly, none of the interviewed political or municipal leaders saw the committees as an important source of political mobilization.

The nonpartisanship of the neighborhood committees would seem to be a positive sign of the construction of true citizen institutions at the margin of partisan politics. However, the absence of partisan involvement also contributed to municipal leaders' general indifference toward the committees. There were no organic channels for committees to get a hearing with public officials. Those who were most successful observed that they often achieved things through "sympathy, relationships, or friendship" with particular officials or just through stubborn determination.[59]

Overall, the municipality succeeded in undercutting the influence of intermediaries and party brokers who represented community residents and in creating a more democratic form of neighborhood organization. However, it failed to create the mechanisms to allow these organizations to relate to the municipality through clear, consistent, institutional channels. In the absence of these channels, the lack of partisan influence in the committees may have been a mixed blessing. On one hand, the committees were largely saved from insertion into partisan politics and were not directly part of clientelistic networks, as had been other organizations in Tijuana in the past. However, the political parties' lack of interest in these committees also translated into the municipal authorities' lack of interest in neighborhood demands. Moreover, no mechanisms existed, inside

---

58. Two of twelve leaders expressed that they were personally close to the PAN and had some involvement in party politics, as did one former leader who is a PAN member (but no longer president of the committee). One past leader had gone on to become a municipal official (subdelegada). Another committee had been close to the PRI, then switched to the PAN, then felt abandoned by both. Yet another was led by a leader of CUCUTAC who had once served briefly as a PRD city council member (though disputes with the PRD had led CUCUTAC to move to the Convergencia, a small party). The rest seemed to lack close ties to any party. In addition to the official committees, there was a PAN committee in one of the neighborhoods; a PRI leader helping residents get land titles (though they later expelled him and started their own independent committee); and the resurgence of PRI committees in both neighborhoods after the victory of the PRI in the August 2004 municipal elections.

59. As one committee president noted, "I can say that they paid attention to us, but because of exhaustion, because sometimes we lasted three or four hours waiting." Other leaders reported that they felt the municipality always wanted something in return from the neighborhood committees, usually small favors like attending public events sponsored by the government. One neighborhood committee leader remarked, "The Delegation [city administrative office] gives support, but it also asks for our support.... We respect the government's decisions since we always have to go ask them for things." In an unusual case, a municipal official asked a committee to help him conduct an electoral poll prior to an election in exchange for help on a project; however, most government requests to neighborhood groups seemed to be less politically charged. Committee president in La Gloria, interviewed by the author, February 19, 2005; El Florido committee member, interviewed by the author, February 13, 2005.

or outside the government, to let the various committees make connections among themselves. The large citywide organizations like CUCUTAC and even the PRI's sectoral organizations had once played this role by bringing together different neighborhoods to discuss common challenges and scale up their demands. By the early 1990s, overarching organizations no longer existed, and the municipal government provided no consistent forum that allowed contact among neighborhood committees.[60] The committees thus remained isolated not only from the political system but also from one another. In short, they were linked neither horizontally among themselves nor vertically to the political system.

The second innovation to build new channels between the municipality and citizens was the Municipal Planning Council (Copladem), which had existed only on paper in previous governments.[61] The second PAN administration, under Osuna Jaime, created a Copladem with thirty members drawn from municipal, state, and federal officials, business organizations, professional associations, universities, and other organized groups.[62] The council also had twelve subcommittees based around key issue areas that brought together representatives of social organizations.[63] The Copladem became a highly visible body during Osuna Jaime's administration because it was the center of a number of disputes between social organizations and the city government. In many cases, these disputes responded to a logic of political confrontation between the PRI and the PAN. However, in other cases, there were legitimate disagreements between citizen members and the administration concerning the government's priorities.[64] The Copladem had no decision-making authority at this time, but it became an important—and highly visible—forum for public debate of municipal policy and a space where the city government, civic organizations, and opposition political parties could meet and interact.[65]

---

60. On rare occasions starting in 1992, the municipality held ad hoc fora for neighborhood committees; no ongoing forum for contact among committees existed.

61. Under the PRI administrations of 1983–86 and 1986–89, the Copladem in Tijuana appears to have been a mere formality without any substantive existence. Under the first PAN administration (Montejo, 1989–92), the Copladem office actually existed, had two staff, and was responsible for holding a series of public forums to get citizen input into the municipal development plan. However, the office did little else during this administration. Guillén, "Gobernabilidad y gestión local en México," 86–92.

62. This was the first council resolution passed under the new administration. *Plan municipal de desarrollo 1993–1995* (Tijuana: Ayuntamiento de Tijuana, 1993).

63. *Informe municipal 1993*.

64. Guillén, "Gobernabilidad y gestión local en México," 90–92; Rosa, interview.

65. This is according to an interviewee who served in the Copladem under Osuna Jaime. She noted that she was one of the few members of the body during that period from a low-income community. Delegational subcommittee member, interviewed by the author, February 29, 2005.

Under the third PAN administration of Guadalupe Osuna Millán (1995–98), the Copladem's structure and functions were greatly expanded. Redesigned under a resolution approved by the city council in 1995, the Copladem now had delegation subcommittees, with thirteen elected councillors in each of the city's (then) thirteen administrative districts (*subdelegaciones*), and with sectoral subcommittees working on fifteen key issue areas, each of which could have up to thirteen citizen members. A city council member chaired each subcommittee to build a link into the official municipal council decision-making process. A municipal development council brought together the delegation subcommittee members to set citywide investment priorities, and a general assembly brought together all subcommittees, city council members, and administration officials to debate overarching municipal priorities.[66] Each of the bodies had a majority of members who were citizens,[67] but government officials were present in each body, and the city council had ultimate jurisdiction over any recommendations made.

The Copladem system had several important design features. It allowed citizens to elect residents from their own delegation to represent them in public investment decisions—that is, spending on roads, bridges, parks, community centers, and other public infrastructure projects—and the system largely empowered these representatives to make these decisions. Moreover, it created two citywide bodies that brought citizen councillors together across neighborhoods, thus building horizontal links between different areas of Tijuana. This also allowed the councillors to address priorities that affected more than one neighborhood (for example, major roads that went through several sectors of the city). In addition, the system engaged organized groups through the sectoral subcommittees, by allowing these groups to have input on the substantive areas on which they were working. In a city with numerous nongovernmental organizations and civic groups working on everything from environmental protection to the welfare of migrants or the treatment of AIDS patients, this structure connected these groups to the policy-making process.[68] Finally, the planning system built in clear links

---

66. In theory, there was also a Governing Council (Junta de Gobierno), consisting of the mayor and city council, that served as the top decision-making organ. However, this was a formality that simply reasserted the council and mayor's final jurisdiction over all decisions.

67. The General Assembly had 74 percent citizen members; the Delegation Subcommittees had 81 percent citizen members.

68. Tijuana has a large number of nongovernmental organizations, primarily devoted to education, child welfare, migration, public health, and addiction treatment. The number of NGOs grew dramatically in the 1990s, reaching 186 in 1999. Many of these organizations had links to the Catholic Church, Protestant

with the city council, since council members chaired each subcommittee, thus ensuring an organic connection between the Copladem and the municipal legislature. This was unlike most participatory planning processes in Brazil, which generally depend exclusively on the mayor and which risk becoming parallel legislative systems that the mayor can use as a counterweight to the city council.[69]

The delegation subcommittees received the most attention and were probably the most successful part of the Copladem system, largely because they had authority over investment decisions.[70] The first election of delegation subcommittees in 1996 involved 7,314 people in the thirteen districts, electing 169 citizen councillors from 336 candidates.[71] This represented barely 2.5 percent of the number of voters who had participated in the 1995 elections, but it was still a significant number of voters.[72] The subcommittees appeared to be quite plural in their composition, with councillors who were close to all political parties and many who had no partisan affiliation at all.[73] These subcommittees were responsible for deciding how to spend between 28 million and 55 million pesos annually on public works, equivalent to between 5 percent and 8 percent of the overall

---

churches, or U.S.-based NGOs. A study by Benedicto Ruíz Vargas in 1999 indicates that 22 percent of the 186 NGOs had started in or before the 1980s. Unlike other Mexican cities, relatively few NGOs were engaged in political or policy-oriented activities, although in the 1990s, a few began to do so, including organizations (and coalitions) dedicated to human rights, women's issues, and advocacy regarding AIDS. Benedicto Ruíz Vargas, "Las ONGs en Tijuana: Un perfil general," *El Bordo*, no. 4 (1999).

69. This was unlike most participatory planning processes in Brazil, which generally depend exclusively on the mayor and risk becoming parallel legislative systems that the mayor can use as a counterweight to the city council. Marcus Melo, "Democratizing Budgetary Decisions and Execution in Brazil: More Participation or Redesign of Formal Institutions?" in Selee and Peruzzotti, *Participatory Innovation*.

70. Mayor Osuna Millán stated that "all projects had to be validated by Copladem," and a published study of the period suggests that the Copladem achieved immense influence as a space for dialogue and decision making on public priorities. According to the director of the Copladem at the time, the process was designed to achieve "equilibrium among the executive, city council, and citizens" and to serve as a meeting place for all three, creating "permanent dialogue [of the executive and legislative branches] with citizens—NGOs and community residents . . . [and] institutional mechanisms for dialogue." Guadalupe Osuna Millán, Tijuana mayor (1995–99), interviewed by the author, April 21, 2005; Rosa, interview.

71. *Plan municipal de desarrollo 1996–1998* (Baja California: Comité de Planeación para el Desarrollo Municipal, 1996).

72. The registration for the election of councillors was held with only three days' notice, which benefited the PAN and administration officials, who knew of the plans and could recruit candidates for citizen councillors ahead of time. However, many candidates sympathetic to other parties, or without any party affiliation, won seats. Guillén, "Gobernabilidad y gestión local en México," 95.

73. Guillén, "Gobernabilidad y gestión local en México," 95–96; Maria de los Angeles Castillo, member of the delegation subcommittee for La Mesa (1996–98), interviewed by the author, February 24, 2005.

municipal budget and 18 percent to 23 percent of its investment budget.[74] Participants in the process remembered it as highly deliberative and a real space of encounter between government officials and citizens.[75] The sectoral subcommittees, which were largely advisory bodies with no funds to distribute, were far less successful, although a few of them had some influence on municipal decisions in the early years and served as a bridge between government officials and NGOs.[76]

The Copladem maintained its official role after 1998, but over time, it lost its capacity to serve as an arena for decision making and as a meaningful channel for dialogue between citizens and government officials. The municipality reduced the percentage of the budget devoted to community investments, thus limiting the scope of the delegation subcommittees' work. Moreover, there were increasing signs that municipal officials had learned how to ensure the victory of candidates close to them in order to maintain control over the budget allocation process.[77] When opposition slates won the elections, they would sometimes find their access to resources slashed.[78] Municipal development council meetings, which

---

74. Author's calculations based on data available in the *Informe municipal* from 1993 to 2002; INEGI, *Finanzas municipales y estatales,* from 1980 to 2002; and Martín de la Rosa Medellín, "La participación social en la obra social comunitaria (el caso Tijuana, B.C.)," in Ziccardi, *Participación ciudadanía y políticas sociales.*

75. Ramón López, former citizen councillor of a delegation subcommittee, interviewed by the author, February 26, 2005; Oscar Escalada Hernández, president of the Network for the Defense of Migrants of Baja California, interviewed by the author, February 23, 2005; and Gabriel Preciado, former deputy director of social development for the municipality during this period, interviewed by the author, April 19, 2005.

76. Several, including the subcommittees on migration, public security, health, urban development, and ecology, were quite active, according to Guillén, "Gobernabilidad y gestión local en México." I attended the migration subcommittee on several occasions in 1996–97 and was impressed by the serious level of discussion between the municipal authorities and NGOs working on migration issues. Interviews with former participants also confirmed their sense that this subcommittee had been quite effective in its early years in terms of getting the municipality to respond to migrant-related concerns.

77. The fourth and fifth PAN governments (1998–2001 and 2001–4) placed far less emphasis on the Copladem structure overall, barely touching on it in their development plans. In 1998, the municipality reduced the number of citizen councillors on the delegation subcommittees from thirteen to five, so as to control them more easily. Interviews with several citizen councillors who had participated in the subcommittees from 2001 through 2004 revealed how much the municipal government had managed to control these bodies. During this period, slates of candidates affiliated with the PAN had won a majority of seats in twelve of the now fourteen delegation subcommittees and all of the seats in ten of them. In El Florido, both councillors and the local government official confirmed that the government had "chosen" the candidates for the winning slate, although one PRI member had managed to win one of the five seats by running a strong campaign.

78. This was the case in La Gloria, for example, when a slate affiliated with CUCUTAC won the local subcommittee election in 2001 and saw the funds for which it was responsible reduced by almost two-thirds (based on data reported in the *Informe municipal* from 2002 to 2003 and during interviews with citizen councillors).

started as a vibrant arena for exchange of views across neighborhoods, gradually turned into docile sessions managed by the mayor and the administration, especially since most members of the subcommittees were now loyal to municipal officials.[79] The subcommittees gradually lost presence and relevance in the community, and by 2004 and 2005, they appeared to have no working relationship whatsoever with the elected neighborhood committees.[80] The sectoral subcommittees followed a similar fate, with most of them losing importance over time.[81] Although the Copladem structure provided new channels for citizens to engage with public authorities on key issues of local policy, it was unable to survive as a relevant institution once political leaders lost interest in it.

79. Citizen councillors reported that the citywide meetings were only called to rubberstamp decisions that had already been made by municipal officials, and since most councillors were handpicked by government officials, there was rarely much dissent. "Everything became confused; who were the members, what were the decisions," noted one councillor who had previously had a more positive experience on the council. "Almost everyone was with the PAN, so all that remained was to vote 'yes' . . . just to legalize and legitimize the decisions." Most decisions passed without debate, but on one occasion, the council members were asked to vote to divert a substantial amount of the Copladem funds to major road projects. This was technically outside the purview of the program, which was supposed to be focused on small- and medium-sized community projects, but it was an election year (2004) and major public works projects had greater visibility. The opposition-supported councillors and city council members voted against the proposal en bloc but were outnumbered. Interviews with three members of the Municipal Council (two from La Gloria, one from Florido, cited previously).

80. In interviews with the leaders of neighborhood committees, not one person indicated a close working relationship with their delegation subcommittee. "I don't know the councillors; I've never heard anyone speak about Copladem," noted one neighborhood committee president. "They never sought us out, and we never sought them out," stated another. Whatever channels might have existed between the neighborhood committees and the Copladem subcommittees in the past appeared to have fallen apart or into disuse by the final PAN administration. Of the twelve leaders interviewed, eight had no direct knowledge of their delegation subcommittee; three knew them but had no ongoing communication with them; and only one was actually in touch with the members. Of those who knew their subcommittee, one leader stated that he had not been allowed to attend the meetings. Another stated that "the councillors have the function of fighting over public works projects. . . . The political parties get together their slates of candidates with their most scandalous people, get their friends and acquaintances involved, register the slate, and whoever gets the most votes wins."

81. One PAN city council member, who chaired the ecology subcommittee, stated that he had simply stopped calling meetings. He complained that the members, representatives of environmental NGOs, only showed up to complain and attack the government. "They have no sense of responsibility at all . . . [just] attacking for the sake of attacking." A PRI city council member stopped holding her subcommittee meetings because she said that the municipal officials in charge of the area would not attend. A PRD city council member, however, observed that his two sectoral subcommittees, on disability and private education, met frequently and appeared to have produced some results. Guerrero, interview; Juanita Pérez, interview; and José Roberto Davalos, city council member (PRD, 2001–4), interviewed by the author, April 1, 2005. On migration issues, it appeared that the state government had largely taken over the role of consulting with NGOs on policy with no real role for the municipal Copladem. Escalada Hernández, interview; Cristina Franco Abundis, director of the Human Rights Program at the Universidad Iberoamericana, interviewed by the author, February 23, 2005.

The final innovation of the PAN governments to build new participatory channels was the creation of the Economic Development Council of Tijuana (Consejo de Desarrollo Económico de Tijuana, CDT), a business/government roundtable designed to spur dialogue and encourage planning between government and the private sector. Set up during the second PAN administration, led by Osuna Jaime, the CDT received equal amounts of funding from the state government, the municipality, and the city's largest business organization, the Business Coordinating Council (Consejo Coordinador Empresarial, CCE). The CDT's most visible function was to develop two long-term strategic plans, one in 1994 and the other in 2003.[82] Based on a model borrowed from Seville, Spain, the plans (each known as "Tijuana Strategic Plan") laid out major priorities for economic development over a twenty-five year period and assigned responsibilities to the different levels of government and to the private sector.[83] These plans were designed to create a more long-term strategic vision than that contained in the three-year municipal development plans and to generate dialogue between government and the private sector about shared responsibilities for development.

Business leaders suggested that the CDT performed relatively well as a space for dialogue between the private sector and municipal and state governments. Overall, they acknowledged that Tijuana's business community is highly fragmented and has little capacity to influence public policy. This is partially a result of the mixture of locally owned and foreign-owned businesses, but it also reflects the fragmented nature of Tijuana society, in general.[84] In this context, the CDT performed an important but limited function in bringing business leaders and public officials together. However, not all of those interviewed were equally enthusiastic about the CDT and its long-range development plan. An opposition city council member and a former government official both noted that in the absence of a strong Copladem with a real participatory planning process, the private-sector-oriented Strategic Plan had supplanted the municipal development plan as the city's blueprint for policy priorities.[85] This, in turn, might mean

82. *Plan estratégico Tijuana 2003–2025; Plan estratégico Tijuana* (Tijuana: Ayuntamiento de Tijuana, 2003).
83. Osuna Jaime, interview. See also the analysis by César M. Fuentes and Noé Arón Fuentes, "Desarrollo económico en la frontera norte de México: De las políticas nacionales de fomento económico a las estrategias de desarrollo económico local," *Araucaria* (Universidad de Sevilla) 5, no. 11 (2004).
84. Antonio Cano, former local legislator (PRI), interviewed by the author, February 23, 2005; Zeferino Sánchez, former municipal official, interviewed by the author, February 24, 2005; Gastón Luken, civic leader, interviewed by the author, February 25, 2005; and Askan Luteroth, civic leader, interviewed by the author, February 23, 2005.
85. Interviews with Juanita Pérez and Rosa.

that the business community was beginning to supplant citizens as the true interlocutors for developing municipal priorities.

Conclusions: Institutional Innovation and Weak Intermediation

The municipality of Tijuana grew significantly in authority and autonomy over the period of PAN governance. Favorable circumstances certainly contributed to this change: the federal government increased transfers to municipalities during these years, and the city had a significant tax base that it could exploit once municipalities were allowed to innovate in tax collection. Tijuana's size and importance within Baja California also let it negotiate over its autonomy with the state government, something few other municipalities could do. However, the city government also took matters into its own hands in seeking out new forms of local revenue. These strategies included modernizing the property tax system, leveraging private investment, suing the federal government, and creating a national mayors' association that could fight for municipal rights. Decentralization was not only a top-down process decided by the federal government but also one constructed bottom-up by the municipality.

Within this context of extensive decentralization, the PAN-affiliated governments of Tijuana, especially in the first nine years after coming to power in 1989, also created several innovative institutions to improve government responsiveness and accountability. Fearing the PRI would recover the city, they sought to break that party's control of corporatist organizations and their political intermediaries. As a party supported mostly by unaffiliated citizens, these administrations had hoped to create a new relationship with their constituents, as individual citizens who would have institutional channels to make demands. Toward this end, they established fair election procedures; improved the representative structure of the city council; and created a series of institutions for citizen participation that included nonpartisan neighborhood committees, a participatory planning structure, and a business/government roundtable.[86] Because of citizen demands, the PAN governments vastly increased the resources devoted to community infrastructure investments and pursued joint public/private ventures for urban development.

---

86. The establishment of election procedures and changes in the council's representational structure were technically both state initiatives, but they were strongly supported by municipal leaders and implemented enthusiastically in Tijuana.

In many ways, these initiatives stand as models of what democratization and decentralization should accomplish: the unleashing of creative democratic energy at the grassroots. The new initiatives implemented under the first three PAN administrations, especially the Copladem planning structure and the neighborhood committees, successfully bypassed political intermediaries to give citizens a more direct voice in public affairs. Similarly, the Tijuana Development Council successfully brought together business leaders and municipal officials to think through long-term opportunities and challenges for the region. Tijuana seemed ideally suited to this kind of innovative participatory governance. It was, after all, one of the cities where the PRI's corporatist structure had sunk the shallowest roots. The city also enjoyed an extensive, though fragmented, civil society, based on small neighborhood organizations, church groups, and nongovernmental organizations dedicated to social assistance. In this environment, PAN mayors initially realized that they had to build a support base for their party by mobilizing individual citizens through institutional channels rather than constituting new clientelistic or corporatist organizations. The improvements in the council structure and functioning and the participatory innovations thus all served to build this relationship.

However, this dense web of citizen-government interaction gradually weakened as the PAN repeatedly won elections and its leaders lost their fear of being thrown out of office. The PAN's historical practices contributed to this: as a party built to resist co-option by the PRI, it had maintained a small, loyal membership. As a result, the party was ideally suited to serve as an incorruptible opposition movement but less so to govern a major city. PAN leaders knew they needed to bring new voices into the policy process, but they also distrusted mass democracy and its potential for corruption. Political institutions reinforced these limitations. Supermajorities in the city council and party-list elections meant that aspiring PAN politicians needed to spend more time negotiating backroom deals with potential supporters within the small party base than attending to citizen concerns.

As a result, later PAN municipal administrations eventually undermined the very channels they had created to make citizens into partners in public efforts. Although the kind of autonomous, diversified civil society that existed in the city was ideal to respond to the participatory initiatives of the first PAN governments, the absence of horizontal links among organizations or with political parties meant that there was no one to defend the advances in democratic government once political leaders lost interest. In the end, PAN officials destroyed most of the influence of the PRI's corporatist organizations, but they created no lasting alterative to link citizens to the government outside of the party system. Indeed, as time went on, they created a form of "weak control," in which they generated their own "intermediaries"—the Copladem councillors and a few successful neighborhood committee leaders—who were willing to do small favors for the government in return for obtaining occasional benefits. These intermediaries, however, did not have an organic relationship to the party. Moreover, government officials did not take them very seriously. This very weak form of clientelism operated at the margins of the municipal government's real decision-making processes, which ran through the PAN's relatively closed party structure.

Under the PRI, citizens had strong ties to the government through the party, though under informal and highly unfair rules that privileged party leaders and community brokers. Under the PAN, citizens had clearer institutional channels for making demands on the government, but government officials paid less and less attention to these demands. The rules of the game were more democratic, but citizens were also more disconnected and isolated from their government than ever before. A highly mobilized and participatory society became increasingly disillusioned with a government that gave only lip service to their concerns and did little to ensure their rights. Many citizens, finding the PAN governments increasingly unresponsive and unaccountable, opted out. Most simply stopped voting, and abstention rates in Tijuana became among the highest in the country.[87] Those who continued to be politically involved finally threw the PAN out of office and opted to return to the PRI and its old style of corporatist government, which at least might take citizens into account.

The 2004 mayoral campaign of PRI candidate Hank Rhon was impressive. He promised a return to the kind of government that paid attention to citizens, and he used his own private wealth to give them a taste of what he meant. During the campaign, if citizens wanted a road, he would often send in heavy equipment to start the work, just to show voters he was serious. But he proved to be an unfocused and ineffective leader. He could not resuscitate the moribund structures of the PRI that had once served as the critical channels between citizens

---

87. The abstention rate in the 2004 elections was 63.7 percent. José Negrete Mata argues that abstention rates rose dramatically not only because the city is highly mobile (some registered voters were not in the city and thus were ineligible to vote on election day) but also because citizens became disillusioned with their options. Given the PAN's technocratic governance style and the perceived corruption of the PRI, they simply disconnected from politics. Negrete Mata, "En busca del votante (tijuanense) perdido: Cultura política, participación y abstencionismo" (Ph.D. diss., El Colegio de la Frontera Norte, 2002).

and the municipal government, and he accomplished few new initiatives. Drug trafficking, which has a long history on the border, grew increasingly violent during his tenure, as well. Some have suggested that this demonstrated his complicity with the drug traffickers; others, his incapacity as a leader; and still others, that he was facing a force beyond the control of any municipal authority. Whatever the truth, voters chose to throw the PRI out in the 2007 elections and return the PAN to power. It remains to be seen whether the PAN's three years in exile will create a sense of urgency for the new administration to renew its ties to citizens.

6 CIUDAD NEZAHUALCÓYOTL: SOCIAL MOVEMENT DEMOCRACY?

In August 2004, Belem Guerrero won the Olympic silver medal in women's cycling, the second medal for Mexico in the 2004 Olympics. The inhabitants of Ciudad Nezahualcóyotl, known usually by the city's nickname, "Neza," were ecstatic. "That's where she lives," one man said as he pointed in the direction of the neighborhood where Belem had grown up. "She always cycles by this way in the morning," said another man as he indicated one of the city's main boulevards.

Belem's victory was highly symbolic for Ciudad Nezahualcóyotl. A large city on the outskirts of Mexico's capital, Neza has always struggled to have an identity of its own. Throughout the 1960s and 1970s, it was known as an extremely poor bedroom community on the fringes of Mexico City, where people from the countryside came to live because they could not afford a place in the capital. Most residents in Neza did not have land titles, and in many neighborhoods, there was no electricity, water, or sewers. Frequent flooding meant that the city's dirt roads constantly turned into muddy pools. The title of a book written about Neza in 1977 called it "a neighborhood on its way to absorption by Mexico City,"[1] although Neza already had almost a million inhabitants. Another book, written by a Jesuit priest who lived there in the early 1970s, noted that "Netzahualcóytol

---

1. The book noted that Ciudad Nezahualcóyotl is a neighborhood on the outskirts of Mexico City defined principally by its social and cultural marginalization. Roberto Ferras, *Ciudad Nezahualcóyotl: Un barrio en vías de absorción por la ciudad de México* (Mexico City: Centro de Estudios Sociológicos, El Colegio de México, 1977). Other works of the 1970s and 1980s similarly approached Neza as a marginalized community of the Mexico City metropolitan area. See, for example, Martha Schteingart, *Los productores del espacio habitable: Estado, empresa y sociedad en la ciudad de México* (Mexico City: El Colegio de México, 1989).

[sic] has no inner life; strictly speaking; it is not a city because it lacks relative autonomy; it is an appendix of a megalopolis."[2]

By the 1990s, however, things had changed. Citizens had begun to organize in the 1970s to demand land titles and basic services, and within two decades, they achieved significant successes.[3] By 2000, almost all properties had land titles, electricity, water, and sewers.[4] Average income had grown to levels well above the national average, though still below that of Mexico City and most neighboring towns. In a generation, Neza's inhabitants had gone from desperately poor to respectably working class. The city had an increasingly strong municipal government and an identity separate from the federal capital next door. As one university professor who grew up in Neza explained, "Our fight in the 1970s was for services; we were proud of being marginal; today our fight is for respect."[5] As part of the struggle for respect, the city government had pitched in to buy Belem her racing bike for the Olympics after Mexico's notoriously elitist Olympic Committee had refused to support her. Her victory was more than an individual achievement; it was an effort by the city to win both respectability and the recognition of Neza's existence.

Eight years before Belem's triumphant race, the inhabitants had taken another step toward winning respect by throwing out the long-ruling PRI. Like most poor and working-class cities, Ciudad Nezahualcóyotl had been dominated by the official party through a web of clientelistic networks that organized people by blocks, neighborhoods, and occupations. The grip of the ruling party began to slip slightly in the 1980s, as strong popular organizations affiliated with leftwing parties began to have increasing success in the struggle for land and services.

---

2. Martín de la Rosa Medellín, *Netzahualcóyotl: Un fenómeno* (Mexico City: Fondo de Cultura Económica, 1974), 4. Interestingly, authors spelled the name of the city two different ways in the 1960s and 1970s.

3. Margarita García Luna chronicled these changes in *Ciudad Nezahualcóyotl: De colonias marginadas a gran ciudad* (Toluca: Pliego, 1992).

4. By 2000, 99.4 percent of homes had electricity, 98.2 percent had running water, and 98.9 percent had sewer connections; additionally, 88.5 percent of the streets were paved. According to the city's municipal development plan, the Canales de Sal neighborhood and a part of Colonia El Sol did not have regularized land titles in 1997, a situation that has now been resolved. *Plan municipal de desarrollo 1997–2000* (Ciudad Nezahualcóyotl: Ayuntamiento de la Ciudad Nezahualcóyotl, 1997). For the data on electricity, water, and sewers, see INEGI, *XII censo*. For the data on pavement, see María del Socorro Arzaluz Solano, "Participación ciudadana en la gestión urbana de Ecatepec, Tlalnepantla y Nezahualcóyotl (1997–2000)" (Ph.D. diss., Centro de Estudios Sociológicos, El Colegio de México, Mexico City, December 2001), 290.

5. Ramón Rivera, native of Neza and a university professor, interviewed by the author, March 4, 2005. Unless otherwise noted, all interviews cited in this chapter occurred in Ciudad Nezahualcóyotl.

In 1996, several of these movements joined together to run a common slate of candidates for mayor and city council under the banner of the PRD. "We were convinced we wouldn't win," according to Héctor Bautista, leader of the largest organization in the coalition, who went on to become mayor of the city a few years later.[6] Yet, to their surprise, they did win, and it gave the Mexican left their first victory in a major city.[7] The PRD, with the same coalition of popular organizations, would go on to consolidate its electoral strength with repeat victories in municipal elections in 1999 and 2003.[8]

Since then, Ciudad Nezahualcóyotl has been the scene of an unusual process of turning a loose coalition of popular organizations into a governing party. The results have profoundly transformed relations between the inhabitants of the city and their municipal government, but not always in easy or predictable ways. In some cases, the PRD governments have shown a penchant for promoting accountable and responsive government, the original demands of the popular organizations that formed the coalition. However, in other cases, they have reinvented, or fallen back on, old strategies of clientelistic control reminiscent of previous PRI governments. The leaders of groups within the PRD have become the new centers of political power, at the top of a dense web of intraparty political factions. The form of democratic governance that has emerged does create more accountability and responsiveness, overall, than existed before. It has also opened up new channels for citizens to relate to their public authorities. However, these advances have taken place by perfecting old patterns of informal intermediation rather than by replacing them with a more direct relationship between citizens and the state.

From Bedroom Community to Major City

The area where Ciudad Nezahualcóyotl now stands was once Texcoco Lake in the State of Mexico, the country's largest state, which surrounds Mexico City on

---

6. Héctor Bautista, a leader of Movimiento Vida Digna, interviewed by the author, Mexico City, March 4, 2005.
7. Neza was the first city of over a million inhabitants governed by the left. The PRD would win Mexico City in 1997 and Acapulco in 1999, as well as several governorships after 1998. But Neza was the first major urban victory for the Mexican left. The PRD had won Morelia, the capital of the state of Michoacán, in 1989, and another party of the left (which later helped found the PRD) won Juchitán, Oaxaca, in the 1980s, but the PRI recovered these medium-sized cities after the initial PRD victory.
8. After the research for this book was completed, the PRD won yet another election in 2006.

three sides.⁹ In the mid-1850s, the government began to dry the lake to prevent flooding, and by 1900, it had become arable land suitable for settlement. The first postrevolutionary government, led by Venustiano Carranza, declared the lands in the former lakebed national property in 1917, and in 1919, it began to sell parcels to settlers. In the 1940s, the federal government promoted the creation of committees for "moral, civic, and material improvement" to help mediate between residents and the government over the installation of basic services.¹⁰ By 1960, the local residents had requested that the area, which now had a population of 73,915, become a separate municipality, a demand that was granted in April 1963.¹¹

The 1960s and 1970s saw an enormous expansion of Ciudad Nezahualcóyotl and of the entire Mexico City metropolitan area. Neza's population increased ninefold in the 1960s and then more than doubled again in the 1970s, leveling off at just under 1.4 million in 2000 in official statistics.¹² In the early 1970s, according to one account, the city had only a handful of phone lines, two post offices, one bookstore, two banks, one firehouse, one Red Cross hospital, and three gas stations. There were no libraries, parks, hotels, theaters, newspapers, or cemeteries.¹³ For Mexicans, the city became a symbol of the worst effects of urbanization.

In the 1980s and 1990s, however, the characteristics of the city changed dramatically. Educational levels increased, as second- and third-generation inhabitants were able to take advantage of opportunities for study in the metropolitan area, and economic fortunes rose noticeably.¹⁴ Nezahualcóyotl had been the capital's poor bedroom community in the 1970s, but by the 1990s, its proximity to the ever-expanding capital meant that it was prime real estate. The city's population leveled off and may even have declined, as the poor sought housing farther

---

9. Mexico City was once part of the State of Mexico, but it became a federal district shortly after independence in 1824. The State of Mexico remains the largest state in the country, however, with 13,096,686 inhabitants; its population is almost double that of the second-largest state, Veracruz, which has 6,908,975 inhabitants, and considerably more than that of the Federal District, with 8,605,239. INEGI, *XII censo*.

10. By 1949, the city had approximately 2,000 inhabitants, a figure that increased dramatically to 40,000 by 1954. In 1953, the state government created the Committee of Urban Neighborhoods of the District of Texcoco to serve as an umbrella organization for the thirteen neighborhoods in the area (which grew to thirty-three by 1959 and thirty-nine by 1960).

11. The history of Ciudad Nezahualcóyotl from the 1850s to 1963 is based on a summary in the *Enciclopedia de los municipios de México* (Mexico City: Instituto Nacional para el Federalismo y el Desarrollo Municipal [INAFED]), available at http://www.e-local.gob.mx.

12. INEGI, *XII censo*; Margarita García Luna and Pedro Gutiérrez Arzaluz, *Nezahualcóyotl: Monografía municipal* (Toluca: Gobierno del Estado de México, 1999), 29 (based on population statistics from previous census calculations).

13. Rosa, *Netzahualcóyotl*, 4.

14. According to figures available from INEGI.

from the capital.¹⁵ There was nowhere left to build in what had become the most densely populated city in the metropolitan area, and greater affluence brought lower birth rates and smaller households.

Despite significant improvements, Ciudad Nezahualcóyotl continued to be predominantly a poor and working-class town that depended heavily on Mexico City and other cities in the region for employment.¹⁶ Indeed, according to the federal government's economic data, only 18 percent of the economically active population of Neza actually worked in the city. Although this statistic almost certainly underestimates the number of people who work in informal employment within the municipality, they point to the city's dependence on the capital for jobs.¹⁷

---

15. More people may be living in the city than official figures indicate. Voter rolls suggest a higher population than census figures do. For example, 900,754 voters were registered in 2003. This was a full 73.5 percent of the official population in 2000, whereas the census suggests that only 65.48 percent of the population was eighteen or older. This difference could be due to registered voters' high level of mobility (with many having left the municipality since registering). This possibility, however, does not seem to be borne out by the evidence: only 7.7 percent of the population in 2000 had lived outside the municipality in 1995, somewhat lower than the average for the state as a whole (10.5 percent), suggesting that Neza has a fairly stable population. Moreover, voting rates in Neza for the 2003 congressional elections (37.8 percent) were very close to the average for the rest of the state (36.5 percent) and to the other major cities in the state (Ecatepec, 35 percent; percent; Naucalpan, 37.6 percent; Tlalnepantla, 40.7 percent; Toluca, 41.8 percent; Chimahualcán, 32.3 percent; and Chalco, 33 percent), which suggests that a large pool of absent voters probably does not exist. This scenario is different from that of Tijuana, which has an unusually high number of registered voters compared to the population figures, but turnout in the 2003 elections was extremely low (28.31 percent of registered voters). This suggests that some registered voters may have moved away, a conclusion that is strengthened by the relatively high number of Tijuana residents in the 2000 census (16.9 percent) who reported that they had been living in another state five years earlier. The population and migrant population are calculated based on the 2000 census (INEGI, *XII censo*) and statistics on registered voters and voting participation. See Instituto Federal Electoral, *La participación ciudadana en las Elecciones de 2003* (Mexico City: Instituto Federal Electoral), available at http://www.ife.org.mx. Census statistics on migrants (the percentage of inhabitants who lived outside the municipality five years earlier) are reported for all inhabitants five years of age and older.

16. In 2000, over half of the working population in Neza reported making less than three minimum wages, the rough equivalent of US$4,140 per year, still a very low wage for the metropolitan area of Mexico City. Few inhabitants, a far smaller proportion than in the state and country as a whole, made over ten minimum wages (roughly US$13,800). These data suggest that most residents are part of the working class and few are middle-class or well-off individuals (based on INEGI, *XII censo*).

17. In the state, 27.4 percent of residents work within their municipality; in comparable municipalities, the figures are 24.6 percent for Ecatepec, 50 percent for Naucalpan, and 54.7 percent for Tlalnepantla. These figures are the author's calculations using the 2000 census (INEGI, *XII censo*) and the 1999 economic census (INEGI, *Imágenes económicos del Estado de México* [Aguascalientes: INEGI, 2001]). The city's municipal development plan for 1997–2000 indicates that 43 percent of the population works in the municipality, 41 percent in Mexico City, and 13 percent in the State of Mexico (*Plan municipal de desarrollo 1997–2000*). However, I have not been able to ascertain the basis for this calculation, and it clearly conflicts with the official federal government statistics.

Political Control and Popular Contestation

The PRI dominated politics in Ciudad Nezahualcóyotl from the city's birth in 1963 until the victory of the PRD in 1996. Every mayor was a member of the PRI, as were all those who sat on the city council until 1982. Even after changes in state electoral rules began to assign seats to opposition parties in that year, the PRI dominated the city council and handily won every municipal election, never holding less than 70 percent of the seats.[18] The PRI maintained this dominance in large part through a strong relationship between the city and state governments, a solid party base of affiliated social organizations, and, in the early years, close ties to the most important economic actors in the city, the real estate developers (*fraccionadores*) who had bought land in Neza to resell it to new settlers.[19]

Similarly, the PRI maintained a tight control of politics throughout the State of Mexico, winning every municipal and state election until the 1980s.[20] Indeed, a single, relatively cohesive political group, known as the Grupo Atlacomulco, dominated the state PRI almost continuously from the 1940s on, providing most of the governors and leading politicians.[21] Although some states, like Guerrero

---

18. Data on seats held by political parties were assembled from several sources. See Moisés Raúl López Laines, *Nezahualcóyotl: Perfil político, análisis y alternativas* (Ciudad Nezahualcóyotl: Imprenta San Diego, 1989); and Emilio Alvarado Guevara, *Yolhueyliztli: Historia de Nezahualcóyotl* (Mexico City: Editorial ARIES, 1996).

19. *Fraccionador* is a term used in Mexico for an individual or company that sells land in parcels. Fraccionadores are often legitimate companies, but evidence from several sources indicates that in Ciudad Nezahualcóyotl few of the fraccionadores had followed legal procedures to obtain land titles—and there was little or no transparency in the land titling system in the State of Mexico in this period. See Rosa, *Netzahualcóyotl*. Concerning the strength of the fraccionadores in local politics, see Emilio Duhau and Martha Schteingart, "El primer gobierno perredista," in Schteingart and Duhau, eds., *Transición política y democracia municipal en México y Colombia* (Mexico City: Miguel Ángel Porrúa, 2001), 166; Rosa, *Netzahualcóyotl*, 11–12; and Ferras, *Ciudad Nezahualcóyotl*, 15. The Asociación General de Colonos (General Association of Settlers), a community organization created with government support in 1957 to represent the area that became Ciudad Nezahualcóyotl, included a state government representative, four representatives of the fraccionadores, and four representatives of the population at large, although two of them were active PRI members close to the state government. This group was the official body that channeled demands for autonomy. It was disbanded when the first city government was elected. However, throughout the 1960s, the fraccionadores ensured the election of mayors who supported the land developers' interests. María Eugencia de Alba Muñiz, "Control política de los migrantes urbanos: Un caso de estudio, Ciudad Nezahualcóyotl" (M.A. thesis, Centro de Estudios Internacionales, El Colegio de México, Mexico City, September 1976), 78–89.

20. This group continues to dominate state politics, though disputes within it and within the PRI itself have become more noticeable since the 1990s. The PAN had a minimal presence in some municipalities and presented its first candidate in gubernatorial elections in 1975 (winning 12.5 percent, the party's best showing until 1993, when it would win 16.5 percent). See Duhau and Schteingart, "El primer gobierno perredista," 176–77.

21. For an extensive analysis of the origins and functioning of the Grupo Atlacomulco, see Rogelio

and Chiapas, experienced competition among leading strongmen and their families, the State of Mexico was dominated by a cohesive, though not homogeneous or always harmonious, political group that maintained close links to national leaders and served as the most important conduit for political power. Although few, if any, political leaders in Neza were part of this group, they depended on their relationships to state leaders for resolving local issues. The chronically weak municipal finances were further compounded by the city's great needs. Since the state government had exclusive rights for granting land titles and providing basic infrastructure, its role was especially significant in this growing city where these primary needs dominated citizens' concerns.[22]

Since the city lived to a large extent under state tutelage, Ciudad Nezahualcóyotl was also used by the state PRI to distribute patronage to politicians from outside the city. Elected representatives and city officials, including mayors and many state and federal congress representatives, were often not even residents of the city. For example, between 1963 and 1990, only five of the nine mayors were city residents.[23] In the one federal election, 1988, only two of the ten candidates for Congress from districts in Neza were residents of the city.[24] During the time when the PRI enjoyed almost complete hegemony in most states, it was not unheard of for outsiders to run for office in Mexican municipalities. Nevertheless, the frequency with which this happened in Neza is quite unusual and speaks to the relative weakness of the local politicians to negotiate their interests vis-à-vis the state government and party structure. The recent creation of the municipality, of course, compounded this since there were few local political leaders who had much stature in the state or national party despite the city's size. The sense that the city was largely an appendage of the state government certainly contributed to its political weakness as well.

The local PRI in Ciudad Nezahualcóyotl depended on a well-structured network of occupationally and territorially based organizations that allowed the

---

Hernández Rodríguez, *Amistades, compromisos y lealtades: Líderes y grupos políticos en el Estado de México* (Mexico City: El Colegio de México, 2007).

22. State governments are to this day responsible for land titles, water, and sewers, and the federal government for electricity (though the state government often serves as an intermediary on requests for the provision of electrical power). In interviews, social leaders active in the 1970s commented that the state government was far more important in terms of successfully meeting citizens' demands than was the municipal government. Odón Madariaga, interviewed by the author, May 21, 2005; Rosa, interview.

23. López Laines, *Nezahualcóyotl: Perfil político*, 85–86. López Laines was a noted PRIista politician and former congressman from the city who produced a critical work on the party's internal practices at the request of the local PRI in order to respond to the party's loss in the 1988 presidential elections.

24. Alvarado Guevara, *Yolhueyliztli*, 181.

party to mediate and, to some extent, control demands between citizens and government authorities. Of the party's three traditional sectors—labor, peasant, and popular—the first two were relatively weak. The National Peasant Confederation (CNC) would gain some influence later in the 1970s by absorbing a social organization that had led a revolt against the fraccionadores, but the absence of industry meant that the labor sector was largely irrelevant. The popular sector, known as the National Council of Popular Organizations (CNOP), brought together associations of owners and workers in the city's many markets, the teachers' union, the chamber of commerce, and the General Association of Settlers (Asociación General de Colonos), an umbrella organization for neighborhood groups. Together they were the backbone of the party. At the same time, the PRI had committees in each sector of the city, which gave the party a geographical base at election time and ensured a party presence in each neighborhood of the city.[25]

The party provided numerous services to local residents through the CNOP-affiliated organizations and the section committees, including legal and financial advice, employment listings, and support for a range of social demands for licenses, land titles, services, and other needs that only the government could resolve. The CNOP organizations thus formed the crucial link between citizens and public authorities under the PRI governments. According to Emilio Duhau and Martha Schteingart, "These organizations linked the daily life of the population in its social, economic, and urban aspects, but they also constituted the channels of support to leaders who occupied the mayor's office, city council seats, and other important positions in the municipality, for many decades."[26]

The PRI, however, was hardly a democratic organization in its internal operation. Though the party provided services through its constituent organizations that served as intermediaries between citizens and public authorities, this was done in return for loyalty, votes, and the support of particular PRI leaders who could claim the ability to resolve problems. The PRI, and the governments it

---

25. This description of the PRI is taken from Duhau and Schteingart, "El primer gobierno perredista," 183–86, and it was confirmed in conversations with leading members of the PRI in the city.

26. Duhau and Schteingart, "El primer gobierno perredista," 186. I was a witness to the CNOP's continued ability to operate as mediator during two afternoons I spent at its office in Ciudad Nezahualcóyotl. During this time, members of various CNOP organizations arrived to get help with such things as contested bills for services and petitions for neighborhood improvements. In one dramatic case, a woman asked for help because the administrator of the city's public hospital, whose services are supposed to be free, had refused to release her sister from the hospital without payment of a substantial sum of money. The CNOP leaders led a march on the hospital to get the woman's sister released.

created, operated in Neza as elsewhere in Mexico, by providing a paternalistic form of intermediation to its loyal members and by refusing to deal with those who chose to go outside the system. When groups tried to break off from the party, the authorities would either try to co-opt them back into the party structure or threaten to write them off.[27] In Ciudad Nezahualcóyotl, the local PRI hierarchy, after much internal negotiation, usually proposed candidates for office to the state PRI, which would make the final decision about who would run. On only one occasion, in 1978, did the local PRI try to elect candidates by allowing members to vote in a primary election; however, the results created so much bitterness among the losing groups that party leaders stepped in to name the candidates in the end.[28] For years on end, a few figures dominated the PRI's candidacies for office and the leadership of the party organizations, although they had to share these with outsiders whom the state PRI wanted to reward.[29] The PRI in Neza created a vertically integrated system of interest intermediation dominated by individual leaders, caciques, who could resolve problems for ordinary citizens in return for loyalty to those leaders. In turn, this system operated within a larger statewide structure of interest intermediation tied to the state's dominant political group.

The lack of horizontal links in Ciudad Nezahualcóyotl during its first twenty-five years also contributed to the PRI's success in controlling dissent and eliminating challenges to its hegemony. Martín de la Rosa Medellín, a Jesuit priest who tried in the early 1970s to organize an autonomous popular movement for change, noted that "horizontal communication is minimal: the city is infinitely atomized; each person or each group fights as hard as possible against daily problems of subsistence, problems that are really common."[30] The atomization of social struggles was compounded by the lack of public spaces, including parks, city newspapers, community radio stations, or local television programs, that could have facilitated deliberation among citizens. In addition, citizens' information often came from Mexico City news sources, and they spent much of their day in jobs in the capital as well. Most of the remaining collective spaces within neighborhoods, markets, and a handful of local businesses were successfully co-opted by the only political party of any strength.

27. Alba Muñiz, "Control político de los migrantes," covers this process in some detail with specific cases. See especially pp. 2–3.
28. Alvarado Guevara recounts this episode in *Yolhueyliztli*, 62–65.
29. López Laines, *Nezahualcóyotl: Perfil político*; Duhau and Schteingart, "El primer gobierno perredista," 156.
30. Rosa, *Netzahualcóyotl*, 4.

However, despite the PRI's seeming monopoly on social and political organization, significant chinks in this control existed. Struggles for land and services developed at the margins of the party, and though these social movements were often co-opted or controlled, their activities laid the groundwork for later cleavages in local politics and the emergence of new political alternatives in the city. The most striking challenge to politics as usual came in the form of a mass struggle against the real estate developers in the late 1960s and early 1970s. In 1953, a group of residents in what would become Ciudad Nezahualcóyotl formed the Frente Mexicano pro-Derechos Humanos (Mexican Front for Human Rights) and threatened to stop paying the fraccionadores for their land titles.[31] This group was suppressed, but in the mid-1960s, several neighborhood leaders began reviving the idea. Though the initial attempt to constitute an alliance that could declare a payment strike failed in from 1964 through 1967, a larger movement emerged around 1969 under the name of the Movimiento Restaurador de Colonos (Settlers' Restoration Movement), known by its initials, MRC.[32] The MRC declared a wholesale payment strike, asking residents of Ciudad Nezahualcóyotl to stop paying the fraccionadores their monthly quotas for the land titles, because so many of the fraccionadores had obtained the titles illegally in the first place. The organization also called on the state government to take control of the land and sell it to the residents at reasonable prices.

The MRC's payment strike spread like wildfire. By 1971, a reported seventy thousand city residents were active in twenty-eight MRC subcommittees.[33] The state government had immediately recognized the need to negotiate with them. The state was in the middle of an election in 1969, and the PRI's gubernatorial candidate, Carlos Hank González,[34] sent a representative to try to contain and, if possible, co-opt the movement. It took three years of negotiation, but the state granted the MRC's principal demands for land titles and basic services in 1972.[35]

31. See Ramón Rivera Espinosa, "Planificación urbana municipal y gestión popular en Ciudad Nezahualcóyotl" (M.A. thesis in Urban Planning, Escuela Superior de Ingeniería y Arquitectura, Instituto Politécnico Nacional, Mexico City, June 2002), 105–6.
32. On the MRC, see Rivera, "Planificación urbana municipal," 107–12; Ferras, *Ciudad Nezahualcóyotl*, 16–19; Alba Muñiz, "Control político de los migrantes," 91–130; Alvarado Guevara, *Yolhueyliztli*, 145–58; and Rosa, *Netzahualcóyotl*, 12–15. This discussion is supplemented with information obtained from the author's interview of MRC leader Odón Madariaga.
33. Rosa, *Netzahualcóyotl*, 12–13.
34. The son of Carlos Hank González, Jorge Hank Rhon, would become mayor of Tijuana in December 2004. See chapter 5.
35. The state government, now led by Hank González, approved a state trust, known as FINEZA, to buy out the fraccionadores at market value, resell the land to residents at a subsidized cost, and install services. Capitalized with 600 million pesos, FINEZA purchased 49,263 lots from the fraccionadores and then

In return for solving the land problem, the MRC leaders joined the PRI; however, they were allowed to join the peasant sector (Confederación Nacional Campesina, CNC) rather than the CNOP so they could maintain a degree of autonomy within the official party.[36] The MRC was by far the largest movement in Neza that took place outside the PRI, and in the end, it successfully negotiated its members' demands in return for loyalty to the party (and eventually positions for its leaders, who became city council members, local legislators, and members of Congress in the late 1970s and the 1980s). Timing and strategy had worked in the favor of the MRC. Following the tumultuous 1960s, President Luis Echeverría and Governor Hank González were trying to reconstruct relations with popular organizations that were willing to negotiate with and ultimately support the PRI.

There were several movements in the 1970s and early 1980s, however, which refused to play by the rules of the game. Though they operated at a much smaller scale, their efforts also laid the groundwork for changes that would take place in the late 1980s and 1990s.[37] One group of Jesuit priests, for example, led by Martín de la Rosa Medellín,[38] started the organization Servicios Populares, A.C. (SEPAC) in 1969 to train community leaders. SEPAC spawned an organization, the Unión de Colonias de Nezahualcóyotl (UNICON), dedicated to fighting for land titles and public services.[39]

---

resold them to residents. Alvarado Guevara, *Yolhueyliztli*, 154–55. By one account (Rosa, *Netzahualcóyotl*, 12), the municipality's annual budget was about 10 million pesos, so it was clearly unable to solve the land problem. Thus, for much of the 1970s, FINEZA became a significant figure of public authority in Ciudad Nezahualcóyotl, rivaling the municipality itself. Ignacio Pichardo, who had been the first negotiator sent by Hank González, became the president of FINEZA, and he later used this position to run successfully for state governor.

36. See Alvarado Guevara, *Yolhueyliztli*, 150–51.

37. The PAN and a few left-wing parties also operated in a limited way. The PAN had a small base in the north of the city, which was comparatively less poor, and also among some residents close to the Catholic Church.

38. Rosa later moved to Tijuana, where he participated in efforts to obtain housing for the city's landless families. He later left the priesthood and eventually joined the first three PAN municipal governments in various roles that had to do with popular participation, including designing the municipality's participatory planning process in the mid-1990s. See chapter 5.

39. On SEPAC, see Rivera, "Planificación urbana municipal," 122–25, and Rosa, *Netzahualcóyotl*. Most of the leaders of current social organizations in Neza who were interviewed for this book cited SEPAC as a significant influence on the formation of the city's independent social organizations. Inspired by liberation theology and the work of the Brazilian educator Paolo Freire, who stressed that people should take development into their own hands rather than be the objects of other peoples' actions, SEPAC eventually lost the support of the more conservative clergy in Ciudad Nezahualcóyotl and separated from the Catholic Church. During the 1970s, SEPAC started a monthly bulletin, *El despertar del Pueblo* (The awakening of the people), a popular film series, food cooperatives, and the city's first popular school.

Another organization, which years before had split from the PRI, the Unión General de Obreros y Campesinos del Estado de México (UGOCM), began a strategy, parallel to the MRC, of forcing the state to intervene against the fraccionadores by pursuing lawsuits and targeted payment strikes.[40] The UGOCM succeeded largely because it kept its actions small and operated with the support of the Partido Popular Socialista (PPS), a small party that PRI leaders used to create the impression of political pluralism. The UGOCM would lose momentum toward the end of the 1970s, but it would reemerge as an important force in the 1990s, when its leader at that time became the first PRD mayor of Ciudad Nezahualcóyotl. Another group, the Frente Popular Independiente (FIPI), was started in 1974 in Neza and Mexico City by students influenced by Maoist thought.[41] FIPI focused on fighting for land titles and services and against the rise in transportation prices. Later called the Unión Popular Revolucionario Emiliano Zapata (UPREZ), the organization was active in national coalitions of the urban popular movement and eventually created a network of "popular schools" for children and youth. The UPREZ would go on to play a decisive role in the 1996 PRD victory and subsequent leftist governments in the city.

Many of these independent groups played only small roles in the struggle for social change in Ciudad Nezahualcóyotl in the 1970s and early 1980s. Their possibilities for action were severely reduced by the almost complete dominance of the PRI and the unwillingness of this party to deal with any organization that did not show it a degree of loyalty. In 1981, however, a state constitutional change allowed for representatives of minority parties to have seats in the city council. Successive legal changes would expand the presence of opposition parties throughout

---

40. The UGOCM argued that the area occupied by the city had been declared communal land by Mexico's liberal President Benito Juárez in 1862 and that President Plutarco Elías Calles reaffirmed that after the Revolution. Consequently, the fraccionadores could not legally have purchased the land. Through targeted lawsuits and payment strikes, UGOCM succeeded in getting a few neighborhoods in the city declared property of the state and resold to residents at a lower price. Rivera, "Planificación urbana municipal," 113–15; Valentín González Bautista, UGOCM leader (and former mayor), interviewed by the author, October 4, 2005.

41. In 1979, following its leader's death by torture, the FIPI divided over whether to participate in the elections, but it reemerged in 1980, joining forces with a local popular school in Neza's Villada neighborhood. By 1987, the organization had metamorphosed once again, acquiring its current name and identity. This brief history of the FIPI/UPREZ is based on the author's interview with Felipe Rodríguez, local congressman, city council member (2000–2003), and historical leader of the UPREZ nationally and in Ciudad Nezahualcóyotl, May 20, 2005; Rivera, "Planificación urbana municipal," 118–19; and the pamphlet printed by UPREZ, "Los siete aspectos que debes saber de la UPREZ." (Seven things you should know about UPREZ).

the 1980s, creating a modest degree of political plurality and providing enhanced support for popular organizations.[42]

An outside observer of Ciudad Nezahualcóyotl in 1987 would probably have seen little change in the ongoing dominance of the PRI and the traditional clientelistic forms of politics. However, the multiple struggles carried out by popular organizations had created political fissures that were being exacerbated by the severe economic crisis Mexico had been suffering since 1982. When Cuauhtémoc Cárdenas bolted from the PRI in 1988 and ran a left-of-center candidacy for president, his campaign brought together these organizations and important groups within the PRI who were concerned about the country's direction. Odón Madariaga, former leader of the MRC, who had since served in Congress and the municipal council, also bolted from the PRI and organized the Cárdenas campaign in Ciudad Nezahualcóyotl. The UPREZ, UGOCM, and the leftist Partido Mexicano de los Trabajadores (PMT), which had developed a small but dedicated following, all joined the campaign as well. To everyone's surprise, Cárdenas won handily in Ciudad Nezahualcóyotl, defeating PRI candidate Carlos Salinas de Gortari by 56.1 percent to 23.4 percent (with a respectable 11.1 percent for the PAN's Manuel Clouthier).[43] Madariaga and one other candidate from Cárdenas' coalition were elected to Congress.

The PRI's first loss in Ciudad Nezahualcóyotl—and by a sizable margin— caused significant reflection within the local PRI.[44] However, the left was unable to capitalize on its victory. Despite the founding of the PRD in 1989, the coalition that had supported Cárdenas's candidacy split and the party received few votes in the next two elections (see fig. 6.1). Nevertheless, these elections and their aftermath proved a turning point for many of the social organizations that had participated. In addition, the 1988 elections forced the state and federal

---

42. The PAN won both opposition seats in 1982. In 1985, when another constitutional change expanded the number of minority seats to three, the PAN repeated in one seat, the PARM (a small party close to the PRI) took another, and a coalition of left-wing parties—the Mexican Socialist Party (PMS)— won the third one. The small but hegemony-breaking presence of the PAN and the Mexican left in the council presaged even bigger changes just around the corner. Information on the political presence of the opposition in the council is based on data in López Laines, *Nezahualcóyotl: Perfil político*, and Alvarado Guevara, *Yolhueyliztli*.

43. María Magdalena Tosoni García, "Acerca de como participan los excluidos en la ciudad de México: La historia de la Colonia Canal de Sales" (M.A. thesis, Facultad Latinoamericana de Ciencias Sociales, Mexico City, 1998), appendix, table 16, based on statistics available at the Centro de Estadística y Documentación Electoral de la Universidad Autónoma Metropolitana.

44. The results are published as López Laines, *Nezahualcóyotl: Perfil político*. Héctor Pedroza, Arcadio López, and Luis Pérez Maldonado (all PRI), interviewed by the author on April 23, 2005.

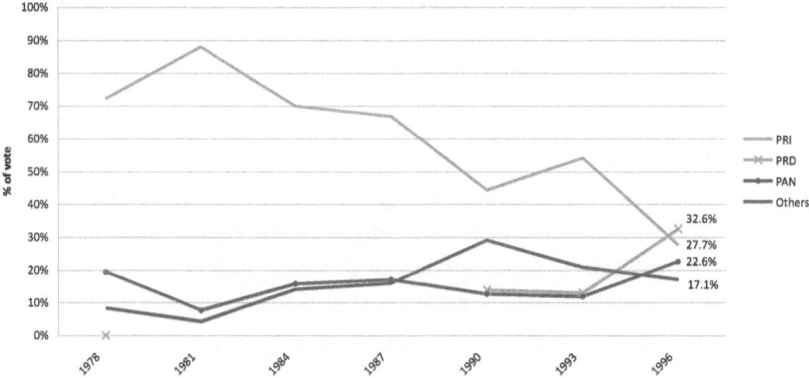

Fig. 6.1 Municipal elections by political party, Ciudad Nezahualcóyotl, 1978–96

Note: Due to the difficulty of obtaining data, the percentage for parties is of valid votes for 1978–87 and of total votes for 1990–96.

SOURCE: Data for 1990–96 compiled from statistics of the Instituto Electoral del Estado de México, available at http://www.ieem.org.mx; earlier years adapted from María Magdalena Tosoni García, "Acerca de como participan los excluidos en la ciudad de México: La historia de la Colonia Canal de Sales" (M.A. thesis, Facultad Latinoamericana de Ciencias Sociales, Mexico City, 1998), appendix, table 16, based on statistics available at the Centro de Estadística y Documentación Electoral of the Universidad Autónoma Metropolitana.

government to change electoral laws to include more representation of minority parties as a means of ensuring legitimacy in the eyes of the public.

One of the organizations that took advantage of the new political climate was the Movimiento Vida Digna (MOVIDIG), born out of the socialist PMT in the early 1980s with the realization that political struggle needed to be "accompanied by the necessity of the stomach."[45] Originally dedicated to the struggle for land titles, MOVIDIG later became known for its extensive distribution of subsidized

45. MOVIDIG came to dominate political life in Neza. It pursued activities like distributing coupons for subsidized food, supplying water to communities left without services during the 1985 earthquake, and obtaining subsidized homes for people who lacked their own property. The leaders of the organization participated in the 1988 campaign for Cárdenas but soon returned to their community organizing work, although with a new commitment to electoral involvement. When the government cancelled the coupons for subsidized food (known as *tortibonos*) after the elections, MOVIDIG switched strategies and began food cooperatives throughout Neza, pooling resources to buy food in bulk and distributing it at low prices to their members. The membership grew until the organization was in every neighborhood of the city. With the success of its cooperative, MOVIDIG ran candidates in 1987, 1990, and 1993 and won municipal council seats under the minority representation rule. Using the salary of the council members, the organization bought a truck and professionalized its operations. This account of MOVIDIG is based on interviews with two of the organization's historical leaders, Héctor Bautista and Cirilo Revilla. The quote is from Revilla, director of public administration in the municipality (2003–6), interviewed by the author, May 19, 2005.

food throughout the city. It also participated actively in elections, as the PMT, winning a seat in three consecutive elections and allowing it to develop a degree of bargaining leverage. In the 1970s and early 1980s, independent movements had rarely been able to make the authorities hear their demands if they did not adopt a degree of loyalty to the PRI. In contrast, in the 1990s, when political competition was a reality (though still highly unequal), PRI governments were willing to deal with opposition-supported organizations to keep them close and, if possible, co-opt them. As Héctor Bautista, historical leader of the MOVIDIG, noted, the communities "where MOVIDIG mobilized were urbanized more quickly.... That is why the social organizations grew, because the PRI gave something [to us]."[46] Although the PRI organizations continued to be the primary channels of influence, the independent organizations had developed a degree of leverage and influence.

In 1996, the principal social organizations, MOVIDIG, UPREZ, UGOCM, and a newer group, the Movimiento de Liberación Nezahualcoyotlense (MLN),[47] decided to launch a joint candidacy in the municipal elections. None of the organizations thought they could win, so they proposed Valentín González Bautista, leader of the tiny UGOCM, to run for mayor, and they divided up the city council candidacies among the larger organizations.[48] González turned out to be a surprisingly effective candidate and the organizations unusually cohesive. In addition, former presidential candidate and PRD founder Cuauhtémoc Cárdenas had just launched his candidacy for mayor of Mexico City, and the high-profile PRD campaign in the capital next door helped raise the profile of the party in Neza.[49] The election produced a surprise result: the PRD won more than one-third of the votes with the PRI and PAN close behind. Under state electoral rules, this meant that the PRD was entitled to the mayor's office and a majority of city council seats. For the first time in the city's history, a party other than the PRI would govern. This change would also coincide with the push in Mexico to strengthen municipal governments. What would these changes mean for democratic governance in Ciudad Nezahualcóyotl? Would it alter the channels that linked citizens and their public authorities? And would it improve the effectiveness of representative government

46. Héctor Bautista, interview.
47. The MLN was formed after the 1988 elections.
48. Héctor Bautista, interview. See also the descriptions by Duhau and Schteingart, "El primer gobierno perredista," 188–89; and Arzaluz, "Participación ciudadana," 301 and 301n.
49. The Mexico City election took place in 1997, several months after the election in Neza, but much of Cárdenas's campaign took place at the same time as that of González. Odón Madariaga, interview.

Empowering the Municipality (1996–2005)?

The story of Ciudad Nezahualcóyotl since 1996 has been one of increasing political pluralism and steadily strengthened municipal structure and finances. The PRD would win municipal elections again in 2000 and 2003, garnering an outright majority of votes in 2003. Neza had truly become a PRD bastion—just at the moment when municipal finances and functions expanded dramatically. The municipality of Ciudad Nezahualcóyotl had always struggled to raise revenue. Since there is little industry and most inhabitants work outside the city, the municipality had few options for leveraging local revenues compared to other cities of its size. Indeed, from 1989 to 1996, total municipal revenue remained almost completely static in real terms (fig. 6.2). Corruption under PRI-affiliated administrations appears to have played a major part in this poor performance. Before 1996, the municipal slaughterhouse, stadium, and zoo produced no income for the municipal government, and it appears that revenue generated from these sources entered the PRI's coffers directly.[50] The PRD-affiliated administrations that governed after 1996 succeeded in increasing locally generated revenue by one-third between 1997 and 2002.[51]

The increase was particularly noticeable in the first three years when the slaughterhouse, stadium, and zoo began to produce revenue. Like many of its Mexican and Latin American counterparts, the municipality has struggled to collect property taxes; fully 42 percent of residents did not pay any taxes on their property in 2003.[52] As a result, the boom in municipal finances that began in 1997 was largely the result of transfers to municipalities, especially Ramo 33, which had come to constitute over 40 percent of municipal revenue by 2002.[53] Given this influx of new transfers, the city's finances more than tripled in *real terms* between 1997 and 2002.[54]

The influx of federal revenues has meant a rapid growth in the municipality's ability to respond to pressing demands without negotiating ad hoc agreements

---

50. Duhau and Schteingart, "El primer gobierno perredista," 201.
51. INEGI, Sistema Municipal de Base de Datos, http://sc.inegi.org.mx/simbad. See also fig. 5.2.
52. *Plan de desarrollo municipal 2003–2006*, 151–52.
53. Ramo 33 funds have oscillated between 41 and 46 percent of Neza's total revenues from 1999 to 2006 (the figure was 35 percent in 1998). Author's calculations based on data from the Instituto Nacional para el Federalismo y el Desarrollo Municipal (INAFED), "Finanzas públicas locales," available at http://www.inafed.gob.mx.
54. In absolute terms, the municipal budget increased almost five times, rising from 217 million to one billion pesos between 1997 and 2002. Author's calculations based on figures in INEGI, Sistema Municipal de Base de Datos.

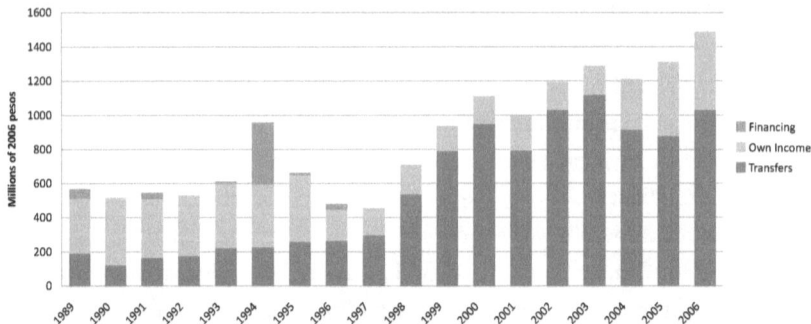

Fig. 6.2 Real municipal income by source, Ciudad Nezahualcóyotl, 1989–2006

SOURCE: Calculations based on data from INEGI, Sistema Municipal de Base de Datos, available at http://sc.inegi.org.mx/simbad, except for 2006, from INEGI, *Ingreso y gasto público en México 2008*.

with the state and federal governments. This has been particularly important in a period of democratic change, where the party in power at the municipal level had few allies in the state or federal government and was often at odds with the dominant political group in the state. A review of yearly reports by mayors of Neza in the early and mid-1990s reveals how much those administrations depended on major investment funds granted by state and federal authorities in order to be able to invest in infrastructure.[55] The formula-based federal transfers that went into effect after 1997 have allowed the city to operate with relative autonomy in setting its own priorities. Because over three-quarters of these funds have been part of the FORTAMUNDF, which can be used for whatever purposes the municipality chooses, the city was able to pay off a major water debt inherited from the PRI governments, and it then had considerable flexibility in setting additional spending priorities.

As in other cities, however, federal transfers have two significant drawbacks. First, although transfers are no longer discretionary at the federal level, state governments set the formula for distributing that money to the municipalities. Consequently, discrepancies in distribution exist within states, but the strict adherence to a formula has made the transfers increasingly equitable, though not perfectly so. Although Ciudad Nezahualcóyotl received less than 40 percent of the state average for per capita federal transfers in 1989–90, today it receives 82 percent

---

55. These annual reports include frequent expressions of gratitude to the federal and state governments for investments in roads, electricity, and water systems. Author's review of the *Informe municipal*.

of the state average and roughly around the same amount as most of the state's other large cities.⁵⁶ Of course, the state government can still delay the transfer of funds, and city officials complain that this is often done to harass the municipal government and make it difficult for them to plan expenditures.⁵⁷ Nonetheless, the decentralization process has been overwhelmingly positive for the municipal government of Neza in terms of enhanced autonomy and authority. They have increased their overall revenues by a significant amount and decreased the degree of control that state and federal governments once exercised over transfers. These changes were especially important for a government run by a party that controls neither the state nor federal governments. For a municipality that has few sources of local revenue, increased federal transfers have also provided Neza with a financial base on par with other, more affluent municipalities.

Strengthening Democratic Representation (1996–2005)

Although the PRD has dominated politics since 1996, elections have been highly competitive (fig. 6.3). The PRD has won all municipal elections (2000, 2003, and 2006) and most federal congressional seats. However, the PRI has maintained a strong base of support and continually threatens to return to power, while the PAN has shown surprising strength, even managing to win, on the coattails of Vicente Fox's presidential campaign, two of the municipality's five federal congressional seats in 2000.⁵⁸ Indeed, since 2000, Ciudad Nezahualcóyotl has been one of those unusual municipalities in Mexico where all three parties actually govern: the PRD in the municipal government, the PRI in the state

---

56. In the 1989–92 period, Neza received one-quarter of the per capita transfers sent to Naucalpan and approximately half of the per capita transfers to Toluca, the state capital. Today, the differences among the three cities are minimal. The discrepancy started to change in 1998 with the creation of Ramo 33 and has improved significantly each year. Author's calculations based on data from INEGI, Sistema Municipal de Base de Datos; INEGI, *XI censo*; *Conteo de población y vivienda 1995* (Aguascalientes: INEGI, 1998); and *XII censo*.

57. In 2005, according to city officials, the state government delayed the transfer of funding to cover a new program for public security to most of its PRD-affiliated municipalities. In response, Mayor Luis Sánchez led a protest in the state capital that lasted for several days. Martín Rosales, chief of staff to Mayor Sánchez, interviewed by the author, May 19, 2005. Notably, public authorities in Tijuana have the same complaint about transfers from their state government, yet both are PAN administrations. At times, these delays may be politically motivated, and at other times, perhaps they reflect bureaucratic inertias and inefficiencies.

58. This chapter only covers the administrations through 2005, however. It should be noted that the PRI did win the municipal election in 2008.

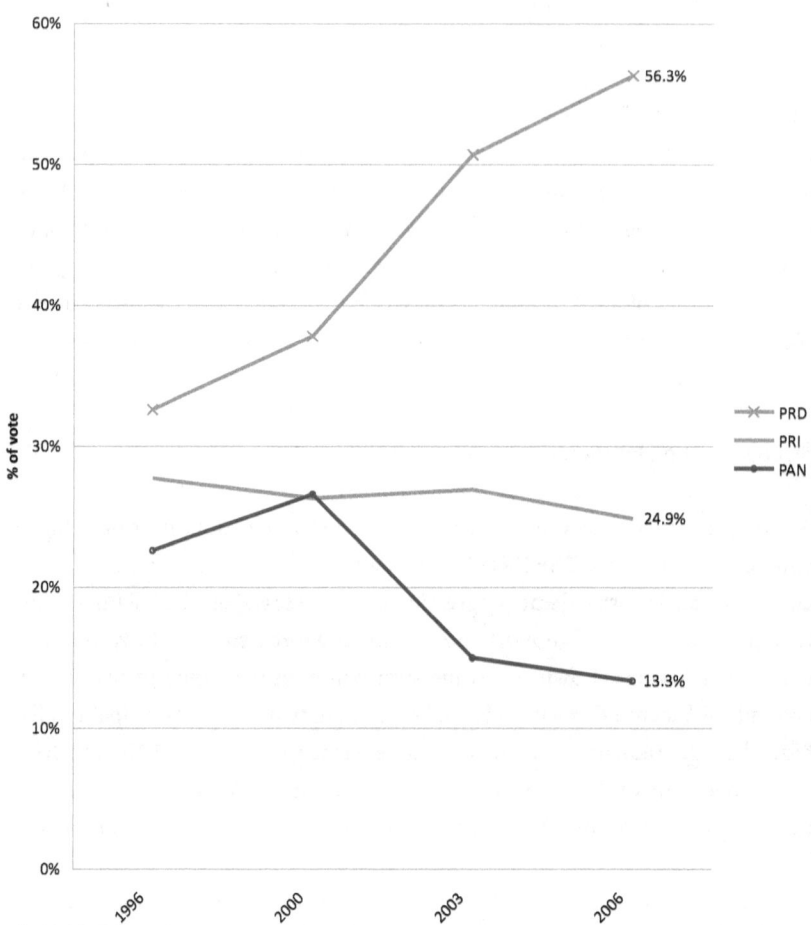

Fig. 6.3 Municipal elections by political party, Ciudad Nezahualcóyotl, 1996–2006

Note: A change in electoral laws in the State of Mexico shifted the electoral calendar ahead by several months. Instead of holding municipal elections in 1999 and 2002, as would have normally happened, the elections took place in 2000 and 2003. This meant that the term of the mayor in 1997–2000 was lengthened by several months. Note that the PRI went into the 2003 elections in a coalition with the Green Party (PVEM), and vote totals reflect the coalition's total.

SOURCE: Instituto Electoral del Estado de México, available at http://www.ieem.org.mx.

government, and the PAN in the federal government. This is a far cry from the pre-1996 period, where the PRI won every municipal election by more than 30 percentage points while controlling both the state and federal governments.

Considerable doubts remain about the impartiality of the state electoral institute, and shortly before the 2005 gubernatorial elections, all of the institute's councillors were forced to resign in the middle of a political scandal, and the state congress appointed replacements. Opposition parties have traditionally claimed that the PRI maintained a tight grip over the institute.[59] Perhaps more important, however, all major parties (and quite a few smaller ones) had continued to win elections in the state. No opposition politicians in Neza seemed to believe that they had lost a municipal election due to fraud.[60]

The PRD held primary elections for its mayoral candidate in the 2000 and 2003 elections, a first for any major party in the city.[61] In 2000, this involved an actual open primary for anyone with a voting card; in 2003, it involved a poll to determine the top two candidates, followed by an actual run-off election between those two candidates.[62] The existence of the primary has served to select candidates with a strong base of support and to give citizens a voice in selecting who governs. As we will see below, the primaries also help determine who runs in the city council elections, which provides for greater citizen engagement in those elections than elsewhere in Mexico.

The first PRD mayor, Valentín González Bautista, had a very plural municipal administration. His party lacked qualified candidates for municipal office, so he relied on technically trained party members and some former PRI officials, many of them from Mexico City. To create confidence, he named a comptroller from the PAN and a director of urban planning from the PRI. This approach

---

59. These forced resignations seem to have pleased all of the major parties. Rodrigo Iván Cortés, congressman and member of the PAN State Council in the State of Mexico, interviewed by the author, Mexico City, March 4, 2005.

60. Author's interviews with four city council members: Carlos Alberto Pérez Cuevas (PAN), April 22, 2005; Héctor Pedroza (PRI), April 23, 2005; César Pedro López Gómez (PRI), April 23, 2005; and Francisco Antonio Ruíz López (PRI), April 23, 2005.

61. My research ended in 2005, so I do not have information on the candidate selection process in the 2006 election.

62. In 1996, of course, no primary was held because the PRD-affiliated organizations had little hope of winning. In 2000, MOVIDIG's leader, Héctor Bautista, in alliance with the MLN, UGOCM, and smaller organizations, defeated UPREZ's leader, Felipe Rodríguez. In 2003, MOVIDIG was challenged by UPREZ, UGOCM, and the MLN in the first round. In the second round, MOVIDIG built a winning coalition with smaller groups, while UPREZ won the support of the MLN and UGOCM. Rodríguez, interview.

created considerable conflict with other groups in the PRD, especially UPREZ and MLN (but also MOVIDIG), which felt excluded from power.[63]

The approach to filling government positions changed dramatically in the following two governments, which instead decided to have a municipal administration made up primarily of PRD members. Héctor Bautista, the leader of MOVIDIG and the second PRD mayor of Neza (2000–2003), complained about González's administration: "I didn't see any difference between a PRIista and a PRDista administration. . . . When I arrived, it was important to give a different profile to the administration; the party members were going to be in the administration."[64] Key positions went to the PRD and especially to members of MOVIDIG. This pattern repeated and intensified in the third PRD government under Luis Sánchez (2003–6), in which almost all top-line positions went to members of MOVIDIG. Sánchez reserved only a few of the less strategic positions, such as ecology and public relations, for people without an affiliation to MOVIDIG, while making sure to install the movement's members in the most sensitive or powerful positions (including secretary of the municipality and the directors of government, finance, administration, and participation, among others).[65]

Electoral laws in the State of Mexico, as in all states, assign a majority of seats in the council to the winning party regardless of the vote total. This has led to a significant degree of overrepresentation of the PRD in many cases and an underrepresentation of the PRI, although this was reduced somewhat by changes in electoral laws.[66] Despite this, divisions within the PRD make for a complicated and occasionally competitive process of decision making within the city council. During the first administration, Mayor González often found himself at odds with UPREZ and MLN and even, for a time, MOVIDIG, after he fired one of its members from his cabinet in 1999. The next two PRD administrations saw fewer obvious divisions among the party's council members, but differences within the

---

63. Duhau and Schteingart, "El primer gobierno perredista," 197; Arzaluz, "Participación ciudadana," 302–4. This information was confirmed in interviews with leaders of PRD-affiliated groups.

64. Héctor Bautista, interview.

65. Revilla, interview. Confirmed in interviews with other municipal officials and current and former city council members. The one notable exception was public security, however, where a director (who did not live in Neza or participate in any of the party's internal groups in the city) was named from a political group within the national PRD.

66. The overrepresentation was 31.4 percent in 1996 and 31.3 percent in 2000, but only 8.4 percent in 2003. The underrepresentation of the PRI also dropped from 14.4 percent in 1996 to 8.1 percent in 2000 and then became a slight overrepresentation of 0.4 percent in 2003. This analysis excludes the mayor as a member of the municipal council and is based on data from the Instituto Electoral del Estado de México, http://www.ieem.org.mx.

party were constantly being negotiated.⁶⁷ According to former Mayor Bautista, "Up to now, the PRD does not exist [as] a militancy, a structure.... They [sic] are the movements."⁶⁸ The party that has benefited most from this state of affairs is the PAN, which established itself as an occasional ally of the mayor on key policy matters during the first and third PRD administrations.⁶⁹ The PRI has had a more difficult relationship with the PRD and a much more marginal impact on policy. According to one PRI council member, "We have been able to have influence, but very little."⁷⁰ Nonetheless, the PRI has often been willing to support major PRD initiatives in return for economic support of initiatives that benefit the PRI base. Moreover, this party has used its linkages to the state government, still controlled by the PRI, to negotiate resources for projects that benefit its base.⁷¹

The PRD has used its open primary system, in part, to assign council seats to its key factions: MOVIDIG, UPREZ, UGOCM, and MLN. According to the results of the primaries, the various factions have negotiated the number of positions each receives within the party's slate for the city council.⁷² In some cases, the major organizations in the PRD have used the quotas they had negotiated in the party list to give spaces to small affiliated organizations.⁷³ Because the major PRD-affiliated groups that originated in Neza have also become the most important political groups within the PRD in the State of Mexico, negotiations for spaces in the council have often reflected alliances at the state and national level. As a result, the local organizations have sometimes ceded spaces to major groups in the national PRD as part of broader political negotiations. Consequently, multiple levels of political negotiation among party factions have increasingly diluted the effect of the primaries on the composition of the municipal council. Whatever effect primaries might have on making the party-list system more representative is thus largely lost.

---

67. Based on interviews with seven current and former members of the city council from all three parties: Alliet Bautista (PRD), April 22, 2005; Antonio Zanabría (PRD), April 22, 2005; Rodríguez (PRD); Pérez Cuevas (PAN); Pedroza (PRI); López Gómez (PRI); and Ruíz López (PRI).
68. Héctor Bautista, interview.
69. Carlos Alberto Pérez Cuevas, coordinator of the PAN in the city council (2003–6), interview; Duhau and Schteingart, "El primer gobierno perredista," 190–91.
70. Interviews with members of the city council.
71. Ibid.
72. However, the system is entirely discretional. For example, UPREZ, which finished second in the 2003 primary, ended up without seats on the council. Rodríguez, interview.
73. This practice is particularly true of MOVIDIG, which gave four seats to small factions in 2003, and of UPREZ, which gave two of its four seats to smaller factions in 2000.

The operation of the municipal council was far less contested than its fragmented composition would suggest. Despite the requirement that city council meetings be public and held at least once a week, they were held sporadically with no announcement or public presence. One council member noted, "The meetings are public, but the meeting room is small and only a few people close to the council members come."[74] The council primarily performed the function of bringing citizen demands to the municipal administration, the real decision maker, and then only in a highly sectarian way. The council did not appear to have become a venue for rational scrutiny of proposals or forging an agreement on policy. Although commissions existed to cover most of the major responsibilities of the council, they rarely, if ever, met, and commission leadership seemed to be used largely to obtain specific benefits for a particular social group or sector of a party.[75] There was significant activity at the outset of the first PRD government, when the council debated and created regulations and even drafted and passed its own internal council regulations.[76] However, activity slowed considerably after that time, despite occasional issues that generated debate.[77]

Perhaps most telling was how the mayor and municipal administration saw the city council and how the council members saw themselves. In the 2003 elections, MOVIDIG chose not to run a single candidate for the council and ceded all of the seats they had negotiated to other small groups close to them. At the same time, they retained almost all of the top administrative leadership positions for themselves. MOVIDIG's leaders consider the administrative positions far more significant than a seat on the council. According to one historical leader of MOVIDIG who served in the administration, "The municipal council sets a general outline of what to do [*lineamientos generales*], but it is not involved in operations."[78] One former PRI council member noted that "by tradition, the city council seats have been centers for receiving demands [*centros de gestión*]." The PAN's former council coordinator observed that "people see us just as people to bring concrete demands to, not as the government" (*la gente nos ve como meros*

---

74. Alliet Bautista (PRD), interview.

75. Commissions, in theory, consist of a president, a secretary, and two to four other members. Except where noted, this paragraph is based on interviews with the current and former council members cited earlier.

76. Apparently suggested by a PAN council member and based on the council regulation of Tijuana (Arzaluz, "Participación Ciudadana," 356 and 356n).

77. One example of an issue that arose during the second administration involved granting land to a private university to set up installations in the city.

78. Revilla, interview.

gestores, no como gobierno). Several PRD council members recognized that they primarily responded to citizen concerns, but that these were usually concrete needs brought to them by neighborhood leaders affiliated with their own group within the party. Major policy issues, they admitted, were usually negotiated among the leaders of the factions before they were brought to the council. In sum, the council served primarily as a way for PRD factions and opposition parties to maintain a quota of influence within the government and to channel demands of their organizations' members to the administration.

New and Old Channels Between Citizens and the Municipality (1996–2005)

The change of party in government in Ciudad Nezahualcóyotl brought about two important institutional innovations that were ostensibly designed to replace traditional forms of clientelism by providing citizens with new channels for relating with their public authorities. The first one, the Municipal Development Council (Consejo para el Desarrollo Municipal, CODEMUN), was designed to oversee municipal investment expenditures under Ramo 33's Municipal Social Infrastructure Fund (FISM).[79] The CODEMUN was to have twenty-five citizen councillors elected in public assemblies in the city's twenty-five districts, and it would also include the mayor (as president), the director of social development (as secretary), and a representative from the city council.

It is unclear how democratic the election of the first CODEMUN was: the election took place with little advance notice, and the PRD won most of the seats, with a handful for the PAN and none for the PRI.[80] However, in some cases, this body proved to be more independent from the mayor than even the municipal council was and far more visible in its public profile. The CODEMUN asserted its right to decide which infrastructure projects would get FISM funds from the municipality, and although the city council had legal authority in this matter, the CODEMUN succeeded in establishing de facto decision-making authority regarding these allocations. The body met once a week in highly public sessions, which were frequently well attended by social organizations that had an interest in the outcome of infrastructure decisions. Equally significantly,

79. See chapter 3 for an extensive discussion of Ramo 33 and FISM.
80. This is noted by Arzaluz, "Participación ciudadana," 346, and confirmed by an interview with a former member of the CODEMUN. Much of the analysis in this paragraph is based on Arzaluz, "Participación ciudadana," 345–71, except as noted.

the CODEMUN began publishing its own bulletin, *Agenda 33*, which reported on infrastructure investments with detailed information about decisions, expenditures, and completion dates. According to one prominent political leader, the CODEMUN "was the 'communications system' between the city government and the citizens" (*era el correo entre el ayuntamiento y los ciudadanos*).[81] Nonetheless, like the municipal council, the CODEMUN also made decisions based on bargaining among factions within the PRD.[82] It was far more public than the council, but its decision-making process was not terribly different in style. Nonetheless, it served the purpose of making decisions on community investments a highly public exercise that citizens could follow closely.

The CODEMUN was not without detractors, who would soon seek to control the body and eliminate its margin of autonomy. Many political leaders, in particular, felt that the council was usurping the authority of the council and had gained too much independence from the mayor. Therefore, the second PRD administration, under Héctor Bautista, sought to minimize its role in investment decisions, even though the same councillors officially remained in office. According to Bautista, the CODEMUN and the Citizen Participation Councils (the second institutional innovation described below) "became an opposition. . . . It was very hard to work with them. . . . I went around them; I went to the municipal council." By 2002, the CODEMUN had stopped meeting entirely.

In August 2004, the administration of Mayor Luis Sánchez decided to revive the council, but he took care to keep it firmly under control by sharing the benefits widely enough that every political faction and party would be happy with a negotiated arrangement. In a late-night meeting with city council members, the mayor offered each political party and its major organizations a quota of seats on the new CODEMUN.[83] The factions were happy to oblige and named their representatives. The PRI took seats related to areas where they felt they were weak and had no other representation. The UPREZ, which had a conflicted relationship with MOVIDIG at the time, was excluded, but the other major PRD factions joined, as did the PAN. In a few cases, it appears that sham elections were held to which only those whose faction was slated to win showed up; in other cases, no assemblies were held and attendance lists were simply fabricated. The

81. Rodríguez, interview.
82. Martín Becerra, interviewed by the author, March 4, 2005, and Arelio Acero, interviewed by the author, November 18, 2005.
83. This information is based on interviews with four city council members and several administration officials. All corroborated the exact same version of events. The PRI council members were especially happy with the negotiated arrangement that allowed them to once again return to the CODEMUN.

sharing of the wealth meant that each party and party organization could guarantee public works projects for its members and clients. A few of the city council members were embarrassed by the lack of transparency, but all recognized that it was a solution that kept everyone happy.

The first PRD administration had also launched another ambitious experiment in citizen participation by creating elected Citizen Participation Councils, known as Copacis (Consejos de Participación Ciudadana). To some degree, these councils had existed for well over a decade and were legally required in each municipality under the state constitution. Under PRI governments, however, the presidents of the Copacis were selected by the PRI's neighborhood organizations (*seccionales*) or party leaders and were charged with providing intermediation between neighborhood concerns and the municipality.[84] In April 1997, however, the new PRD government opened the process to the public by holding open elections in ninety-six small districts, each made up of a few blocks. Each Copaci would have five members, including a president, secretary, and three councillors, all elected together on a single list. Only a fraction of registered voters participated: approximately 25,000 voters, or 8 percent of the 312,724 citizens who had voted in the mayoral elections a few months before. This was still a significant number for a first-time vote for neighborhood authorities who still had few clear functions. In 2000, the number of voters rose to 33,000 and then to 66,248 in 2003, a full 22 percent of those who voted in the mayoral election of the same year. In each election, 80 to 90 percent of the districts had two or more lists competing.[85]

Although these were nominally nonpartisan elections, each party ran its own slate of candidates in the districts. The PRD, in the first Copaci election, tried to reproduce the alliance of factions that had brought it to power a few months earlier by negotiating common party lists in each district, but in many cases the specific groups in the party ended up facing off against one another with different lists. This tendency for different PRD groups to compete against one another

---

84. Based on interviews with three neighborhood leaders who participated in Copacis before 1997.
85. Gerardo Salazar, "La participación ciudadana organizada" and "Diagnóstico de los consejos electos 2003–2006," both unpublished documents; and internal municipal documents obtained by the author. Vote totals for 2003 cited in *Plan municipal de desarrollo 2003–2006* (Ciudad Nezahualcóyotl: Ayuntamiento de la Ciudad Nezahualcóyotl, 2003), 132. The 2000 estimate is based on the assertion in the *Plan* that the 2003 election represented a 98 percent increase in voting. All other figures are estimates based on a sample of Citizen Participation Councils (seventy-three out of ninety-six for 1997 and twenty-seven out of seventy-nine for 2003) from internal municipal documents.

would increase in each successive Copaci election.[86] Although parties were officially not allowed to get involved in what was supposed to be an election for nonpartisan citizen councillors, only a handful of lists won that were not backed by a faction or candidate affiliated with one of the parties. As in the case of the city council and the CODEMUN, disputes among the PRD factions dominated the Copaci elections as well.

Extensive interviews with neighborhood leaders, party operatives, and administration officials, as well as internal municipal documents, confirm that the councils have largely been partisan organizations, despite the legal framework that forbids parties from getting involved in their election.[87] Indeed, slates in Copaci elections are usually put together in complex negotiations among the key political factions in the PRD and PRI, or smaller factions use them to show their strength to the larger organizations.[88] Municipal officials echoed this view, noting that Copacis are primarily political organizations, which help to measure the strength of different groups affiliated with a party.[89]

The politicization of the Copacis would seem to provide damning evidence that they are mere manifestations of political competition without a role in linking citizens to public affairs in any meaningful way. However, these councils do appear to play an important role as official intermediaries between neighborhood residents and local leaders. These councils deal with demands that are the

---

86. Almost three-quarters of the districts (73 percent) surveyed in one internal municipal study revealed competition among two or more lists, and almost half (48 percent) had more than two lists competing. Author's calculations are based on data on the 1997 Copaci election in Salazar, "La participación ciudadana." Salazar, an anthropologist, would become the municipal government's coordinator of citizen participation shortly after the 1997 elections.

87. This included interviews from February through October 2005, with fourteen neighborhood leaders in eleven neighborhoods, including eleven who were serving or had served as leaders of Copacis, plus interviews with seven city council members and several administration officials.

88. One leader of a small faction in the PRD noted, for example, that having a Copaci "reaffirms the political space that I have" and allows him to negotiate other demands with the municipality. A PRI Copaci leader noted that serving on a Copaci is a "platform to a political career." Still another Copaci leader stated that "the councils are tied to political parties; they work with them, through them." And yet another noted that "here one cannot talk really about a Copaci made up of citizens—all are politicians." Four Copaci leaders, interviewed between February and October 2005.

89. Municipal documents about the Copacis invariably refer to them by their party affiliation and the specific faction to which they belong within the party. Héctor Bautista, the former mayor, observed that the Copacis "come out of political agreements; in many cases, they do not represent citizens.... They are spaces of [political] projection." The municipal director of public security stated that he saw little reason to work systematically with the councils because they were "a type of political expression.... In many cases they have a political tilt." MOVIDIG leader and municipal official Cirilo Revilla similarly commented that "we do that Copaci thing because it is a legal requirement.... The real leaderships are different." Héctor Bautista, former mayor, interview; Jorge Amador, director of public security, interviewed by the author, February 20, 2005; and Revilla, interview.

bread-and-butter issues that affect people's quality of life: broken water pipes, flooding, insecurity, permits for vendors and for festivals, broken street lights, and the paving of roads. Without an exception—and regardless of party affiliation—every interviewed neighborhood leader saw the Copacis as an important avenue for resolving community concerns by enabling people to get their demands heard by decision makers. At the same time, they all recognized that these organizations existed alongside traditional forms of intermediation within the different factions of the PRD and the PRI.[90] It was clear that the government tended to listen more to PRD-affiliated Copacis, and these were generally effective because they could leverage support from leaders of their party faction in the council or in the administration. However, even the PRI Copaci members felt that they were effective and able to get a hearing on most issues.

Copacis were clearly most active in the first period of PRD government, under Valentín González Bautista (1997–2001), when municipal officials met frequently with the councils and conducted a series of health campaigns with them.[91] His commitment to participation may have come in part out of his convictions as a social leader. However, it also seemed to be the result of his tenuous position in the mayor's office. González Bautista was elected mayor by a narrow margin from a small faction in the PRD, and he knew he needed to reach out to citizens in creative ways if he were to be successful. Much like the early PAN mayors in Tijuana, he felt the need to mobilize citizens through participatory channels to gain legitimacy. After the next two PRD mayors won election by larger margins, they gradually abandoned the emphasis on the Copacis. These next two mayors were also both from MOVIDIG, by far the largest PRD-affiliated organization, which meant that they had an extensive network of organizers already on the ground in every neighborhood even without the Copaci system. These mayors lowered the councils' profile and stopped meeting regularly with them. However,

90. One PRI Copaci president stated, after noting the city government's lack of interest in the councils, "I am the government." He also said that even though municipal officials often preferred to ignore the Copacis, they had to respond to them. As he and others observed, the Copacis have official stationery with the seal of the municipality, which they can use to present demands to the corresponding agency of the municipal government, and the agencies are required by law to respond. This particular leader said that 80 percent of the demands he presented had been met. Other Copaci leaders, of both the PRI and the PRD, concurred with this interpretation. They felt that they were elected neighborhood authorities, and municipal officials were obliged to listen to them. Another PRI council president noted that Copaci development "depends on how innovative a person is," though she added that "the government plays ball with groups of councillors that are of their party." Copaci leaders, interviewed by the author, March to June 2005.

91. During this period, a director of citizen participation in the municipal government also reported directly to the mayor. Former Mayor González Bautista noted that "participation was the basis of everything we did." González Bautista, interview.

the Citizen Participation Councils survived because the law afforded them a degree of legitimacy and because many of the Copaci leaders were tenacious in making sure that the government listened to them.

Despite the success of the Copacis in establishing themselves as official interlocutors between citizens and the government, they were by no means alone in this role. Indeed, as the interviews with city leaders indicate, the most significant grassroots leaderships were those tied directly to the factions within the PRD and the PRI. Leaders of MOVIDIG and UPREZ in the PRD and the CNOP in the PRI indicated in interviews that they had representatives in each neighborhood who were charged with providing links between citizen concerns and the faction leaders, who in turn would bring these concerns to the attention of the government.[92] In many cases, these organizations have offices within neighborhoods where they can respond to the demands of citizens. In other cases, citizens can go an organization leader's place of business or home (which usually has a sign outside with the organization's name) to request assistance.

On balance, the predominant channels for intermediation between citizens and the government remained the informal structures of these party-affiliated organizations, each tied to a historical leader of a social movement in the city or to the PRI's CNOP. However, Copacis have gained a small foothold as an institutionalized channel for intermediation as well.

Conclusions: Competitive Clientelism?

The victory of the PRD in Ciudad Nezahualcóyotl both coincided with and contributed to a significant growth in the city's authority and autonomy. The advent of increased federal transfers multiplied the income of a municipality that had subsisted on debt and infusions of resources from the state government. After 1996, the PRD administrations were able to pay off their inherited debt and embark on ambitious initiatives to invest in the city's development. Moreover, by closing gaps in the municipal treasury, from which previous administrations had siphoned off city funds for partisan purposes, they increased the municipality's locally generated revenue. However, these achievements also faced serious limitations. With most of its residents working outside the city limits or in informal jobs within the city, the municipality lacked a tax base of its own that it could

---

92. Interviews with Rodríguez (UPREZ/PRD); Héctor Bautista and Revilla (MOVIDIG/PRD); and Pedroza and Pérez Maldonado (CNOP/PRI).

tap. Therefore, although the municipal government grew significantly, in terms of the level of municipal per capita expenditure, it still remained far below other large cities in Mexico.

As decentralization took root in Neza, the city was embarking on an ambitious experiment in democratic governance. For the first time in the history of Mexico, a coalition of popular organizations was taking over a large city government, and it was committed to creating a new model of participatory democracy. Some of these efforts were—at least initially—a clear break with the past. The municipal council rose in importance as disputes among factions created genuine strategic debates in the municipal council, significantly raising its importance, and open primary elections allowed citizens to decide the party lists. The government empowered the Municipal Development Council (Codemun), an elected citizens' organization, to make decisions on the use of some investment funds and directed dozens of Citizen Participation Councils (Copacis) to serve as the municipality's official conduit for citizen demands.

The reality of these changes was far less ambitious than it first seemed, however. The municipal council soon receded from view as the different groups within the PRD reached elite pacts on how to govern together, while the results of primary elections were often superseded by negotiations among party leaders. The mayor negotiated a backroom deal with the municipal council to appoint new members of the Codemun in lieu of an open election, and the now-tamed body ceased to publish information on public investment as it had once done. Real decision-making power came to be held by the leaders of the party factions within the PRD, who strategically negotiated most major issues before they ever reached the municipal council or the Codemun. The local leaders of the PRI and the PAN maintained some influence by deploying their relationships with the state and federal governments, which were controlled, respectively, by their parties. Meanwhile, the Copacis, which had appeared to be an ambitious experiment in citizen participation, soon lost their visibility and had to compete with informal power brokers from the different party factions, who reclaimed their role as the principal intermediaries between citizens and the municipality. Given the significant deficits in public services and the uneven access to the legal system, political brokers played a vital role in helping citizens make their rights effective. Few if any autonomous organizations existed, and almost all collective efforts in the city were in some way tied to groups affiliated with one or another of the parties. By 2005, the political landscape of Neza was one of constant bargaining among the three main political parties and among the major factions within them.

Although this style of minimalist democratic governance fell far short of the democratic ideal espoused in 1996, it was a significant advance beyond the authoritarian, top-down politics that had dominated the city before the PRD's arrival. Citizens had highly competitive elections and an equally competitive market of political intermediaries. They had recourse to Copaci leaders, council members, Codemun members, designated neighborhood representatives of the different PRD-affiliated organizations, section presidents in the PRI's grassroots structure, and dozens of other intermediaries, all of whom made some claim on political influence and provided ways to articulate interests and process demands. Citizens had few formal institutional channels for influencing public decisions and almost no autonomous spaces outside the parties, but they were not hostage to a single group or set of groups with exclusive control over political power. And although the leaders of the party factions had final say in most policy decisions, they had to take into account their own members as well as the range of other actors who legitimately represented voices in the city—smaller PRD-affiliated organizations, PRI-affiliated organizations, the PAN, and even the Copacis.

A dense web of social and political interactions, mediated by hundreds of community brokers representing different parties and party groups, tied leaders and constituents together in a kind of complicity of governance. This, in turn, assured a degree of responsiveness to citizen demands and perhaps some accountability as well. Although formal institutional channels mattered far less for decision making than the informal channels, the latter had at least been multiplied and democratized significantly. Indeed, the fact that the organizations that represented citizens' views were invariably tied to political parties helped ensure that they had influence in the decision-making process and gave citizens an ongoing, albeit indirect, voice in public decisions.

In June 2005, the State of Mexico held gubernatorial elections. The PRI won almost half the votes in the state and more than double the votes of the PRD's gubernatorial candidate, a little-known businesswoman named Yeidckol Polevnsky. The PRD won only one municipality in the entire state but did so by a large margin: Ciudad Nezahualcóyotl. In 2006, the PRD would win the municipality once again with an overwhelming majority. The PRD's method of governance might be far from perfect, but it appeared to have won the sympathy of the voters for the time being. And there was still that sense of pride in Neza, too—the pride that was associated with having thrown out the once all-powerful PRI. The voters were not about to let the PRI back in again—at least not quite yet.

PART 3
CONCLUSIONS

7 PATHWAYS OF DEMOCRATIC CHANGE

The Mexican political system that took root during the twentieth century, following the Mexican Revolution, was built on dual pillars, of both centralized formal power in the state and a diffuse network of informal power built on patronage politics. National political leaders guaranteed the stability of the government by co-opting power centers outside the state that threatened its existence and by creating a set of clear channels for resolving conflicts among competing regional and local leaders. Based on a single hegemonic party, Mexico's political system became one of the most durable in Latin America, largely because it achieved a set of shared understandings among competing political leaders and groups and their successful incorporation into a web of informal power through which state functions were exercised. The state centralized formal power in the national government, but left considerable decision-making ability to local political leaders, who served as intermediaries for citizens in return for their loyalty to the official party. Even state programs—from education to social welfare—were often delivered through these chains of intermediation rather than by the federal government itself (or through a combination of both public and private intermediation).

Within this context, municipal governments were quite weak. They comprised a minimal percentage of all public expenditures and depended on highly discretionary investments of resources from the federal and state governments. However, municipal governments were frequently important arenas for the negotiation of demands and the delivery of services, even if many of these had to be coordinated with federal and state authorities.[1] Mayoral candidacies were

---

1. This conclusion contrasts somewhat with Grindle, *Going Local*, 34–35, who suggests that municipalities were largely irrelevant before 1994.

eagerly sought after as stepping-stones in a political career (or as recognition after a long career of service to the party), but mayors and municipal council members were hardly alone as political intermediaries in municipalities. Party leaders inside and outside of government, including members of Congress, union officials, delegates of federal and state agencies, and influential personalities within the PRI's sectors, all functioned as intermediaries who played a role in maintaining the control by the official party. Although this was an authoritarian system, it did have mechanisms of responsiveness and accountability built in, since effective intermediaries had to deliver goods to their constituents and could lose influence if they did not.[2] Local mobilizations often succeeded in ensuring greater responsiveness and accountability, as long as they did not question the system itself.

Changes in the past two decades have sharply transformed the Mexican state and its relationship with citizens. The dual processes of democratization and decentralization have made competitive elections common throughout the country while also devolving a significant amount of formal power to local and state governments. These twin processes have generated a form of "democracy close to home" that, in many ways, differs substantially from the authoritarian centralism of earlier decades. Gone are the days of a single hegemonic party. This study confirms that municipal elections are largely perceived as free and fair (though not without some flaws). Most municipalities have experienced alternation of the parties in power, and almost all have more than one party that competes regularly with a real chance at winning.[3] Moreover, municipalities have regained a degree of authority and autonomy that they have not had for decades. They comprise almost one-tenth of all public expenditures (up from 1 to 2 percent in the early 1980s) and have much more stable sources of income than in previous decades. Municipalities now receive transfers according to more or less consistent formulas, and for urban municipalities, property taxes and other local fiscal revenues have grown considerably. Municipalities have even begun to develop

---

2. Jonathan Fox argues that accountability mechanisms exist even in authoritarian political systems. For a highly nuanced discussion of this in rural Mexico, see Fox, *Accountability Politics*.

3. See the evidence presented in chapter 3 that most municipalities are sites of significant electoral competition. Grindle, in *Going Local*, notes that even where the PRI remains dominant, other parties almost always compete actively. Electoral rules in Mexico, of course, continue to be contested, and several local elections, including the 2003 and 2006 elections in Baja California, have ended up in the electoral courts. Even the 2006 presidential election was the subject of considerable debate regarding the fairness of the process; however, for the most part, local elections now take place without the kind of conflict that was common in the 1990s.

greater capacities for managing their responsibilities, although with Mexico's no-reelection rule, the short, three-year tenure of mayors and their administrations limits greater professionalization and long-term planning.[4]

Despite the dramatic transformations that democratization and decentralization have brought to formal institutions, important continuities also exist that undermine the potential for democracy "close to home" to produce greater responsiveness and accountability. Although all three cities analyzed in this book have competitive elections, representative institutions do not appear to be the primary means for making demands, nor do they ensure accountability at the local level in any of them.[5] Similarly, even though all three municipalities have experimented with institutions to promote citizen participation in public decision making, none of these attempts has managed to become fully sustainable.[6]

Instead, in each city variations on the kind of informal power relations that existed prior to democratization continue to be the primary form of linkage between citizens and the municipal government. Citizens continue to depend on intermediaries in the political system to bring demands to the municipal government, which, in turn, depends on these intermediaries to maintain contact with citizens. In most cases, the intermediaries involved are embedded within the political parties and represent a mixture of formal and informal representation, but with the latter predominating.

Moreover, the three cities have developed significantly different patterns of democratic governance. Formal institutional differences in representation and municipal structure are relatively minor and do not appear to account for these differences. The stock of social capital prior to decentralization and democratization seems to have some weight in the outcomes. However, as we will see below, the different configurations of informal power appears to have the greatest explanatory weight. Because informal power remains the dominant means of linking citizens and the state, it should not be surprising that it also helps shape the outcomes of political change that is moving Mexico toward responsive and accountable government. Let us look first at how informal power has persisted and then at its effect in shaping democratic outcomes.

---

4. Grindle, *Going Local*, 70–72; Cabrero Mendoza, *Innovación en gobiernos locales*.
5. Cf. Guillén, "Democracia representativa y participativa."
6. For a more thorough discussion, see Andrew Selee, "An Alternative to Clientelism? Participatory Innovation in Mexico," in Selee and Peruzzotti, *Participatory Innovation*. For a review of other cases of participatory innovation in Mexico, see Selee and Santín, *Democracia y Ciudadanía*, and Alicia Ziccardi, ed., *La tarea de gobernar: Gobiernos locales y demandas ciudadanas* (Mexico City: Instituto de Investigaciones Sociales, UNAM, 1995).

The Persistence of Informal Power

Why do elements of the old authoritarian order survive even in a period of democratic opening? Even more specifically, how has informal power survived in a period of intense transformation of formal institutions? The findings appear to point to a set of self-reinforcing mechanisms that prevent the new formal institutions from displacing older informal forms of political intermediation. This has profound consequences for responsiveness and accountability. In turn, informal intermediate institutions help maintain a pattern of indirect citizenship that prevents the emergence of democratic citizenship, and ensure that most citizen demands continue to be negotiations over private goods rather than participation in efforts to ensure the provision of public goods or to set the direction of public policy. There are several possible hypotheses that may explain why informal power persists despite the advent of competitive democracy.

The first hypothesis for the persistence of informal power has to do with socialization. Both politicians and other citizens grew up in a political system that was based on informal intermediation and negotiations over private goods. Perhaps change will require a generational shift for it to become consolidated? Although this explanation is a popular one among people who observe events on the ground,[7] it does not seem to square fully with what we know about political and social change. Although informal rules help structure people's expectations about political behavior, changes in the way that institutions operate also appear to change people's expectations. The consolidation of participatory budgeting in cities in Brazil appears, in some cases, to have undercut clientelistic networks by creating alternate channels that work better for citizens.[8] Although socialization may represent a drag on institutional change, clearly changes in institutions can produce transformations in behavior.

A second plausible hypothesis is that municipalities' antiquated formal structure for representation produces few incentives for political leaders to reach out to citizens in new ways.[9] Rules that elect municipal councillors by party lists—where the only visible candidate is the mayor—and ensure supermajorities for the winning party appear to have undermined the effectiveness of the councils. Council members generally owe their nominations to the mayor or party leaders,

---

7. The academic literature rarely cites this explanation, but it is used by politicians to explain their continued role as clientelistic intermediaries and by civic leaders to explain why they negotiate.

8. See Abers, *Inventing Local Democracy*.

9. Guillén, "Democracia representativa y participativa."

so the councillors tend to be largely subservient to the mayor. There are, of course, exceptions when the majority party is divided on issues, but these appear to be rare cases, as we have seen in the previous chapters. The prohibition on reelection further undermines the responsiveness and accountability of council members and the mayor by providing incentives for upward accountability to party leaders who make decisions on future candidacies. The prohibition on independent candidacies and the high barriers to entry in the leading political parties mean that party leaders (both the formal and informal ones who hold decision-making influence) play a significant role in local elected officials' calculations. For council members, the strong incentives for upward accountability are accentuated by the lack of incentives for downward accountability.

These formal rules played an important role in buttressing the old authoritarian system. Supermajorities guaranteed the PRI a dominant role and majority control in the council while diluting the presence of the second largest party. The prohibition on independent candidacies forestalled challenges from popular individuals who were not career politicians, and the prohibition on reelection and the election via party lists guaranteed upward accountability from the candidates to party leaders.[10] Candidates for council thus owed their place on the list to patrons higher up in the party, sometimes to the mayoral candidate, but frequently to leaders of other groups who were successful at negotiating to get their followers on the list. Council members and the mayor would have to remain loyal to those above them in the party if they hoped to get a nomination to a future position after their three-year term expired. In a system based on the building of cohesion among competing leaders and groups, this form of upward accountability helped ensure a degree of hierarchical control and loyalty to the party and its leaders. However, the persistence of these rules, designed for a period of one-party dominance, has gone a long way to undermining hopes that municipal councils and even mayors would be downwardly accountable to citizens and function as meaningful channels for citizens' demands (beyond those of particular factions).[11]

---

10. Party list systems are very common in Latin America—and in other recent democracies, including several in Africa. In a few cases, however, their worst effects are somewhat mitigated by having low barriers to entry into parties (e.g., Uruguay). In these cases, elections are through party lists, but party hierarchies have little control over who is a candidate. Colombia recently abandoned party list voting altogether in municipal elections with seemingly positive effects for democratic governance. Large municipalities have become vibrant centers of democratic innovation, often driven by independent candidates who have won local elections in cities like Bogotá and Medellín.

11. For an eloquent development of this argument, see Guillén, "Democracia representativa y participativa." It is perhaps surprising that there has been little comparative work done on municipal electoral

Nonetheless, this does not appear to be a complete explanation. Because their political future depends in part on showing that they have performed well while in office (or, at the very least, maintained a degree of order), municipal mayors do have some incentives to be responsive to constituents under the current system, although councillors do not. In addition, federal and state representative structures have changed considerably (if not completely), making them more formally responsive and accountable. Yet this does not seem to have undercut the informal channels that tie politicians to citizens.[12] Therefore, the antiquated structure of municipal representative institutions is likely a contributing factor to the persistence of informal power, but this is not the sole explanation.

Still another possibility has to do with the weakness of civil society. One variation on this hypothesis suggests that the lack of strong popular or nongovernmental organizations in Mexican municipalities undermines the potential for change, because citizens continue to approach the municipality primarily as petitioners rather than as participants in public processes.[13] A second variation might suggest that although civic organizations may exist, they lack the horizontal and vertical linkages that would allow them to be important advocates for citizen preferences in the municipal arena.[14] This seems plausible because the one-party hegemonic system that existed for decades managed to absorb most popular organizations and resist the building of large coalitions that might have threatened its existence. The result has been a civil society that is far more atomized than those found in some other Latin American countries.

---

rules despite the vast (but quite separate) literature on both local governments and electoral institutions. A cursory review of the literature on local governments in Latin American, African, and Asian countries suggests that many countries face the same situation: rules that are carried over from an authoritarian past and never revised to address the possibilities for democratic change. As I will argue below, political elites often continue to employ these old rules, even in the process of democratic change. Cf. Ribot, *Waiting for Democracy*, who also points to this problem, especially in Africa, and Crook and Manor, *Democracy and Decentralisation*, who also mention it.

12. This research did not specifically address the federal and state level, but as the previous chapters show, federal and state elected officials are among the intermediaries acting in the municipal arena, especially in regard to state and federal programs.

13. Cf. Grindle, *Going Local*, especially 175 and 181–82. This argument bears resemblance to that of Robert Putnam, in *Making Democracy Work*, on the need for social capital.

14. For an argument about this in Peru, see Gerd Schönwälder, *Linking Civil Society and the State: Urban Popular Movements, the Left, and Local Government in Peru, 1980–1992* (University Park: Pennsylvania State University Press, 2002). Fox, in *Accountability Politics*, also indicates that this is a concern in Mexico; however, he argues that horizontal and vertical linkages do sometimes develop. In fact, he notes that the state of Oaxaca has some of the most active popular organizations in Mexico, and yet it is one of the country's most authoritarian state governments.

However, the period of political change in Mexico in the 1980s and 1990s considerably altered patterns of civic organization and to some degree allowed horizontal and vertical linkages to emerge.[15] Of the cases presented in this book, Tijuana has a long history of strong civic engagement. Although most of the large popular organizations are now disarticulated, the city still has a strong base of nongovernmental organizations. Even more markedly, Ciudad Nezahualcóyotl continues to have some of the most active popular organizations in the country, and they interact regularly with one another and build coalitions around common issues. Indeed, it is hard to walk more than a few blocks in any neighborhood in Neza without passing by the offices of one of the many popular organizations that bring citizens together. Moreover, most of these organizations have close vertical ties to political leaders in one party or another, so they are hardly isolated from political decision making. The existing organizations seem to function partially as civic associations and partially as political party organizations. Still, in general, Mexico's civil society organizations are more atomized and have less autonomy than might be the case elsewhere in Latin America.

This suggests a fourth hypothesis, closely tied to the third, that looks at the role of the state in preventing greater autonomous civil society activity and in preserving the central role of informal power. As noted previously, the Mexican state historically structured its relationship with citizens through a complex pattern of informal intermediation, which determined not only citizens' channels for demand making but also the delivery of many public services, social programs, and infrastructure investments. The Mexican state frequently carried out its functions through private channels or through a combination of public and private channels. To a large extent, even with political competition and alternation, the state's structure remains largely unchanged. The cases of the development planning councils in Neza and Chilpancingo are telling: because no party had a full monopoly of political power, the mayors would divide up public works projects among the political parties (and their key factions and faction leaders) according to their relative weight in the municipality. Essentially, each of the major political groups in the city was allowed to deliver projects to their clients as determined by their ability to demonstrate influence. This system was highly functional, because it allowed party faction leaders to negotiate the distribution

---

15. Alberto Olvera, "Civil Society in Mexico at Century's End," in Middlebrook, *Dilemmas of Political Change*.

of resources and it avoided major conflicts, but it also undermined the capacity of the municipality to act in a coherent and strategic manner for the public good.

Prior to the 1980s, these negotiations over the distribution of public resources and programs took place almost exclusively among PRI leaders, who served as the intermediaries for the transmission of demands and delivery of projects. Today, all political parties have learned how to take part in this way of doing business. Therefore, even where strong civil society organizations exist, as in Neza, they are tied to the prevailing system of informal intermediation or they are left out of the allocation of government benefits. Even in Tijuana, which has the weakest forms of intermediation, the old style of informal power remains the most important way to link citizens and their government, although citizens have difficulties linking to decision makers.

The organization of the Mexican state along informal lines has outlived the hegemonic party system for which it was designed. This continuity suggests the system's great functionality for political leaders and the great difficulty that exists in attempting to change it. The dependence on informal channels has been particularly useful in maintaining stability. Almost all decisions (at least on a local level) are constantly negotiated. No one is ever fully satisfied with the outcome, but no one is ever completely left out either. This privileges a degree of consensus that helps to maintain order and a degree of inclusion, although it often comes at the expense of good policy and democratic procedures. This finding also suggests that the Mexican state has little capacity to deliver services or enforce the rule of law, not because of inherent inefficiencies, but because the state is designed to operate through political brokers rather than directly with citizens. What some observers have called "corruption" or the "ineffectiveness" of the Mexican state is actually an inherent part of its design.

Some politicians have tried to change this. In particular, the first mayors elected in Tijuana and Neza from then-opposition parties undertook valiant efforts to create formal structures for mediating between citizens and the state.[16] They did so because they believed it was the right thing to do: the popular organizations that make up the PRD in Neza had long fought for the inclusion of civil society organizations in public affairs, and the PAN in Tijuana had a strong belief in the right of individual citizens to take part in public decisions. In both cases, they also had political incentives to do this. The first opposition mayors started their

---

16. In the case of Tijuana, it was not the first PAN mayor, although he took a few halting steps, but the second and third mayors from that party.

terms with a small political base and limited capacity for informal intermediation, so the creation of formal channels also allowed them to reach out to citizens more effectively and build political support.

However, as both parties consolidated their dominance in those cities and developed their own leaders capable of informal intermediation, they abandoned the formal structures in favor of a system that resembled the PRI's old structure. In both cases, they had to contend with and include the intermediaries of other parties (as the recent PRI governments in Chilpancingo have had to do as well), but they found the old ways, which had never truly disappeared, to be far more politically useful than were the formal structures that had tied their hands. All of the municipalities studied here have had long periods of single-party governance. Of course, mayors in municipalities with more frequent party alternation might have greater incentives to change that government's relationship with its citizens. Nevertheless, given mayors' short terms in office and prohibition on reelection, these municipalities are unlikely to be able to make permanent changes.

Different Pathways of Political Change

The three municipalities analyzed in this book are following significantly different pathways of political change. The formal institutional changes brought about by democratization and decentralization were fairly similar across the three cases, and we find relatively minor differences in the way these have been adapted locally in the three cities. Yet the divergent outcomes suggest that we need to understand democratic transitions not only through the optic of formal institutional changes at the national level but also through the way that informal political relations between state and society are transformed in local spaces during a period of democratic transition. A study of only three municipalities—all of them urban—can hardly hope to shed light on all possible scenarios in Mexican municipalities;[17] however, this study points to three different trajectories that appear to offer at least some of the alternate models for democratic change that Mexican municipalities are following. Both the history of state-society relations and the identity of the governing party appear to play a significant role in determining these trajectories.[18]

---

17. For rural municipalities, see Fox, *Accountability Politics*. It is very likely that small rural municipalities face even greater challenges for achieving responsive and accountable government.

18. The nature of state-level politics, which receives comparatively less treatment in this book, also

Chilpancingo demonstrates a pattern that may be close to that of other cities where the PRI still remains dominant. The municipality's relationship with citizens continues to be dominated by informal power relationships within the PRI, particularly through PRI-affiliated organizations and local party leaders, who maintain contact with PRI leaders within neighborhoods. Increasingly, the PRD has developed a base of leaders on the ground, and other parties have done so to a lesser extent. Participatory planning systems are used to validate decisions that were already made through complex negotiations among the PRI leaders and outside groups and are ultimately brokered by the mayor. It is, in short, a hierarchical system predicated on informal power dominated by PRI intermediaries but with an increasing inclusion of non-PRI intermediaries in the negotiations.

The contours of this system are largely determined by the nature of the PRI itself, which continues to be a mass-based party built on mobilizing citizens through corporatist organizations and clientelistic networks within the party.[19] The PRI operates through a network of intermediaries who resolve issues for citizens at the community (or workplace) level and who, in turn, respond to higher level intermediaries within the party hierarchy that are part of the PRI's territorial or occupational organizations.[20] As more people fall outside these channels of intermediation, this system is increasingly less effective than it once was, but it still works sufficiently well to win elections in municipalities like Chilpancingo where the opposition is relatively weak. The continuity of this system in that city has been reinforced by the nature of state politics in Guerrero, which, until recently, was governed by the PRI with a handful of dominant political families that had especially strong influence.

Ciudad Nezahualcóyotl, on the other hand, represents a significantly different pathway of change, where popular organizations that once opposed the PRI's dominance became the city's government as a coalition under the PRD. In Neza, the PRD has operated as a highly decentralized coalition of organizations, even after three administrations under that party, and although the largest organization, MOVIDIG, has consolidated its preeminence, it still needs to negotiate

---

has an important secondary effect on local developments since state governments have important weight in municipal politics, and state political leaders outside the municipality are generally important intermediaries within the larger political system

19. On the recent history of the PRI, see Crespo, *PRI: De la hegemonía a la oposición.*

20. In theory, the party's territorial organizations should be the ones that manage neighborhood relations, but in practice, many unions have intermediaries on the ground in neighborhoods throughout Chilpancingo and elsewhere in Mexico.

continuously with other large and small organizations that have independent bases of support. The leaders of the PRD-affiliated organizations have acted as informal intermediaries for citizens' demands and for the delivery of public benefits. However, because the party is based on a coalition, it is far less hierarchical than the PRI, and it survives by constantly renegotiating pacts among its affiliated organizations. This coalition-type behavior seems to mirror the behavior of the national PRD, which is often described as a collection of "tribes" rather than a coherent political party.[21] The PRI and PAN also maintain brokers on the ground and occupy spaces in the municipal council, which they use to negotiate benefits, often availing themselves of their ties to the state and national governments that are in the hands of those two parties.

The political system in Neza essentially has been a dense and competitive marketplace of intermediation, where citizens continue to relate to public authorities through political brokers, but where they have ample choices about which brokers to choose. Citizenship remains largely indirect, but democracy has given citizens multiple avenues for influence and information. This multiplication of channels has built a significant degree of responsiveness and accountability into relationships with political intermediaries, who have been compelled to deliver goods to citizens or risk losing influence. The municipality created a participatory planning structure and then co-opted it, but the government was unable to eliminate the elected neighborhood committees because these had close ties to the popular organizations. Ironically, this participatory initiative survived largely because it is embedded in the political fabric of the municipality; a truly independent citizens' body would almost certainly have been eliminated or ignored. In short, Neza contains a mixture of forms of intermediation, most of them informal but highly plural and competitive, which ensures a significant degree of responsiveness and accountability.

In Tijuana, in contrast, early PAN governments sought to undermine the PRI's long-standing clientelism by creating its own formal channels for citizen participation in public policy. They sought to strengthen the central role of the city council and, under it, structured mechanisms for participation that gave citizens meaningful direct input into public decision making as well. Nonetheless, the council appears to have weakened over time vis-à-vis the mayor. Moreover, PAN leaders eventually abandoned the participatory initiatives and, without eliminating them, simply chose to ignore their decisions. To the extent possible,

---

21. On the PRD, see Bruhn, *Taking on Goliath*.

they stacked the participatory planning process with their own allies and bypassed the elected neighborhood committees, which remained largely outside partisan politics. As a result, citizens ended up with few intermediaries, formal or informal, who had real influence with public authorities. Thus, a form of "weak clientelism" emerged, in which PAN party leaders were the only significant decision makers; however, in neighborhoods throughout the city, they had tenuous relationships with their allied intermediaries in the formal and informal structures.

The system that has emerged in Tijuana suggests a substantially different pathway of democratic change. It is, on one hand, more normatively democratic than the system in Neza, in that it allows a greater degree of direct citizenship through elections without the interference of strong clientelistic networks. However, the absence of strong formal mechanisms for intermediation has meant that citizens also feel largely disconnected from the political process, and they have become increasingly disengaged from politics in general. This process largely reflects existing tensions within the PAN leadership nationwide.[22] It is the one major party that has resisted becoming a mass political party, opting instead for a small base of party members who share common ideological underpinnings. At the same time, party leaders believe they should engage individual citizens in public affairs through institutional channels. In the case of Tijuana, the vision of a participatory democracy lost out over time to the practice of an efficient government directed by the party faithful. Undoubtedly, the repeated victories in municipal elections also made the party less concerned about reaching out to citizens. In the end, the PRI's clientelistic networks were replaced by weak forms of intermediation tied only loosely to the top leaders of the PAN.[23]

In short, it appears that the two cities with the greatest stocks of social capital, Tijuana and Ciudad Nezahualcóyotl, have enjoyed better outcomes in terms of

---

22. On the PAN, see Shirk, *Mexico's New Politics,* and Mizrahi, *From Martyrdom to Power.*

23. Although it falls outside the scope of this study, one form of strong informal power in Tijuana deserves brief mention here: organized crime. As I noted in chapter 2, under the one-party hegemonic system, the rule of law was largely maintained through informal arrangements. Tijuana, as is the case for many border cities around the world, was the site of significant contraband traffic for most of the twentieth century, including marijuana and heroin produced in the nearby state of Sinaloa. As cocaine trafficking routes from South America shifted toward Mexico and the country developed its own methamphetamine production, drug traffickers increasingly used Tijuana as a transshipment point for their largest market, the United States. The city's largest drug-trafficking organization, run by the Arellano Félix family, appears to have developed informal understandings with municipal authorities in order to maintain its monopoly over the trade. It is unclear whether these understandings were primarily with law enforcement agencies or were with politicians as well. Nevertheless, these arrangements were similar to other informal power arrangements in the city—informal understandings forged through intermediaries.

responsiveness and accountability. Despite what social capital theory might predict, however, civic associations' linkages to political power turn out to be almost as important as the mere existence of these associations. In Mexico's political system, in which political parties have a monopoly over representation, independent civic associations, such as those that predominate in Tijuana, appear to be less effective than those that are tied closely to channels of informal power, as are the associations in Ciudad Nezahualcóyotl. This may not be normatively appealing to those who dream of a system of liberal democracy in which individual citizens influence political decisions and hold their authorities accountable for their actions. But in a political system dominated by informal power, rather than by formal institutions, a dense associational life closely linked to partisan politics may actually be more effective than an active and autonomous civil society. At least in the short term, it appears that it is not merely the stock of social capital that matters for responsive and accountable government but also the horizontal and vertical linkages that citizens have to the state and to political actors.

In the short run in terms of enhancing responsiveness and accountability, the most effective pattern of political change appears to be that found in Ciudad Nezahualcóyotl, where civic associations are dense and have historically developed with some autonomy from the state, but where they maintain linkages to political leaders with influence in municipal decision making. The second most effective pattern appears to be in Tijuana, where civic associations are quite active and densely representative but only weakly linked to political parties or the municipality. In Chilpancingo, fewer civic associations operate and they are almost entirely dependent on political parties, and they appear to be far less effective for generating responsive and accountable government. In short, formal institutions and social capital certainly influence outcomes for democratic governance, but equally important is the way linkages between citizens and the state are constructed.

It is beyond the scope of this study to determine which of these pathways to democracy is likely to lead to the best long-term outcomes. Will Chilpancingo develop a more competitive political process that breaks down the traditional forms of informal power that still dominate local politics? Will the embryonic forms of responsiveness and accountability built into Neza's competitive market of intermediaries lead to demands for more direct forms of citizenship? Will the weak intermediation of Tijuana eventually liberate citizens so that they can demand an effective municipality that listens to their demands and engages them in the policy process? To understand the evolution of Mexico's democratic process, it will be vital to follow these divergent trajectories in order to know how democracy actually operates on the ground.

All Political Theory Is Local

The kind of political system emerging in Mexico's municipalities is far more democratic than that which existed ten, fifteen, or certainly thirty years ago. The advent of competitive elections has given citizens real options for selecting their public authorities, and this has provided a degree of responsiveness and accountability far beyond what existed under the one-party hegemonic system that prevailed for many decades. There are clear signs that municipal elections are competitive, and mayors, if not council members, feel obligated to perform well in office in order to advance their political career.

However, the kind of democracy that exists in Mexico's municipalities still falls short of the normative ideal of a responsive and accountable democratic government. Most Mexicans relate to their municipal authorities through brokers tied to one of the major political parties. As a result, citizenship also remains indirect and mediated through these forms of informal power. Indirect citizenship, in turn, serves to privatize public relationships, by forcing citizens to make their demands as requests for private favors instead of the enforcement of rights and by allowing the state to distribute public goods as private concessions. Although elections have helped ensure a minimal degree of responsiveness and accountability at election time, they have not undermined the basic structure that binds citizens and the state between elections.

Across different municipalities, however, significant differences exist in the way processes of informal intermediation are emerging. These represent alternate pathways to democracy that need to be understood because they suggest divergent ways that democracy is being achieved in municipalities throughout a single country. In some cases, old patterns of informal power are becoming slightly more competitive but still hierarchical; in other cases, these channels of informal power are becoming more dense and developing a more horizontal structure that ensures a competitive market for intermediation; and in still others, the channels are weakening and being replaced by less intense forms of intermediation. Although no cases analyzed here met the criteria for fully democratic citizenship, there are shifting patterns of informal power that may hold the seeds for the emergence of more democratic relationships in the future.

Although this study has focused exclusively on Mexico, this finding suggests that any process of democratic change anywhere in the world is likely to have significant variations in its outcomes across localities, and only by understanding these can we hope to understand the quality of democracy in a country as a whole. These different pathways owe their existence less to differences in formal institutional structures or stocks of social capital than to the ways that informal power shapes the relationship between citizens and the state. In countries undergoing processes of decentralization in which local governments are empowered, these effects are certain to be magnified.

There are many reasons why informal power perseveres even in the midst of a democratic transition. Outdated municipal structures and the atomization of civil society undoubtedly have played a part in Mexico. However, the most important factor appears to be the organization of the Mexican state itself, which has long relied on informal forms of intermediation to maintain order, channel demands, and deliver goods and services. This state structure helped ensure stability in Mexico throughout much of the twentieth century by privileging consensus among political leaders who might otherwise have been in conflict. Even as Mexico has become a competitive polyarchy, however, this structure has survived. Without any question, there have been advances in constructing a state that can operate in direct relationship with its citizens. The consolidation of generally free and fair elections at all levels is perhaps the clearest sign of this. So, too, is the implementation of formulas for transfers of funds to states and municipalities and a few social programs that bypass intermediaries.

However, the dominant logic of the Mexican state appears to still be one of informal power. This has profound implications for the strength of the state and its capacity to deliver what citizens want and need. It also, of course, has implications for the nature of democracy and the meaning of democratic citizenship. These are, of course, challenges that are common to all democracies throughout the world—developed and developing, old and new—that struggle to balance the capacity of the state to perform its functions with the need to respond to powerful interests outside the state. In the end, it turns out that all politics is local and so, too, is all political theory.

Index

All locations are in Mexico unless otherwise noted. Page numbers in *italics* refer to illustrations.

Acapulco, Guerrero state, PRD in, 132 n. 7
Acatitlán Ramón, Daniel, 84 n. 31
accountability, 16, 40, 66, 167. *See also* municipal governments, accountability and responsiveness in; responsiveness
  in Chilpancingo, 95–96, 175
  decentralization's effects on, 3, 4, 7–9, 18–20
  democratization's effects on, 1, 18–20, 165
  informal power relations and, 13, 15, 21, 166
  in Neza, 132, 173, 174–75
  in Tijuana, 100, 115, 126
Acero, Arelio, 154 n. 82
Acevedo, Josefat, 83
Africa, 14–15, 167 n. 10
Aguirre, Julio César, 86 n. 43, 88 n. 48, 89 n. 52, 90 n. 56, 93 n. 67
Alarcón Abarca, Saúl, 79, 86, 86 n. 41, 90 n. 55, 91, 91 n. 62
alcabalas, 30, 34
alternation, political, 164, 169, 171
Álvarez, Juan, 77
Amador, Jorge, 156 n. 89
AMMAC. *See* Asociación de Municipios de México (Mexican Association of Municipalities, AMMAC)
apellidos, 79–80, 87. *See also* families, elite
Araujo Hernández, Jesús, 83
Arellano Félix family, 174 n. 23
Argentina, 11 n. 32, 29 n. 10
Asociación de Municipios de México (Mexican Association of Municipalities, AMMAC), 111
Asociación General de Colonos (General Association of Settlers), 135 n. 19
associational life, 7–8, 9, 19. *See also* social capital; social movements; state-society linkages
Astudillo, Héctor, 73, 75

Authentic Party of the Mexican Revolution (Partido Auténtico de la Revolución Mexicana, PARM), 43–44, 142 n. 42
authoritarianism
  in developing world, 9, 10
  informal power relations and, 4–5, 16
  in municipal governments, 7, 41, 160, 164, 167
  postrevolutionary, 38–46
authority
  centralizing, 31 n. 18, 36
  in Chilpancingo, 76, 86–87
  decision-making, 20, 31, 153–54
  municipal governments', 1, 69, 109, 111–12, 164
  in Neza, 139 n. 35, 147
  in Tijuana, 105, 109, 126
Autonomous University of Guerrero, 83
autonomy. *See also* municipal governments, autonomy of
  in Baja California, 104
  in Chilpancingo, 76, 86–87
  of civic organizations, 154, 175
  in federalism, 29 n. 10
  in Neza, 131, 135 n. 19, 146, 147, 154
  in state governments, 10, 54, 61–62
  in Tijuana, 101, 105 n. 18, 109, 111, 126
Auyero, Javier, 11 n. 32

Baja California, state of, 100 n. 6, 101, 111. *See also* Tijuana, Baja California state
  elections in, 112–13, 164 n. 3
  PAN in, 43 n. 65, 52, 102, 106, 108, 112–29
  PRD in, 112, 116 n. 48
  PRI in, 104–5, 112, 113
Banobras loans, 109, 110, 111
bargaining, 10, 14, 20. *See also* intermediaries/intermediation; negotiations

Index

basic services. *See also* public works
  in Chilpancingo, 84, 92
  demands for, 14, 45, 170
  in Neza, 130, 131, 139–40, 141, 159
  provision of, 8, 50, 136 n. 22, 163, 169
  in Tijuana, 99, 103–4, 105, 106–7, 118
Bautista, Alliet, 151 n. 67, 152 n. 74
Bautista, Héctor, 132, 132 n. 6, 143 n. 45, 144, 144 nn. 46, 48, 149 n.62, 150, 150 n. 64, 151, 151 n. 68, 154, 156 n. 89, 158 n. 92
Becerra, Martín, 154 n. 82
Berriozábal, Chiapas state, 67
Bolivia, decentralization in, 2 n. 3
bracero program, 102 n. 8
Bravo, Nicolás, 77
Brazil, 10 n. 25, 20 n. 57, 29 n. 10
  participatory budgeting in, 6, 122, 166
brokers. *See* intermediaries/intermediation
Business Coordinating Council (Consejo Coordinador Empresarial, CCE), 125
business organizations, 15 n. 42, 27 n. 1
  in Chilpancingo, 74, 79 n. 15
  in Neza, 138
  in Tijuana, 109, 116, 120, 125
Bustamante Cruz, Tomás, 74 n. 3, 78 n. 12

Cabañas, Bertín, 88 n. 48, 93 nn. 67, 70, 94 n. 71
cabildos. *See* municipal councils
Cabrero Mendoza, Enrique, 53 n. 21, 68 n. 60
caciques
  in Chilpancingo, 80–81
  PRI alliances with, 41–42, 73, 138
  regional, 28, 33, 34, 36
Calles, Plutarco, 35, 36
Campbell, Tim, 109 n. 25
Cano, Antonio, 125 n. 84
Cárdenas, Cuauhtémoc, 51–52, 56 n. 26, 84, 108, 142, 143 n. 45, 144
Cárdenas, Lázaro, 38–39
Carranza, Venustiano, 133
Catholic Church, 15 n. 42, 32 n. 19, 34 n. 32, 140 nn. 37, 39. *See also* de la Rosa Medellín, Martín
caudillos, end of, 41–42
CCE. *See* Business Coordinating Council (Consejo Coorinador Empreserarial, CCE)
CDT. *See* Economic Development Council of Tijuana (Consejo de Desarrollo Económico de Tijuana, CDT)

CEEGRO. *See* State Electoral Council of Guerrero (Consejo Estatal Electoral de Guerrero, CEEGRO)
Central Bank, 35 n. 35
centralization, 1–4, 10. *See also* decentralization
  informal power relations and, 27–46, 169
  state, 28–34, 45, 49, 163–64, 169
  Tijuana's avoidance of, 102–3
Cervantes Delgado, Alejandro, 82 n. 24
Chalco, Mexico state, 134 n. 15
changes
  democratic, 6–7, 167 n. 11, 174, 177
  institutional, 18–19, 47–54, 126–29, 153, 165, 166
  political, 3, 9, 61, 104–8, 166, 171–76
  social, 33, 166
Chiapas, state of, 15, 136
Chihuahua, state of, PAN victories in, 52
Chilpancingo, Guerrero state, 5, 73–97
  accountability and responsiveness in, 95–96, 175
  autonomy in, 76, 86–87
  contestation in, 82–83, 95–97
  decentralization and democratization in, 23, 95–97, 175
  decision making in, 86–87, 96, 172
  development committees in, 91–94, 169
  education in, 74, 83, 84
  elections in, 73, 74–76, 80–81, 81, 87–88, 89, 96–97
  elites in, 76, 79–80, 82, 87, 97
  employment in, 75, 79
  federal funds' transfers to, 85–86, 86, 91, 92–93
  history of, 74 n. 3, 76–79
  infrastructure in, 75, 82, 85, 92
  intermediaries in, 76, 81, 95
  mayors in, 169
  municipal council in, 76, 80, 86, 87, 89–90, 93–97
  municipal government in, 76, 85–87, 95–97
  neighborhoods in, 83–84, 94, 95–97
  PAN in, 90–91, 94 n. 71, 96 n. 73
  political hegemony in, 79–84, 95
  population of, 78, 86
  poverty in, 74, 75, 76, 78, 79, 83, 84, 85, 86 n. 39, 87
  PRD in, 75–76, 84, 87–88, 90–91, 94
  PRI in, 21–22, 74–76, 80, 83, 84, 86, 87–89, 91–97, 171, 172
  resistance movements in, 82–84
Chimahualcán, Mexico state, 134 n. 15
circularity, elite, 40, 41–42, 49

cities. *See* municipal councils; municipal governments; *and individual cities and towns*
citizen councillors, 52, 54, 88, 112, 121–22, 123 n. 77, 123 n. 78, 124 n. 79. *See also* Citizen Participation Councils (Consejos de Participación Ciudadana, Copacis)
Citizen Participation Councils (Consejos de Participación Ciudadana, Copacis), 154, 155–60
citizens. *See also* Citizen Participation Councils (Consejos de Participación Ciudadana, Copacis); decision making, citizen involvement in
  accountability to, 5, 66
  demands of, 16, 47, 49 n. 2, 90 n. 55, 95, 166, 167, 172, 173–74, 176
  empowerment of, 8, 13, 31 n. 17
  intermediaries between the state and, 7, 14, 28, 39, 46, 69, 96, 108, 163, 169–70, 173
  mobilization of, 5, 38, 43, 127, 144, 164, 172
  municipal governments' relationships to, 115–28, 132, 136 n. 22, 137, 152–58, 165
  participation in government, 1, 67–70, 91, 96, 100, 115–16, 121
  preferences of, 11, 20, 43
  states' relationship to, 3–5, 9, 13, 48, 175, 177
citizenship, 32–33, 46
  democratic, 15, 166, 177
  direct, 174
  indirect, 9–16, 28, 42, 46, 166, 173, 176
  rights of, 2, 4, 30–31
  state building and, 28–34
  universal political, 31, 46
Ciudad Juárez, Chihuahua state, 68, 99 n. 3, 101 n. 7, 131, 132
Ciudad Mendoza, Veracruz state, 68
Ciudad Nezahualcóyotl, Mexico state (Neza), 5, 130–66
  accountability and responsiveness in, 132, 173, 174–75
  autonomy in, 131, 135 n. 19, 146, 147
  basic services in, 131, 139–40, 141, 159
  Catholic Church in, 117 n. 50, 140 n. 37
  citizen participation in, 68, 169
  clientelism in, 68, 142
  decentralization in, 159, 172–73
  decision making, 150, 152–53, 159
  democratic governance in, 132, 147–53, 159–60, 175
  economy of, 131, 134 n. 16, 139 n. 35
  education in, 141
  elections in, 135 n. 20, 138, 143, 144, 147, 148, 149, 151, 152, 159
  employment in, 134 n. 17
  food cooperatives in, 143 n. 45, 144
  history of, 132–34
  infrastructure in, 136, 146, 153–54, 159
  intermediaries in, 132, 138, 170
  land titles in, 130, 131, 135 n. 19, 136, 139–40, 141
  left-wing parties in, 132, 140 n. 37, 141, 142
  marginalization in, 130 n. 1, 131
  mayors in, 135 n. 19, 136, 144, 149, 150, 157, 169, 170–71
  municipal council in, 131, 135, 144, 149–53, 158–59, 160
  municipal government in, 131, 135, 144, 145 n. 54, 151–53, 158–59, 160
  neighborhood committees in, 137, 173
  PAN in, 135 n. 20, 140 n. 37, 142 n. 42, 144, 147, 151, 159, 160, 173
  population of, 101 n. 7, 133 n. 10, 134 n. 15
  PRD in, 22–23, 132, 141, 143–45, 147, 149–51, 153–55, 157–60, 170, 172–73
  PRI in, 131, 135–60
  proximity to Mexico City, 130–31, 133
  revenues for, 145–47, 146, 153
  social movements in, 135–60, 169, 170
civic organizations, 13, 33. *See also* business organizations; social movements
  autonomy of, 47, 154, 175
  Federal funding for, 52–53
  horizontal-vertical linkages in, 5, 8, 19, 138–39, 168–69
  in Tijuana, 116, 121
civil society, 33, 138, 168, 177
clientelism, 4, 9, 11, 12–13, 20 n. 57, 46. *See also* corporatism
  in Neza, 131, 132, 142, 153
  PRI's use of, 42, 43, 45, 66–69, 172, 173
  in Tijuana, 100, 115–16, 119
  weakening of, 68, 76 n. 5, 128, 166, 174
Clouthier, Manuel, 142
CNC. *See* National Peasant Confederation (CNC)
CNOP. *See* National Council of Popular Organizations (CNOP)
CODEMUN. *See* Municipal Development Council (Consejo para el Desarrollo Municipal, CODEMUN)
Colombia, elections in, 167 n. 10
colonias, 78, 83, 94, 104 n. 15

comités de desarrollo. *See* development committees (*comités de desarrollo*)
Comités de Vecinos. *See* neighborhood committees (Comités de Vecinos)
Comité Unión de Colonos Urbanos de Tijuana, A.C. (Committee Union of Urban Residents of Tijuana, Civil Association, CUCUTAC), 106, 107, 116, 119 n. 58, 120, 123 n. 78
commissions, 35 n. 35, 152 n.75
Committee for a Free and Sovereign State of Baja California (Comité Pro-Estado Libre y Soberano), 104, 105 n. 18
Committee of Urban Neighborhoods of the District of Texoco, 133 n. 10
Communist Party (Partido Comunista Mexicano, PCM), 44
competition, political, 22, 44, 88, 94, 95–96, 107, 144, 156, 169, 173. *See also* elections, competitive
CONAGO. *See* National Conference of Governors (Conferencia Nacional de Gobernadores, CONAGO)
conflicts. *See* contestation
Congress, federal, 44, 48, 56, 57–58, 147
Congress of Anáhuac, 77
Consejo Popular de Colonias (Popular Council of Neighborhoods), 83–84
Conservatives, 31, 33, 77
constitutions
  of 1824, 29–30
  of 1857, 31, 32, 34 n. 32
  of 1917, 34 n. 34, 37, 38, 66, 81; changes to, 37n45, 40, 50, 58, 60–61
  state, 41 n. 57, 44, 58, 81, 141
contestation. *See also* dissent
  in Chilpancingo, 75, 76, 82–83, 95–97
  in Neza, 135–44
  political, 37, 43, 45, 47, 49
control, 75, 104–8, 135–44
Copacis. *See* Citizen Participation Councils (Consejos de Participación Ciudadana, Copacis)
Coplade. *See* State Planning Council (Consejo de Planeación para el Desarrollo Estatal, Coplade)
Copladem. *See* Municipal Planning Council (Consejo para la Planeación Municipal, Copladem)
corporations. *See* business organizations
corporatism. *See also* clientelism
  in Chilpancingo, 73–97
  PRI's structure of, 42, 126, 127, 128, 172
  weakening, 99–100, 101, 115–16

corruption, 127, 128 n. 87, 145, 170
Cortés, Rodrigo Iván, 149 n. 59
crisis of 1928, 36 n. 40
CUCUTAC. *See* Comité Unión de Colonos Urbanos de Tijuana, A.C. (Committee Union of Urban Residents of Tijuana, Civil Association, CUCUTAC)
CUDs. *See* Single Development Agreements (Convenios Únicos de Desarrollo, CUDs)
Cuquío, Jalisco state, 67

Dahl, Robert A., 17 n. 48
Damián, Píoquinto, 88 n. 47
Damián Huato, Píoquinto, 87–88
Davalos, José Roberto, 124 n. 81
decentralization, 1–25, 31 n. 18, 47–70, 164. *See also* centralization; New Federalism
  accountability and responsiveness through, 7–9, 18–20
  in Chilpancingo, 3, 95–97, 175
  democratization's link to, 1–25, 49, 164
  economic effects of, 53, 64
  formal channels of, 20, 171
  of municipal governments, 17 n. 47, 18–19, 52, 69–70, 177
  in Neza, 159, 172–73
  of states and municipalities, 59, 61
  in Tijuana, 100, 126–27
decision making, 4, 159, 172
  authority for, 20, 31, 153–54
  in Chilpancingo, 86–87, 96, 172
  citizen involvement in, 20 n. 57, 67–68, 160, 165, 170, 173, 175
  through Copladems, 121, 123
  formal, 4, 12, 160
  in Neza, 150, 152–53, 159
  state and municipal, 60–61, 69, 163
  in Tijuana, 108, 111–12, 128
de la Madrid, Miguel, 49–50, 51
de la Rosa Medellín, Martín, 109 n. 26, 117 nn. 50, 51, 120 nn. 64, 70, 125 n. 85, 136 n. 22, 138, 140
de los Angeles Castillo, Maria, 122 n. 72
demands. *See also* citizens, demands of
  for basic services, 14, 45, 170
  negotiating, 43, 93, 163
  political, 28, 38, 45, 90
democracy, 19, 166, 176
  close to home, 1, 164, 165
  decentralization's effects on, 1–25
  demands for, 45, 47, 173

internal, 112–14, 118
liberal, 98–129, 175
multiparty, 1, 59
participatory, 91, 174
social-movement, 130–66
democratic governance, 19, 22–23, 61, 165
  in Chilpancingo, 23, 175
  decentralization's effects on, 1, 3, 6, 7–9
  in Neza, 132, 147–53, 159–60, 175
  in Tijuana, 99–100, 126–27
democratization, 17, 47–70
  accountability and responsiveness through, 5, 18–20
  changes during, 3, 61, 165
  in Chilpancingo, 23, 95–97, 173
  decentralization's links to, 6–9, 16, 49, 164
  institutional changes through, 18–19, 171
  of municipal governments, 52, 53, 69–70
  in Tijuana, 100, 127
developed world, 2, 10 n. 28, 28, 177
developing world, 1, 2, 3, 9–10, 177
development committees (comités de desarrollo), 91–94, 95, 169
Díaz, Porfirio, 33–34, 40, 66, 78
Díaz Cayeros, Alberto, 56 n. 25
dissent. See also contestation; political parties, opposition
  in Chilpancingo, 76, 83–84
  control of, 28, 36, 45 n. 70, 75, 138–39
  in PRI, 76 n. 5, 108
drug trafficking, 129, 174 n. 23
Duhau, Emilio, 137

Eaton, Kent, 18 n. 52
Ecatepec, Mexico state, 134 nn. 15, 17
Echeverría, Luis, 140
Economic Development Council of Tijuana (Consejo de Desarrollo Económico de Tijuana, CDT), 116, 125–26, 127
economy
  crises in, 32, 47, 49–50, 51, 57, 106, 111, 142
  decentralization's effects on, 53, 64
  growth of, 31–33, 38, 44, 46, 78, 99, 103–4
  indicators of, 32 n. 19, 33 n. 30
  liberalization of, 4–5
education
  in Chilpancingo, 74, 83, 84
  decentralization of, 3 n. 4, 54 n. 22
  in Neza, 141
  public expenditures for, 35, 52 n. 15, 61–62

Ejército Popular Revolucionario (EPR), 83
ejidos. See land ownership
elections. See also Chilpancingo, Guerrero state, elections in; Ciudad Nezahualcóyotl, Mexico state (Neza), elections in; political parties; voters
  in Baja California, 112, 164 n. 3
  competitive, 1, 17, 64–67, 75, 88, 112, 115, 147, 155, 160, 164–65, 176
  federal, 112, 118 n. 54, 136
  free and fair, 17, 20, 65, 164, 177
  gubernatorial, 149, 160
  in Guerrero state, 84, 87–88, 96–97
  indirect, 31, 42
  laws regarding, 50–51, 52, 66, 88, 150
  mayoral, 30
  in Mexico City, 144 n. 49
  municipal, 34, 39, 43, 49, 54, 56, 164, 176
  party-list, 48, 65–66, 114–15, 127, 155–56, 166, 167
  presidential, 39, 51–52, 59, 105, 164 n. 3
  reforms of, 32–33, 52, 112–15, 142–43
  single-party, 16, 47
  state, 39, 52, 54 n. 23, 105, 134 n. 15, 136, 149
El Florido, Veracruz state, 117 n. 53
Elías Calles, Plutarco, 141 n. 40
elites, 8, 31. See also families, elite
  in Chilpancingo, 78, 79–80, 82, 87, 97
  circularity of, 40, 41–42, 49
  competing, 36–37
  pacts with, 36 nn. 40, 43, 37, 38, 48, 159
  political, 45–46, 48, 167 n. 11
  regional, 29–30
  revolutionary, 35, 36
employment
  in Chilpancingo, 75, 79
  in Neza, 134 n. 17
  in Tijuana, 102 n. 8, 103–4, 107
Ensenada, Baja California state, 106
EPR. See Ejército Popular Revolucionario (EPR)
Escalada Hernández, Oscar, 123 n. 75
Escalante Gonzalbo, Fernando, 29 n. 7, 32 n. 25
Europe, 10 n. 26, 98 n. 2
expenditures, public, 3 n. 4, 62. See also investment, government
  through Copladems, 121, 122–23, 124 n. 79
  federal, 27, 28, 49–50
  in Neza, 153–54, 159
  as percentage of GDP, 46, 52 n. 15
  state and municipal, 1, 27–28, 61–62

FAISM. *See* Fund for the Support of Municipal Social Infrastructure (FAISM)
families, elite, 37, 42 n. 58, 172, 174 n. 23. *See also* elites
   in Chilpancingo, 73, 78 n. 12, 81, 88–89, 96
   in Tijuana, 101
Federal Electoral Institute, 52, 54, 65
federal government, 32 n. 21. *See also* expenditures, public; municipal governments, federal funds' transfers to; Ramo 26; Ramo 33; Solidarity (social program); state governments, federal funds' transfers to
   budget of, 46, 58, 59
   electoral reforms by, 112–13
   fiscal powers of, 37–38, 53 n. 21
   municipal governments' relationship with, 37, 51, 168
   state governments' relationship with, 32, 37, 81 n. 22
federalism, 29–30, 31, 32, 56–57, 60–62
Fernández, Rubén, 60 n. 37, 111 n. 32
Figueroa family, 73
FINEZA, 139 n. 35
FIPI. *See* Frente Popular Independiente (FIPI)
FISM. *See* Municipal Social Infrastructure Fund (FISM)
food cooperatives, 143 n. 45, 144
formal power relations
   centralization of, 4, 10, 27, 163–64
   intermediation through, 91–94, 166
   relationship to informal, 13, 48, 95–96, 160, 171
FORTAMUNDF. *See* Fund for Strengthening Municipalities and the Federal District (FORTAMUNDF)
Fox, Jonathan, 164 n. 2
Fox, Vicente, 59, 147
fraccionadores, 135 n. 19, 137, 139, 141
Franco Abundis, Cristina, 124 n. 81
free trade agreements, 98 n. 2, 102
Freire, Paolo, 140 n. 39
Frente de Lucha de las Colonias Populares (Front for the Struggle of the Popular Neighborhoods), 84 n. 31
Frente Mexicano pro-Derechos Humanos (Mexican Front for Human Rights), 139
Frente Popular Independiente (FIPI), 141
Fund for Strengthening Municipalities and the Federal District (FORTAMUNDF), 58, 146
Fund for the Support of Municipal Social Infrastructure (FAISM), 58, 67. *See also* Municipal Social Infrastructure Fund (FISM)

Gato Felix, Héctor, murder of, 98 n. 1
General Association of Settlers (Asociación General de Colonos), 137
González Bautista, Valentín, 141 n. 40, 144, 149, 150, 157, 157 n. 91
González Casanova, Pablo, 40 n. 55, 42 n. 60
government, 39 n. 52, 78 n. 12, 79 n. 15, 163. *See also* federal government; municipal governments; regional governments; state, the; state governments; subnational governments
   accountability and responsiveness of, 1, 4, 7
   Castilian model of, 28–29
   revenues for, 38
governors, state
   in Baja California, 106
   federal authority over, 4 n. 5, 40–41, 81 n. 22
   in Guerrero, 80–81, 86–87, 95
   party affiliations of, 55, 56 n. 26, 60
Greens (revolutionary group), 80
Grindle, Merilee S., 164 n. 3
Grupo Atlacomulco, 135
Guerrero, Arnulfo, 114 n. 40, 115 nn. 45, 46, 123 n. 75, 124 n. 81
Guerrero, state of, 44 n. 69. *See also* Chilpancingo, Guerrero state
   elections in, 84, 87–88, 96–97
   elites in, 79–80, 135–36
   governors of, 80–81, 86–87, 95
   PRD in, 76 n. 5, 87 n. 44, 96
   PRI in, 73–74, 76, 96–97, 172
guerrilla movements, 44 n. 69, 74, 83

Habitat (social program), 59, 85, 86 n. 39
Hagopian, Frances, 11, 12
Hank González, Carlos, 139, 140
Hank Rhon, Jorge, 98, 100 n. 5, 118 n. 57, 128–29, 139 n. 34
health care
   decentralization of, 3 n. 4, 51 n. 12, 61
   public expenditures on, 52 n. 15, 61–62
hegemony, political, 4, 16, 28, 38–46, 66, 142 n. 42, 170, 171. *See also* single-party politics
   in Chilpancingo, 79–84, 95
Hermosillo, Sonora state, citizen participation in, 68
human rights organizations, 83, 139

inclusion, 115, 170, 172
inflation, 50, 57, 111. *See also* economy, crises in
informal power relations, 9–16, 19, 61, 176. *See also* politics, informal

accountability and responsiveness in, 13, 15, 20, 21, 166
centralization and, 27–46, 169
  in Chilpancingo, 87
citizen-state linkages, 3–5, 13–16
  intermediation through, 91–94, 165
  in Neza, 159, 175
  persistence of, 48, 166–71, 172, 177
  political, 45–46, 66, 163
  relationship to formal, 13, 48, 95–96, 160, 171
infrastructure, 33
  in Chilpancingo, 75, 82, 85, 92
  funding for, 33, 53, 58, 59
  in Neza, 136, 146, 153–54
  in Tijuana, 99, 104, 110, 118, 121
innovations. *See* changes
institutionalization, 11, 36 n. 43
institutions, 34, 46
  changes to, 18–19, 47–54, 126–29, 153, 165, 166
  in Chilpancingo, 87–91
  formal, 3–5, 9, 10, 165–66, 171, 175, 177
  participatory, 67 n. 52, 68–70
  political, 2, 96
  representative, 8, 165, 168
  in Tijuana, 112–15, 119
intermediaries/intermediation. *See also* caciques; leaders, political, as intermediaries; negotiations
  in Chilpancingo, 70, 81, 95
  Copacis as, 156–58
  formal/informal channels of, 4–5, 9, 46, 67, 91–94, 171, 173–74, 176–77
  in Neza, 132, 138, 170
  by PRI, 15, 95, 105, 107–8, 169–70, 172
  in Tijuana, 100, 115–29, 170
investment, government, 111 n. 3, 118, 146, 153–54, 159. *See also* expenditures, public

Juárez, Benito, 31–32, 77, 141 n. 40
Juchitán, Oaxaca state, PRD in, 132 n. 7

Katz, Travis, 109 n. 25
Knight, Alan, 36 nn. 40, 43
Krauze, Enrique, 32 n. 21, 40

labor, 35 n. 35, 39, 137
La Gloria, Veracruz state, 117 n. 53, 123 n. 78
land ownership, 33, 34, 35, 50
land titles
  in Chilpancingo, 84

demands for, 45
  in Neza, 130, 131, 135 n. 19, 136, 139–40, 141
  in Tijuana, 104 n. 15, 105, 106–7, 116, 118
Latin America, 10, 15, 169. *See also* individual countries
  decentralization in, 1, 4
  democratization in, 6, 20
  political parties in, 47, 167 n. 10
  public expenditures in, 28, 46
law(s), 30 n. 12, 34 n. 32, 35, 92, 111–12. *See also* constitutions; rule of law; rules
  electoral, 50–51, 52, 66, 88, 135, 143, 150, 164 n. 3, 167 n. 11
leaders, political. *See also* governors, state; mayors; presidency
  as intermediaries, 11, 13, 14–16, 33, 95, 160, 163–64, 165, 168
  local, 30, 48, 49, 100, 163, 169–70
left-wing political parties, 44–45, 68
  in Baja California, 108, 116
  in Guerrero, 84
  in Neza, 132, 140 n. 37, 141, 142
  in Tijuana, 102, 106
León, Guanajuato state, 39 n. 52, 68
Ley Lerdo (Lerdo Law) of 1856, 34 n. 32
Leyva Acevedo, Efraín, 79, 91 n. 60
Liberals, 31, 32–33, 77
liberation theology, 140 n. 39
local governments. *See* municipal governments
López, Arcadio, 142 n. 44
López, Ramón, 123 n. 75
López Gómez, César Pedro, 149 n. 60, 151 n. 67
López Laines, Moises Raúl, 136 n. 23
López Portillo, José, 49, 51 n. 10
Lozena, José Luis, 78 n. 37, 92 n. 63, 93 nn. 67, 69, 70, 94 n. 72
Luken, Gastón, 125 n. 84
Luteroth, Askan, 125 n. 84

Madariaga, Odón, 136 n. 22, 139 n. 32, 142, 144 n. 49
Madero, Francisco, 34
Madison, James, 9 n. 22
Magaloni, Beatriz, 16, 56 n. 25
Maldonado, Braulio, 104, 108 n. 22
Mallon, Florencia, 31 n. 18
Mamdani, Mahmood, 14–15
Mann, Michael, 10 n. 26
"Manos a la Obra" (Hands to Work, Tijuana), 118
manufacturing, 79 n. 16, 102, 103

Index

mayors, 4 n. 5, 111, 163–64, 176
  in Brazil, 122
  in Chilpancingo, 80, 82, 86, 87, 95, 169
  development committees' relationship to, 51 n. 11, 93
  election of, 30, 56 n. 26, 65–66, 166
  municipal councils' relationship to, 114, 115, 167, 168
  in Neza, 135 n. 19, 136, 144, 149, 150, 157, 169, 170–71
  party affiliations of, 56, 56
  reelection prohibited, 37 n. 45, 165, 171
  states' power over, 40–41, 50, 75, 80–81
  in Tijuana, 98, 108, 111, 114, 127, 170–71
  women as, 65 n. 49, 80
McConnell, Grant, 9 n. 22
media, 15 n. 42, 102 n. 9
Méndez, Belem Guerrero, 130, 131
Mercado Durán, Miguel Ángel, 88 n. 47
Mexicali, Baja California state, 43 n. 65, 106
Mexican American War (1846–1848), 100 n. 6
Mexican independence (1810–1821), 29–30, 77
Mexican Revolution (1910–1920), 34–37, 40, 66, 78
Mexican Revolutionary Party (Partido Revolucionario Mexicano, PRM), 39
Mexican Socialist Party (PMS), 142 n. 42
Mexico, state of, 133 n. 9, 135–38, 160
Mexico City, Federal District
  Neza's proximity to, 130–31, 133
  population of, 133 n. 9
  PRD control of, 56 n. 26, 59, 132 n. 7, 144 n. 49
  Tijuana's distance from, 101–3
Meyer, Lorenzo, 28 n. 4, 29 n. 9, 32 n. 19, 36
Meza Andraca, Aurora, 80
middle class, 33, 34, 43
Migdal, Joel S., 10
migration. See Tijuana, Baja California state, migrant population in
MLN. See Movimiento de Liberación Nezahualcoyotlense (MLN)
mobility, 103, 107, 134 n. 15
mobilization
  citizen, 5, 38, 43, 127, 144, 164, 172
  political party, 49 n. 2, 95, 119
  popular, 49, 83
  social, 9, 13
  of voters, 16, 102
Molinar Horcasitas, Juan, 4 n. 5
Montejo, Carlos, 99, 100, 108, 109, 112, 117, 120 n. 61

Morelia, Michoacán state, 132 n. 7
Morelos y Pavón, José María, 77
Moreno, Mario, 89, 93, 97
MOVIDIG. See Movimiento Vida Digna (MOVIDIG)
Movimiento de Liberación Nezahualcoyotlense (MLN), 144, 149 n. 62, 150, 151
Movimiento Restaurador de Colonos (Settlers' Restoration Movement, MRC), 139–40, 141
Movimiento Territorial de Chilpancingo (Territorial Movement of Chilpancingo), 83 n. 30
Movimiento Vida Digna (MOVIDIG), 143–44, 149 n. 62, 150, 151, 152, 154, 157, 158, 172–73
MRC. See Movimiento Restaurador de Colonos (Settlers' Restoration Movement, MRC)
municipal councils, 30, 41, 164, 176. See also Ciudad Nezahualcóyotl, Mexico state (Neza), municipal councils in
  accountability and responsiveness of, 167, 168
  in Chilpancingo, 76, 80, 86, 87, 89–90, 93–97
  elections of, 37 n. 45, 48, 66
  opposition parties on, 51, 90–91, 95–96, 114, 151–53
  party-list selection of, 65–66, 114–15, 127, 159, 166, 167
  states' power over, 50, 80–81
  supermajorities on, 50, 115, 127, 166, 167
  in Tijuana, 114–15, 121, 122, 126 n. 86, 152 n. 76, 173
  women on, 65 n. 49
Municipal Development Council (Consejo para el Desarrollo Municipal, CODEMUN), 58, 66, 67, 153–54, 159
municipal governments. See also Ciudad Nezahualcóyotl, Mexico state (Neza), municipal government in
  accountability and responsiveness of, 5, 8–9, 48, 70, 164, 167, 168, 171 n. 17, 176
  authoritarianism in, 7, 41, 160, 164, 167
  authority of, 1, 69, 109, 111–12, 164
  autonomy of, 1, 29, 30–31, 37, 50 n. 5, 61–62, 69, 85, 86–87, 109, 164
  in Chilpancingo, 76, 85–87, 95–97
  citizens' relationships to, 115–28, 132, 136 n. 22, 137, 153–58, 165, 172
  decentralization's effects on, 17 n. 47, 18–19, 52, 61, 69–70
  decision making by, 69, 128
  democratization's effects on, 18–19, 52, 69–70
  electoral competition in, 64–69, 176

empowerment of, 1–25, 47–48, 109–12, 144, 145–47, 177
federal funds' transfers to, 57–59, 61–62, 64, 69, 82 n. 24, 85–86, 100, 109, 126, 145–47, 164, 177
federal government's relationship with, 32, 51, 168
opposition parties in, 43–44, 51, 54 n. 24, 56–57, 67
policy-making by, 48, 60–61
political affiliations in, 57
PRI control of, 59, 65, 66
public expenditures by, 1, 27, 53, 61–62, 66–67, 85 n. 36, 90 n. 55, 91, 159
responsibilities of, 80 n. 20, 145, 163
revenues for, 8, 37–38, 50, 63, 80 n. 20, 86, 110, 145, 158–59
rural, 33–34, 64, 65, 78, 171 n. 17
Solidarity Municipal Funds program, 53–54
states' relationship with, 34, 37, 43, 50, 58, 60–61, 81, 82, 95, 146, 158
in Tijuana, 117 n. 53
weaknesses of, 49, 163
Municipal Planning Council (Consejo de Planeación para el Desarrollo Municipal, Copladem), 51, 58, 66, 67, 91, 92–93
in Tijuana, 116, 120–25, 127, 128
Municipal Social Infrastructure Fund (FISM), 153–54. See also Fund for the Support of Municipal Social Infrastructure (FAISM)
MUP. See Urban Popular Movement (Movimiento Urbano Popular, MUP)

National Conference of Governors (Conferencia Nacional de Gobernadores, CONAGO), 60
National Council of Popular Organizations (CNOP), 137, 140, 158
National Electrical Commission, 35 n. 35
National Fiscal Convention, 60
National Peasant Confederation (CNC), 137, 140
National Power Commission, 35 n. 35
National Revolutionary Party (Partido Mexicano de los Trabajadores, PMT), 142, 143–44
National Revolutionary Party (Partido Nacional Revolucionario, PNR), 36, 37–39. See also Mexican Revolutionary Party (Partido Revolucionario Mexicano, PRM)
National Union of Education Workers (Sindicato Nacional de Trabajadores de la Educación, SNTE), 84

Naucalpan, Mexico state, 134 nn. 15, 17, 147 nn. 56, 57
Navarrete, Clementino, 83 n. 30
negotiations, 43, 45, 49 n. 2, 80, 172. See also bargaining; intermediaries/intermediation
informal, 12, 15 n. 42, 93
political, 54, 151, 156, 159, 169–70
Negrete Mata, José, 128 n. 87
neighborhood committees (Comités de Vecinos). See also Citizen Participation Councils (Consejos de Participación Ciudadana, Copacis)
in Chilpancingo, 83–84, 94, 95–97
in Neza, 137, 173
in Tijuana, 104 n. 15, 116–20, 124 n. 80, 127, 128, 129, 174
New Federalism, 56–57
Neza. See Ciudad Nezahualcóyotl, Mexico state
nongovernmental organizations (NGOs), in Tijuana, 121, 123, 124 n. 81, 169
North, Douglass C., 34

Oaxaca, state of, 168 n. 14
Obregón, Álvaro, 35, 36
O'Donnell, Guillermo, 11
oil companies, expropriation of, 39
organizations. See business organizations; civic organizations; human rights organizations; neighborhood committees (Comités de Vecinos); social movements; and individual organizations
Osuna Jaime, Héctor, 109, 110, 110 n. 30, 111, 113–14, 118, 118 n. 54, 120, 120 n. 65, 125, 125 n. 83
Osuna Millán, Guadalupe, 109, 121, 122 n. 70

pacts
elite, 36 nn. 40, 43, 37, 38, 48, 159
political, 39, 47, 173
social, 52
PAN. See Partido Acción Nacional (PAN)
PARM. See Authentic Party of the Mexican Revolution (Partido Auténtico de la Revolución Mexicana, PARM)
participatory democracy, 8, 127, 157 n. 91, 159, 174
particularism, 4, 11, 14
Partido Acción Nacional (PAN), 5, 43, 149. See also Ciudad Nezahualcóyotl, Mexico state (Neza), PAN in; Tijuana, Baja California state, PAN in

Partido Acción Nacional (PAN) (*continued*)
   in Baja California state, 43 n. 65, 52, 102, 106, 108, 112–29
   in Chilpancingo, 90–91, 94 n. 71, 96 n. 73
   on CODEMUN, 153, 154
   election victories, 49, 52, 56 n. 26, 59
   in Guerrero state, 84
   in municipal governments, 67, 68
   subnational political activities, 58
Partido de la Revolución Democrática (PRD), 5. *See also* Ciudad Nezahualcóyotl, Mexico state (Neza), PRD in
   in Baja California, 112, 116 n. 48
   in Chilpancingo, 75–76, 84, 87–88, 90–91, 94
   on CODEMUN, 153, 154–55
   on Copacis, 155–56, 157, 158
   election victories of, 56, 59, 132 nn. 7, 8
   founding of, 52, 142, 144
   in Guerrero, 76 n. 5, 87 n. 44, 96
   in municipal governments, 67–68
   in Tijuana, 119 n. 58, 124 n. 81
Partido Revolucionario Institucional (PRI), 5, 15, 116, 157. *See also* Chilpancingo, Guerrero state, PRI in; Tijuana, Baja California state, PRI in
   in Baja California, 104–5, 112, 113
   clientelism in, 42, 43, 45, 66–69, 172, 173
   on CODEMUN, 153, 154
   corruption under, 128 n. 87, 145
   dominance of, 40–46, 52, 65, 164 n. 3, 167
   election results for, 49, 56, 149
   in Guerrero state, 73–74, 76, 96–97, 172
   intermediation by, 39, 95, 105, 107–8, 169–70, 172
   internal structure of, 66, 105, 120, 126, 127, 128, 171
   in Neza, 131, 135–60
   opposition to, 76 n. 5, 84, 108
   weakening of, 59–61, 68, 160
Party of the Poor, 83
patronage, 11, 12, 42, 136, 163
PAU. *See* Plan de Plan de Activación Urbana (Urban Activation Plan, PAU)
PCM. *See* Communist Party (Partido Comunista Mexicano, PCM)
peasants, 32, 35, 39, 137
Pedroza, Héctor, 142 n. 44, 149 n. 60, 151 n. 67, 158 n. 92
Pérez, Juanita, 114 n. 40, 124 n. 81, 125 n. 85
Pérez Cuevas, Carlos Alberto, 149 n. 60, 151 nn. 67, 69

Pérez Maldonado, Luis, 142 n. 44, 158 n. 92
Peronism, 11 n. 32
personalism, 12, 69
Peruzzotti, Enrique, 8
Pichardo, Ignacio, 139 n. 35
Plan Chilpancingo, 82 n. 24
Plan de Activación Urbana (Urban Activation Plan, PAU), 110–11
planning processes, participatory, 116, 121–22, 125, 126, 140 n. 38, 172, 173–74. *See also* citizens, participation in government; Municipal Development Council (Consejo para el Desarrollo Municipal, Codemun); Municipal Planning Council (Consejo de Planeación para el Desarrollo Municipal, Copladem)
plurality, political, 41, 47, 59, 94, 141, 142, 145, 149–50, 173
PMS. *See* Mexican Socialist Party (PMS)
PMT. *See* National Revolutionary Party (Partido Mexicano de los Trabajadores)
PNR. *See* National Revolutionary Party (Partido Nacional Revolucionario, PNR)
Polevnsky, Yeidckol, 160
policy making, 20 n. 57, 166
   in Chilpancingo, 89–90
   state and municipal, 1, 48, 49, 60–61, 66–67
political parties, 2 n. 3, 9, 42, 46, 175. *See also* elections; leaders, political; single-party politics
   competition between, 94, 95–96
   election results, 81, 89, 107, 113, 143, 148
   mass, 39, 172, 174
   minority, 50, 90, 112, 143
   in municipal governments, 57
   opposition, 43–44, 47–48, 52, 54, 87–88, 90–91, 102, 149, 153, 170–71
politics. *See also* competition, political
   informal, 12, 69, 100, 163
   local, 42, 51, 139
   multiparty, 1, 59, 66
   partisan, 59, 60, 93, 96, 119, 122
   state-level, 171 n. 18, 172
   traditional, 4, 11, 160
polyarchy, 17
poor people, 12–13, 45, 52. *See also* Chilpancingo, Guerrero state, poverty in
   neighborhoods of, 59, 106 n.21
   in Neza, 131
   rural, 33–34, 64
   in Tijuana, 106
Popular Socialist Party (Partido Popular Socialista, PPS), 43–44, 141

power, 31 n. 18, 43, 49, 159. *See also* formal power relations; informal power relations
  hierarchy of, 8, 12–13, 16, 172
  metaconstitutional, 4 n. 5, 87
  political, 41, 107, 175
  presidential, 42 n. 60
  states', 35 n. 36, 164
PPS. *See* Popular Socialist Party (Partido Popular Socialista, PPS)
PRD. *See* Partido de la Revolución Democrática (PRD)
Preciado, Gabriel, 123 n. 75
prefects, 30, 32, 34, 37, 80, 81
presidency, 4 n. 5, 42 n. 60, 53–54, 59, 90 n. 55. *See also* elections, presidential; and *individual presidents*
PRI. *See* Partido Revolucionario Institucional (PRI)
private goods, 166, 176
PRM. *See* Mexican Revolutionary Party (Partido Revolucionario Mexicano, PRM)
protests. *See* contestation
PRT. *See* Trotskyite Workers Revolutionary Party (PRT)
Public Education Department (Secretaría de Educación Pública), 35
public goods, 1, 8, 14, 20, 166, 170, 173, 176
public works, 90 n. 55, 91, 92–93, 109 n. 25, 124 n. 79. *See also* basic services

Ramo 26, 57, 58
Ramo 33, 57 n. 29, 58, 62, 67, 153
  in Chilpancingo, 85, 86 n. 39, 91, 92–93
  in Neza, 145–47, 153
  in Tijuana, 100, 111
Ramos Romero, Rigoberto, 85 n. 38, 86 n. 42, 88 n. 48, 90 nn. 56, 57; 91 n. 58, 93 n. 67, 94 n. 71
recentralization, 18 n. 52, 53–54
Reds (family group), 80
reelection, prohibition against, 40, 48, 66, 80, 165, 167, 171
reforms
  constitutional, 37n45, 40, 50, 58, 60–61
  for decentralization, 1, 48, 49, 50–51
  electoral, 32–33, 52, 112–15, 126 n. 86
  land, 35, 39
  state, 54, 55–58
regidores (council members), 30, 65 n. 49. *See also* municipal councils
regional interests, 9, 28–30, 31 n. 18, 32, 36 n. 43, 61

representation
  in Chilpancingo, 87–91
  informal mechanisms for, 11, 175
  municipal structures for, 65, 69–70, 166
  in Neza, 147, 149–53
  in Tijuana, 114 n. 41
resistance. *See* contestation
resources, distribution of, 12, 45, 169–70. *See also* basic services; investment, government; public goods
responsiveness. *See also* accountability
  in Chilpancingo, 95–96, 175
  decentralization's effects on, 3, 4, 7–9, 18–20
  democratization's effects on, 1, 18–19, 165
  informal power relations and, 13, 15, 20, 21, 166–67
  municipal governments', 5, 8–9, 48, 70, 164, 168, 171 n. 17, 176
  in Neza, 132, 173, 174–75
  in Tijuana, 100, 115, 126
Revilla, Cirilo, 143 n. 45, 149 n. 65, 152 n. 78, 156 n. 89, 158 n. 92
rights. *See* citizenship, rights of
Riker, William H., 29 n. 10
Rivera, Ramón, 131 n. 5
Rodríguez, Abelardo L., 101, 151 nn. 67, 73; 154 n. 81, 158 n. 92
Rodríguez, Felipe, 141 n. 41, 149 n. 62
Rondinelli, Dennis, 17 n. 47
Rosales, Martín, 147 n. 57
Ruffo, Ernesto, 106, 108, 116
Ruíz López, Francisco Antonio, 149 n. 60, 151 n. 67
Ruíz Vargas, Benedicto, 121 n. 68
rule of law, 10, 11, 14, 46, 170, 174 n. 23
rules. *See also* law(s)
  fiscal, 60, 111
  formal, 12 n. 33, 37, 167
  informal, 48, 166
  political, 65–66, 69, 80, 115, 128, 140
rural areas. *See* municipal governments, rural
Rus, Jan, 15

Sabato, Hilda, 31 n. 15
Salazar Adame, Florencio, 79, 82 n. 24
Salinas de Gortari, Carlos, 52, 54 n. 22, 84, 98, 108, 142
Sánchez, Luis, 147 n. 57, 150, 154
Sánchez, Zeferino, 125 n. 84
San Luis Potosí, San Luis Potosí state, 39 n. 52
Schteingart, Martha, 137

Secretariat of Social Development (Secretaría de Desarrollo Social), 53 n. 19
SEPAC. *See* Servicios Populares, A.C. (SEPAC)
services. *See* basic services
Servicios Populares, A.C. (SEPAC), 140
sindicos (municipal councils), 30, 65 n. 49. *See also* municipal councils
Single Development Agreements (Convenios Únicos de Desarrollo, CUDs), 51
single-party politics, 1, 36, 70, 102, 167, 171. *See also* hegemony, political
    weakening of, 47, 59–61, 69, 164
SNTE. *See* National Union of Education Workers (Sindicato Nacional de Trabajadores de la Educación, SNTE)
social capital, 7–8, 19, 165, 166, 174–75, 177
social movements, 44–45
    in Chilpancingo, 74, 75, 76 n. 5, 83
    in Neza, 130–66, 170
social services. *See* education; health care
society. *See* civil society; state-society linkages
Solidarity (social program), 52–54, 57, 85, 91, 111
    Municipal Funds initiative, 53–54, 66
spending, government. *See* expenditures, public
stability, maintenance of, 31, 45, 163, 170, 177
state, the. *See also* citizens, intermediaries between state and; government
    centralization of, 28–34, 45, 49, 163–64, 169
    citizens' relationship to, 3–5, 9, 13, 48, 175, 177
    formation of, 10, 23, 48–49
    power groups and, 15 n. 42
    reforms in, 54, 55–58
State Electoral Council of Guerrero (Consejo Estatal Electoral de Guerrero, CEEGRO), 88
state governments, 29–30, 46, 136 n. 22, 168. *See also* governors, state; municipal governments, states' relationship with
    constitutions of, 41, 41 n. 57, 44, 58, 81
    decentralization's effects on, 54, 61, 69–70
    federal funds' transfers to, 51, 57, 58, 59, 61–62, 177
    federal government's relationship with, 32, 37, 81 n. 22
    policy-making by, 48, 60–61
    power of, 35 n. 36, 164
    public expenditures by, 1, 61–62
    revenues of, 37–38, 62 n. 40
State Planning Council (Consejo de Planeación para el Desarrollo Estatal, Coplade), 51
state-society linkages, 23, 151, 171, 175
Stepan, Alfred P., 29 n. 10
Stevens, Evelyn P., 45 n. 70
strikes, 44 n. 69
subnational governments, 6–7, 38. *See also* municipal governments; state governments
    fund transfers from federal government, 57, 59, 64
    PAN's activities in, 57–58
    structure of, 10, 17 n. 47, 28, 48
suffrage. *See also* voters
    universal, 30–31
    women's, 37 n. 45, 80
Supreme Court rulings, 60–61, 111

Tatahuilcapán, Veracruz state, 68
taxes
    federal, 77 n. 8
    income, 35 n. 35
    municipal, 37–38, 64, 85, 110, 112 n. 34, 126, 158–59
    property, 50, 109, 112 n. 34, 145, 164
    state, 37–38, 77 n. 8
teachers' movement, 84
Televisa (Mexican television), 15 n. 42
tequila crisis (1994–1995), 57
Texoco, Mexico state, 133 n. 10
Tijuana, Baja California state, 5, 22, 23, 98–129, 134 n.15, 174 n. 23
    accountability and responsiveness in, 100, 115, 126
    autonomy in, 105 n. 18, 126
    basic services in, 99, 103–4, 105, 106–7, 118
    business community in, 125–27
    Copladem in, 120–25, 127, 128
    decentralization and democratization in, 99–100, 126–27
    decision making in, 108, 111–12, 128
    economy in, 99, 103–4, 106
    elections in, 98, 101–2, 105–6, 107, 108, 112–15, 113, 118 nn. 56, 57, 119 n. 58, 122 n. 72, 126 n.86
    employment in, 102 n. 8, 103–4, 107
    history of, 100–104
    infrastructure in, 99, 104, 110, 118, 121
    intermediaries in, 100, 115–29, 170
    land titles in, 104 n. 15, 105, 106–7, 116, 118
    left-wing parties in, 102, 106
    mayors in, 108, 111, 114, 127, 170–71
    migrant population in, 101 n. 7, 102 n. 8, 103, 106, 123 n. 76, 124 n. 81

municipal council in, 114–15, 121, 122, 126 n. 86, 152 n. 76, 173
municipal government in, 117 n. 53
neighborhood committees in, 104 n. 15, 116–20, 124 n. 80, 127, 128, 129, 174
NGOs in, 121, 123, 124 n. 81, 169
PAN in, 22, 43 n. 65, 98–100, 102, 105–6, 107, 109–29, 123 n. 77, 124 n. 81, 128, 147 n. 57, 170, 173–74
planning processes in, 68, 140 n. 38
population of, 99, 100, 101 n. 7, 103, 105, 117 n. 53
PRD in, 119 n. 58, 124 n. 81
PRI in, 98, 99, 101–8, 116, 118 n. 57, 119 n. 58, 120, 124 n. 81, 126, 129, 173
revenues for, 100, 109, 110, *110*, 111, 126, 147 n. 57
Tijuana Strategic Plan, 125
Tilly, Charles, 13–14
Tixtla, Guerrero state, 77
Tlalnepantla, Mexico state, 134 nn. 15, 17
Toluca, Mexico state, 134 n. 15, 147 n. 55
Torreblanca, Zeferino, 75
tortibonos (food coupons), 143 n. 45
towns. *See* municipal councils; municipal governments; *and individual cities and towns*
Treaty of Guadalupe Hidalgo (1848), 100 n.6
Trotskyite Workers Revolutionary Party (PRT), 84, 106

UGOCM. *See* Unión General de Obreros y Campesinos del Estado de México (UGOCM)
UNICON. *See* Unión de Colonias de Nezahualcóyotl (UNICON)
Unión de Colonias de Nezahualcóyotl (UNICON), 140

Unión de Colonias Populares de Chilpancingo (Union of Popular Neighborhoods of Chilpancingo), 83
Unión General de Obreros y Campesinos del Estado de México (UGOCM), 141, 142, 144, 149 n. 62, 151
Unión Popular Revolucionario Emiliano Zapata (UPREZ), 141, 142, 144, 149 n. 62, 150, 151, 154, 158
unions, 83–84, 105, 116, 172 n. 20
United States (U.S.), 29 n. 10, 30 n. 14, 31 n. 16, 98 n. 2, 102–3
UPREZ. *See* Unión Popular Revolucionario Emiliano Zapata (UPREZ)
Urban Popular Movement (Movimiento Urbano Popular, MUP), 84

Vásquez, Genaro, 83
Vaughan, Mary Kay, 35 n. 36
Venezuela, decentralization in, 2 n. 3
Veracruz, state of, 133 n. 9
Villahermosa, Tabasco state, 65 n. 45
voters. *See also* elections; suffrage
mobilization of, 16, 102
participation rates of, 31 n. 15, 113, 118 n. 56, 128 n. 87, 134 n. 15, 155

Weingast, Barry, 56 n. 25
Weldon, Jeffrey A., 4 n. 5
women, 37 n. 45, 80
working classes, 22, 131, 134

Zanabría, Antonio, 151 n. 67
Zavala, Catalino, 108 n. 22, 116 n. 48
Zedillo, Ernesto, 54, 56–57
Zumpango, Guerrero state, 77

www.ingramcontent.com/pod-product-compliance
Lightning Source LLC
Chambersburg PA
CBHW031551300426
44111CB00006BA/273